D1173224

BREAKING THROUGH

BREAKING THROUGH

ALLAN McDOUGALL

AM PUBLISHING

Published by

First Edition
Copyright © 2011 by Allan McDougall
All Rights Reserved

No portion of this book may be reproduced or transmitted
in any form whatsoever, including electronic, mechanical or any information
storage or retrieval system, except as may be expressly permitted in the
1976 Copyright Act or in writing from the publisher.

Requests for permission should be addressed to:
Allan McDougall
allan@ampublicspeaking.com

ISBN: 978-0-9850514-0-2
Library of Congress Control Number: 2011932483

AM Publishing
P.O. Box 22111
Pittsburgh, PA 15222

Printed in the USA

Dedicated to everyone who believed in me before I believed in myself.

Table of Contents

FOREWORD

WHEN I FIRST MET ALLAN MCDOUGALL, I was intrigued by his story. Growing up in the lush farm country of southwestern Ontario, Canada, he suffered a nightmare youth filled with myriad abuses at the hands of his parents, his teachers, school bullies and life itself. That abuse does not compare, however, to the anguish Allan caused himself through toxic relationships and excessive drinking.

After two decades of alcohol abuse, Allan discovered that alcohol was not really his problem. It was merely his answer to a much deeper problem. He was living a substandard existence created by the limited beliefs of others that he had also accepted. As a hard rock miner in Canada for many years, Allan continued to live that existence which resulted in driving him away from his true self. Due to an unanticipated intervention, Allan discovered that he could create his own life. Through perseverance, hard work and faith he was able to turn his life around. *Breaking Through* tells the almost surreal story of the many challenges that he faced, how he defeated those challenges and how he then took back his power.

Breaking Through is a book that engages you instantly but is hard to forget. Without pretense, Allan provides us with provocative insights, raw emotions and heart-breaking dilemmas. It is not, however, a story about overcoming substance abuse. Instead, Allan shows in painful detail the emotional torment behind a grim adolescence. Thankfully, out of this dark place grew a genuinely edifying lesson about overcoming the self-inflicted abuses of fear, doubt, self-hatred and lack of forgiveness. These are the barriers that keep many people from accomplishing their goals and dreams, from discovering the greatness that they have within themselves.

What impresses me about Allan is that you would never suspect his story if he did not tell it. When you go through things in life, they can make you bitter, or they can make you better. Allan decided in his heart of hearts that his past would not define him. He literally turned a lemon into lemonade. He became a better person. He is an asset to the world rather than a liability. He has a story and a voice that is being heard. He is committed to changing lives until he takes his last breath. This is something that we both have in common.

This book will change your life. Through speeches, keynote events and workshops, Allan shares his story and his experiences to inspire others to dig down into the core of their being and find the richness that lives there. For as much as he has accomplished so far in his life, Allan has not yet reached his maximum potential or the impact he will have on this world.

If you take anything from this life-affirming survival guide, know this: if Allan can do it, so can you. There is always a path to your greatness if you fight to find one. Take these lessons to heart and you will create opportunities to make true change in your life, discover your voice and live your purpose.

In pursuit of your greatness,

Les Brown,
Motivational speaker, author, radio personality

FOREWORD

PREFACE

IT WAS A HAZY JULY EVENING IN 1992 in Sudbury, Ontario, Canada. North of Lake Huron and Georgian Bay, families in the city of 120,000 were out on their lawns taking advantage of the all-too-brief summer season. Around 7:30, I received a phone call. The voice on the other end sounded disturbed. I recognized Louise's voice. She and I were friends from my time in the adult education program at Cambrian College.

"Allan, I need your help. Could you come over to our house right away? Marcel is in trouble."

I hung up and drove over. It was warm when I walked into the back yard but emotions would soon ignite an inferno. Marcel was having a barbecue. He was drunk and in no mood for visitors, let alone me, a recovering alcoholic of five years. Louise introduced us and Marcel's face, ruddy from the sun, turned deep crimson. His wife excused herself and left us alone to talk; matters went downhill from there.

The intensity of our conversation reached a flash point when Marcel threw me against a fence and put a knife to my throat. In an instant he could have ended my life. His face was so close to mine that I could almost taste the whiskey on his breath. I could not avoid the hatred in his eyes. At that moment I could smell and see something else—fear. Fear, you see, had been my constant companion from as early as I could remember. When it didn't have me in a hammerlock, it was always in the shadows waiting for its next opportunity.

As Marcel pinned me against the fence, I was thrown back to my childhood, standing in front of 52 kids in a one-room school in southwestern Ontario. Each year, from Grade 3 on, we had to stand in front of the class—the whole school, really, Grades 1 to 8—and give a speech. Oral composition it was called, and I dreaded it more than anything in my life. It was always one of the worst days of my life. I had a terrible speech impediment, and each year, as soon as I started my presentation, I began to stutter something awful.

"Mr. McK--K--Kay and f--f--f--ellow st--st--st--students, the t--t--t--topic I have ch--ch--ch--chosen i--i--i--s-- . . . ." At that point, I would burst into tears. That fear that I felt every year on Oral Composition Day was the same fear that I saw in Marcel's eyes that night.

"I could kill you, you son of a bitch," he seethed.

Maybe it was the crystal clarity induced by the knife at my throat. There is nothing like a real threat to your survival to bring you into the moment. Regardless, I said, "Marcel, you are absolutely right, you could. But let me tell you something—I went through a terrible divorce four years ago and my ex-wife got everything, even the barbecue. I haven't had a good barbecued steak in years. Would you mind if we did this after we eat?" I was somewhat outside myself as the words passed my lips. My voice was calm, clear, concise.

We stood there looking at one another. Time stopped.

For a moment, Marcel's eyes turned perplexed and then he said, "You know, Al, you are crazier than I am."

He put the knife down. We went over to the table and I ate one of the best steaks I ever had. I am not sure if that was because Marcel was a good cook or I had been just scared to death and was simply happy to be alive.

Later, as the sun was setting and the air began to cool, so did the atmosphere in Marcel's backyard. When I close my eyes even today, I have a picture postcard memory of this life-altering ordeal. That night, I drove Marcel to a detox center and left him in a safe environment. I took the weapon out of his car; he had planned to do some harm that night. At that point, the rifle was safer in my hands than his. To this day, Marcel has never had to have another drink of alcohol. I send him postcards when I travel and visit him in his retirement home when I am back in Sudbury and he has told me that I am in his will.

For 22 years, I worked as a hard rock miner in Canada, pulling riches from the earth: nickel, copper, gold, platinum, lead and others. Every day I went thousands of feet under the ground. I hoisted a 110 pound drill and fought Mother Earth in sweltering heat for her mineral wealth. I drilled and blasted the pyrrohtite, sweated in near darkness, avoided several close calls myself and lost friends who were not so lucky.

However, no matter the riches I uncovered deep within the earth or the wages I accrued over the years, the riches I discovered when I went deep within myself, the 18 inches from my head to my heart, have proven much more valuable, not only to me but to my world.

This is the story of my struggles, the victories I tasted and the defeats I suffered along the way. I tell it to convey the message that there is always hope, there is always the possibility for change and redemption. My life is living proof.

Allan McDougall
Pittsburgh
Spring, 2011

CHAPTER 1

A Boy Living in Fear

Nobody's family can hang out the sign,
"Nothing's the matter here."
–Chinese Proverb

My whole childhood, all my school years, were driven by fear.

I grew up on a dairy farm about a mile from the tiny hamlet of Auburn, in southwestern Ontario, 12 miles from the eastern shore of Lake Huron. The land there is fertile and mostly flat but punctuated by gently rolling hills. Forests that had stood since the last ice age have mostly been cut down for farmland. The Maitland River meanders southward past Auburn and empties into the lake at the town of Goderich. Most people in Auburn were farmers and even today the land remains a patchwork of neat fields and open spaces.

A long gravel lane ran north from the county highway up a gentle hill to the big old farmhouse where we lived. Halfway up the lane on the left was our barn and on the right was the chicken coop. A large drive-in equipment shed also stood off to the left of the house. Some years, Dad planted the vegetable garden down by the chicken coop, other times up closer to the house. He didn't want to plant it in the same location for too many years or the yield would suffer. A fence and gate was at the end of the driveway and opened into the front yard.

Acreage on the farm was utilized either for grazing land for the cows or hayfields for their winter feed. We also grew oats and barley. At the north end of the property there was a stand of maple trees and a gravel pit where we sold gravel to construction companies for road building.

Dad sailed about 70 feet off a cliff into that pit one winter while riding a "flying saucer," one of those metal discs with handles that kids played with in the snow. He bought it for us one Christmas, but being safety conscious, he wanted to try it out before turning us loose. Dressed in his big brown parka with the hood tied tight around his head and a big Christmas cigar in his mouth, he looked like a gingerbread man as he began a gentle slide down a small hill. Before he knew what was happening though, the saucer picked up speed and in what seemed like a second, he was racing out of control. Over the cliff he went in a cloud of snow. My sister Bernice and I could not believe what we had just witnessed—Dad disappearing in a white cloud!

We ran to the edge and peered over. We saw him spinning wildly and turning somersaults helter-skelter but still grasping the handles. Finally, the saucer came to a stop and Dad sat there, upright but completely still, probably meditating on what had just happened. His cigar looked like an exploding cigar after the charge goes off. He couldn't open his eyes because of the snow packed behind his glasses. I came very close to making yellow snow without taking off my overalls and long johns, I was laughing so hard.

Our farmhouse was built around 1900. It had two stories and was built of dull yellow brick; there wasn't much red clay in the area. A cement porch ran across the front. A covered veranda ran along the left side of the house, and that is where, depending on the season, Dad shook off the snow, mud or dirt, and removed his barn clothes before coming inside. There was a couch and a chair and when neighbors came over to talk to my dad, they would sit out there. Sometimes Dad slept on that couch when he needed to get away from my mother.

We mostly used the veranda's side entrance rather then the front door because that is where the kitchen was and where most family life took place. Our kitchen was massive, larger than any other room in the house. Inside the entrance to the right were stairs leading to the

The family farm where I grew up.

My boyhood home. Except for the TV antenna and the newly relocated chimney, it looks much as I remember it.

basement. Down there was a good-sized cistern that held rainwater collected from the gutters along the eaves. We used a hand pump next to a sink to draw water for the laundry and for sponge baths.

To the right of that sink was a large pantry with doors at either end that opened up into the kitchen. The pantry held our dry goods and I remember riding my tricycle in and out of the doors as a child. When I got a bit older, well, really, when my sister Bernice got older and needed some privacy, the pantry became my bedroom. Like every farming kitchen I have ever entered, we had a couch in there. Behind the kitchen and attached to the house was a wood shed large enough to hold our firewood for the winter. A clothesline attached by a pulley to the shed ran out to a pole in back where Mom hung the laundry. I remember peering out the window and counting the clothes as Mom clothespinned them to the line and pushed them out into the sunlight.

Towards the front of the house facing the highway was a parlor that we never used unless someone important was coming. My mother's side of the family was known for their musical talents. We had a player piano that was used during family get-togethers and we had fun with it. The unused front entrance opened onto a staircase leading to the second floor and on its left were two bedrooms. Bernice's and mine faced the front and, because the hallway door to our room had been blocked off, we had to walk through Mom and Dad's room to get to ours.

The upstairs had three large bedrooms and above these, an attic, and all were mainly storage. We almost never went up there and certainly never slept there. A grim family joke was that we had air conditioning in the winter and heating in the summer. Spring and fall were short respites from either blazing heat or freezing cold. It was 95 degrees in summer and minus 40 in winter with only a month of pleasant temperatures in between.

The sole source of warmth for the entire house was a wood stove in the kitchen. We didn't have a furnace. During winter, it was so cold that frost formed on the inside of the windows. We kept our school clothes for the next day under the blankets to keep them warm for the morning. Years later, we managed to get an oil heater for the parlor.

We never needed an alarm clock; my father lighting the stove in the morning always woke us. He would pour some gasoline into a small salmon can and throw it on the smoldering embers from the previous night's fire. The explosion lifted the lids clear off the stove and their clanging back onto the stove top accompanied by a few words of profanity from Dad never failed to wake the family. Looking through the frosty bedroom window it was not unusual for Bernice and me to see three and four foot long icicles hanging from the frame. I used to marvel at the exquisite patterns that the frost formed on the inside of the window panes.

I still have a vision of my mother sitting in front of the wood stove every night in winter. She would open the oven door, and resting her calves on it, stick her feet inside to keep them warm and off the ice-cold floor. Sometimes we had to leave water dripping from the kitchen faucet to keep the pipes from freezing; otherwise, my dad would have a difficult time thawing them.

At the bottom of the stove was an ash drawer where we would collect the ashes at the end of the day's burn and dump them in a pile outside. We'd use the cinders for traction when our car got stuck in the snow. My mother also used them in her flower beds and they really made the flowers bloom.

Indoor plumbing was a luxury we would not experience until we moved off the farm and into the village when I was 15. Until then, I would follow my dad's footprints in the snow as he broke trail to our two-seater outhouse. Otherwise, we had chamber pots under the bed. We took our weekly baths in a tub out on the lawn and in winter went to our Grandma's house in the village. That was the era and that was our economic status; even in a poor agricultural community, we were considered very poor.

The emotional atmosphere at home was usually just as harsh as the winter weather. The nurturing that any child needs was not forthcoming from my parents. Certainly, it was not adequate for what I needed. That is just the way it was. Those were the cards I was dealt and as you will see, I didn't play my hand well for many years.

Breaking Through

CHAPTER 2

CHILDHOOD CHALLENGES

If we are to make the future good,
we'll learn what the past can teach us.
–ANONYMOUS

FOR NINE MONTHS, a baby is cared for and nourished in the dark warmth of its mother's womb. Its place in the world is secure, tethered like a flower to a stalk rooted firmly in the soil. Life flows from soil to roots to plant to flower, which one day blooms to the delight of the world.

I entered this life on August 3, 1950 at 12:01 a.m. On the fourth day after I came home from the hospital, my mother refused to feed me any longer. She couldn't seem to cope with the idea of having a son. My sustenance cut off, I had to live for a time with my grandparents at a very early age. I have no recollection of that; however, I'm sure it had a lasting effect on the feelings I had with rejection, a bud ripped from the soil that gave it life and cast aside.

My mother, were she to give birth today, likely would be diagnosed as suffering from postpartum psychosis. That is the closest comparison I can make and it set the stage for my childhood. During my early years, I truly felt that I had no safe place, no place in which to sink roots.

I was born with asthma and in a short time developed a severe case. My earliest memories are of struggling to breathe. It's a horrible feeling not knowing whether your next breath is coming. Progressively, my asthma got worse. One night around the age of four, I had a terrible attack. I could hardly breathe. After what seemed an eternity, my parents finally drove me to the hospital. In the hospital parking lot my breathing stopped. The doctor hurriedly gave me a shot of adrenaline to the heart and told my mother, "This is the last hope. Either he will stay like he is or he will begin to breathe again." Though I was very young, I remember that event. For whatever reason, I have been blessed with a good memory.

During the frequent winter snowstorms, the lane to our house became impassable and we had to leave the car on the highway down by the gate. The wind whipping around me made me lose my breath and I would gasp and wheeze as I trudged for what seemed like miles up to the house. Often, Dad would have to carry me as I struggled and fought for air. Those times were terrifying. The simple act of breathing was, for me, a chore.

When I began speaking, I developed a severe stuttering problem. I often say that I talked like Mel Tillis, the country and western singer who has a speech impediment when he talks but who sings beautifully. Unfortunately, I never learned to sing, so I had to learn how to control my stuttering. I was not able to do that well, and whenever I became anxious or fearful, which was often, my stutter was quite pronounced. Being small in stature and a stutterer gave me very low self-esteem. Self-esteem is simply the opinion a person holds of himself. When it came time for me to begin school, my opinion of myself was not good. Immediately, I became the perfect target for bullies on the school grounds.

To top it off, when I was about seven, Bernice discovered a spot on the back of my head where no hair was growing. I told my mother but she didn't do anything about it for another week.

"It's nothing. It'll go away," she insisted.

When things did not improve, we went to the family doctor and I was diagnosed with ringworm. I contracted it from the cows on our farm. Ringworm is a fungus and was quite prevalent in the 1950s and 60s.

The remedy was very outdated by today's standards; it consisted of

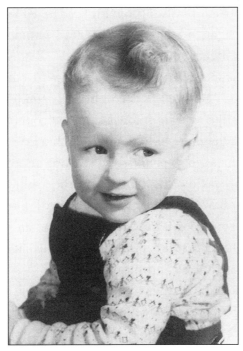

Me at age 2.

putting slices of potato on the affected area during the day to draw out the fungus. At night, we would bathe the area and peel off the scabs that had formed during the day and then drain off the accumulated fluid. I had to wear a head bandage to school, and the nightly ritual of bathing, peeling scabs, draining fluid and bandaging potato slices to my head went on for the better part of a year. I am laying claim to being the original "Mr. Potato Head," but as of yet have not received any royalties.

The potatoes did not do the job and the infection burrowed deeper into my skull. Bernice was looking at it one day and told Mom that it was getting worse. Had it broken through the skull and into my brain, it could have been fatal. Finally, my parents listened to her and they took me to a specialist in a larger city about 40 miles south with a more modern hospital.

The doctor looked at my scalp, put my head under a machine, turned on an ultraviolet light and the fungus was dead within five seconds.

"It will never bother you again," he said.

Can you imagine my relief?! I was overjoyed but also extremely angry that we hadn't gone to this doctor in the beginning. I had suffered needlessly for nearly a year from something that could have been cured in five seconds. Why did I have to go through all those tears when it could have been handled so painlessly? I couldn't believe it!

The infection was directly centered in the back of my head and today, I still don't have much hair growing there. I'm fortunate to have lots of hair that grows down the back of my head and covers the spot quite nicely. I'm lucky that it happened to me where it did.

Generally though, I was a panicky little boy.

My mother coped with my problems by screaming a lot. She always had a terrible anger problem and couldn't handle the stresses of her life. Somewhere inside her, too close to the surface, were wounds that the salt from a single tear of a little boy could inflame most painfully.

Mom would come into our bedroom at night and glare down with wide eyes that seemed so full of hatred. "Now, don't you get sick tonight, don't you get sick!" she would command angrily. Her side of the family couldn't handle the thought of sickness. It carried a stigma of weakness. I can still see her eyes and feel the malevolence as she put the fear into me not to get sick. It is hard to describe the look of those blazing eyes. If I could paint them, they would have flames of bright orange shooting out. My mother would get right in my face and command, "Don't you get sick tonight!"

Along with everything else I had going on, naturally, it didn't take long to develop all types of childhood diseases. I had them all: chickenpox, whooping cough, pneumonia and double pneumonia. It was a terrible time in my life.

Mom lived her whole life in or around Auburn and came from a family that had built successful lives for themselves. Her siblings had good jobs back in a day when one income was enough to raise a family and secure a comfortable retirement to enjoy the grandkids.

Her brother Aubrey bought a farm, raised and trained Clydesdales for show across North America and had contracts with Anheuser Busch. Her brother Stewart earned a master's degree, set up a successful education program in Kenya and when he returned, worked his way up through the education system and retired as Director of Education for Middlesex County in Ontario. Today, he runs a very successful consulting business.

She had a sister, Amy, and Aunt Amy's was "the place" for family gatherings of all kinds. Amy was a teacher and always had music playing in her home. A few years ago after her husband Huey had passed away, I dropped by unexpectedly one beautiful Lake Huron summer morning. The doors to her house were wide open and her favorite song, Elvis Presley's "I Don't Have a Wooden Heart," was blaring. She couldn't have known I was coming, and as I peered in I saw Aunt Amy sashaying dreamily across the kitchen floor, holding a broom, possibly dancing with the memory of her late husband.

As I said, my mother's side of the family was musically inclined and remains so today. Mom loved to play our piano. She could read music and as a teenager accompanied the rest of the Toll family orchestra; everybody in the family played one or more instruments. For most of her adult life, she played piano in church and Sunday school. When my kids visited, they begged her to play and she taught them simple ditties. Music seemed to furnish a welcome refuge from the anger that otherwise buffeted her life.

Her brother, my Uncle Stewart, was 18 years younger than my mother and she had to leave school to help raise him because of a medical condition that her mother suffered from. Not being able to complete her education was a frustration she carried throughout all of her days. Perhaps that is what lay under her outright demands that we never be ill. Something else my mother carried was the idea that money meant happiness, yet money was something she was not destined to have.

As a young man, my father was raised on a farm an hour's drive north of Auburn. When he was 15, my dad was working in the fields with his father who suddenly collapsed with a heart attack and passed away that night. My father and his older brother could not run the farm by themselves. My grandmother sold it the next year and thereafter, Dad and his brother made money by working out of their car shearing sheep. They ended up in Auburn where they got steady work as hired hands with local farmers.

Now a widow, Grandma McDougall, as I knew her, got a job as a housekeeper for another widower on a farm about 25 miles away. Since he willed her the farm when he passed away, I always suspected there was more than housekeeping provided. Every summer we spent a week at her farm with my cousins. Dad's brother Elmer had eight children and Bernice and I were envious of them because they had so many siblings to play with. They were envious of us because there were fewer siblings to share toys with and we probably had our own rooms. If they only knew. As the saying goes, "The grass is always greener on the other side of the fence. But you still have to cut it!" Grandma McDougall sold the farm and moved to another town about 20 miles from Auburn.

Once a month or so, we would drive to Grandma McDougall's house and I always enjoyed these trips. At some point Dad would say, "Come on, Allan, let's go for a walk." We would saunter down two blocks to a bowling alley and roll a few games while the women caught up on their news.

One year, we were visiting at Thanksgiving. My dad brought a "turkey lifter," essentially a stainless steel rack, which was just out on the market. He was very proud of his new gadget as he lifted the 25 pound, beautifully basted turkey out of the oven until his turkey lifter failed and the bird went spinning across the floor like a curling stone across the ice towards its target. Mom came to the rescue by emitting a scream that, fortunately, did not break any wine glasses.

A few years after my dad began working in Auburn, the farmer who employed him retired and had sold him the dairy farm. Throughout his life, my dad always loved people, but was never able to save money. He didn't fritter it away and he didn't drink; there simply was never much of it. Our poverty was another source of frustration for my mother. She took it out on Dad, my sister and me.

We were driving in the car one day when I was about 8, my dad, Grandma McDougall and my mother in front and me in back. Grandma had sold her inherited farm and my mother saw this as a way for our family finally to get ahead. Money was important to her and she was always looking for ways to ameliorate the shame of poverty. The money would do the family good, she asserted. Why not give half to her son, my dad, now? A conversation ensued that rapidly escalated into a furious tantrum on my mother's part. She was always a yeller and screamer but flying down our country highway at 50 miles an hour added a new dimension. After a good bit of fighting and hollering, my mom screamed that if my grandmother would not accede to her demands, she would throw herself out of the car and then made a grab for the door handle. I sat in the back seat, dumbstruck by what I was witnessing.

My grandmother, a very strong woman, ignored my mother's erratic behavior and did not give in to her demands. Not being so strong, the episode left me traumatized for many years.

My mother's outbursts could be spitefully destructive. One winter, to keep our lane open, Dad bought a plastic housing for his tractor that would allow him to use a snow blower to clear the snow. He and Mom argued about spending the money but Dad eventually bought it anyway. When my mother found out, she was outraged to the point that she took a pitchfork and tore holes through each of the plastic windows, rendering the housing useless. If Dad wanted to use the tractor, he had to do so with no protection from the howling winds. Still, he often preferred to be out there rather than indoors facing my mother's icy stare and her volatile temper.

My parents often argued heatedly. To stop my mother's screaming, my sister would hold me up as an infant in front of them. Upset by their acrimony, I would begin to scream and cry. After some time, my own cries would register with my mom that she was creating stress in the family and that sometimes calmed her down.

Those episodes I don't remember but I don't doubt my sister's account, based on what I saw later on. I would be in bed and hear loud voices and then my mother screaming on the other side of the wall. More than once I opened the door to their room to find my dad sheltered behind their dresser in the corner and my mother standing in front, yelling and punctuating each point of the debate with a wave of a large kitchen knife. She would turn her glare on me and warn, "Don't you ever let a word get out about what you just saw!"

From as early as I can remember, my mother used to tell me, "I'm a very unhappy woman. If you weren't here, if you hadn't been born, then I would be much happier and I wouldn't have to live with your father."

Given the age difference with my sister—Bernice is six years older than I—I suppose it is altogether possible that my arrival was not a planned one.

Paradoxically, I experienced separation anxiety. I feared that my parents would leave me whenever I went to Sunday school and used to plead with Mom and Dad, "I'll see you when I get home. Will you be here when I get home?" They both had to confirm that, yes, they would.

I had the same separation anxiety my first couple of years in elementary school. I was scared that they would not be there when I got home and I would have to fend for myself. As much as I think that's silly now, it was a big part of my early years.

A cousin reminds me that when I came to their house for a visit I would cry with the most lost, mournful wail. I might be okay for two or three days, but then my separation anxieties would hit and I would carry on until my mother drove out to get me, which normally sparked an angry tirade.

On our way to church. Dad, Mom, my sister Bernice and me.

Whenever I was mischievous, my dad would try to take my side and lessen my mom's wrath. "Listen, Marjorie," he would say, "don't punish Allan. He's been so asthmatic and sick all his life. Whenever he gets feeling good enough to get into some mischief, don't punish him. He is always so sick." My mother did not necessarily follow that advice.

Bernice often served as my protector, both at home and for the one year we were in the same schoolroom. In fact, she was the closest thing to a touchstone in my young life. Feeling rootless, I often grafted myself to her, desperate almost for any sort of positive emotional nourishment. Sometimes though, a sibling rivalry developed, mostly from my end.

My sister had frizzy hair, and on the farm we had burdocks that grew along fences or in corners of fields. When we walked by them they stuck to our clothes and that's how they pollinated. Once, she was outdoors studying and I didn't think that was a good thing because she received positive recognition for being studious. My mother thought that if she was studying then I should be studying, too. There wasn't much I hated more than studying.

I became upset with Bernice, and thought, "I'll get her. I'm going to mess up her day because she's messed up mine."

I went down to the chicken coop by the garden and collected a pile of burrs about the size of a soccer ball. She was lying on the grass studying, being the good little girl, when I snuck up from behind and mashed those burrs into her thick hair. Needless to say, that went down harder on me than it did on her. As frizzled as her hair was, so was my behind.

Bernice was always afraid that people were hiding under her bed. Every night before she went to sleep, she looked underneath it to see if the boogeyman was waiting there for her.

One morning, I was feeling mischievous, so while she was still sleeping, I got up and grabbed an old jacket, filled it full of pillowcases, old socks and underwear and stuck it under the bed. I left the elbow of the arm bent so that if she looked down she would see an elbow only, not the rest of the jacket. I positioned it just right then ran outside and banged on her window to wake her up. She saw me in the window, I put my best look of horror on my face and pointed under her bed. She looked at me and looked at the jacket and looked at me and looked at the jacket, so she knew it wasn't me. She fully suspected that there was a boogeyman under the bed because she could see his arm and was horrified.

Although it was fun for five minutes, here, too, things did not work out well for me after she ran out and told Mom. "Wait till your father comes in from the barn," was always a downer. Although my dad was soft and a really gentle man, he did get angry a couple of times, and rightfully so, but never said too much. He became more angry with me when I was sixteen, seventeen, eighteen with my drinking antics than anything I did as a youngster.

Whenever I did things that got on Mom's nerves, she would

threaten me with, "I'm taking you up to Mrs. Molden's and dropping you off!"

That meant she intended to take me to the home of a skinny old woman in the village who looked like a witch. She always wore a train engineer's cap and straight white hair fell out from under it, framing a long pointed nose and chin. She lived with her son, and in reality, was probably a very nice woman, but I never got the chance to find out. My mother would put me in the car when I misbehaved and drive to the front of Mrs. Molden's house. She would park, go around to my door and threaten to drop me off, telling me I'd have to live with them. The threat would freeze me and I'd beg her not to, anxiously promising to behave. These upsets were often followed by panic-induced asthma attacks.

Such were circumstances in the suffocating emotional atmosphere I breathed during my formative years. Outside, during the warmer months, Mother Earth was at her nurturing best; the fertile rolling hills, dairy cows lounging languidly in the fields, the warm sun pulling her bounty up to sustain all creation. Sometimes, sitting on our sun porch with Dad, I would catch a glimpse of the peace and contentment surrounding us. Eight inches behind the brick wall at my back, however, an erupting volcano was always just one mishap away. Both Dad and I did not just walk on eggshells, we walked on pullet eggshells, which are even more fragile.

BREAKING THROUGH

CHAPTER 3

No Solace in School

I'm always ready to learn,
although I do not always like being taught.
—Winston Churchill

THE CIRCUMSTANCES OF MY EARLY YEARS were not a recipe for confidence building. Picture a kid coming from a very poor family—my parents didn't even have electricity until the year I was born—who is asthmatic and so can't play with other kids during the years when sports are so important, who has a bad stuttering problem and who has to go to school with potato slices bandaged to his head. Could there be a more perfect target for schoolyard bullies?

The older boys would push me around and because of my shortness of breath I was never good in sports. I remember reading books about people who were good in sports but poor in the classroom and I also read books about people who were outstanding academically but who did not excel in sports. Well, I was poor in both. I was always the last one picked for baseball or soccer. The familiar refrain was, "Come on, McDougall, it's our turn to have you on the team today. We will probably lose."

It wasn't as though school was an escape from home. What was worse, my school was located only about an eighth of a mile from our farm, so it was always in sight as a constant reminder.

Union School Section #5 was the classic one room, red brick country schoolhouse. Fifty or so kids from the village and surrounding farms

Looking past our barn at the one-room schoolhouse I attended through Grade 8. The quonset hut was built much later.

attended from Grades 1 to 8, learning the rudiments of the "Three Rs." Most students would grow up and carry on the family farm or learn a blue collar trade in high school. There was a bell on top with a rope that hung down inside the library but I don't ever recall it being used. We were always summoned in from recess or noon hour by a handheld bell.

To one side of the schoolhouse, there was a soccer field and on the other was a baseball diamond with burlap potato bags for bases. Behind the school stood two teeter-totters set in cement alongside a swing set. There was also an area where we did track and field with a crude pit for the running broad jump and various other events. The schoolyard perimeter was ringed by trees and a chain-link fence fronted the highway so an absent minded kid couldn't chase a ball out onto the road.

Two steps led up to a formidable entrance. It was a big solid door and my sister told me that she was nervous walking to school because she worried about getting that big thing to open and if she failed, being stuck outside. It never occurred to her that she could simply turn around and walk home. Sometimes I wished that door would have become stuck for me so I could go home.

Once inside, our nostrils were filled with the smell of dustbane. That was a green chemical, sort of like kitty litter, that they used to spread on the wood floors after school to hold down the dust in the classroom while sweeping. Two of the Grade 8 students were paid fifty cents a week to sweep the school, clean the blackboard, clap the erasers and wipe the windows down. Straight ahead from the front door, steps led down into the basement. That is where the furnace and bathrooms were and where we sometimes played during recess on rainy days.

To the left and right, staircases ran up to the classroom. Halfway up was a landing and along the walls were shelves where we could put our lunch pails. Mine was a little tin lunch pail and it always had a cowboy like the Two Gun Kid or the Lone Ranger on it. It held a little thermos of milk and my sandwiches. At the top of the stairs was the cloak room. That's where we hung our winter gear, the coats, boots, mittens and toques, those knitted woolen beanies that Canadian kids have worn forever.

During the school day, the cloakroom was jammed to overflowing and as disorderly as fifty kids could make it. Sometimes, the odor of snow melt mixed with scorched woolen scarves and mittens hung too close to the heating register would drift through the building. Dealing with all this clothing was quite an ordeal and the Grades 7 and 8 students helped the younger kids get their boots on and laced up and their scarves on so they wouldn't freeze to death on the way home. There was no bus service in those years. Usually a parent or two came down from the village and filled their cars with students and took everyone home.

Off the cloak room, another door opened into the classroom, revealing eight or nine rows of old wrought iron desks bolted to the floor. The scarred, umber-colored desk tops didn't lift like they do now. A little shelf underneath furnished a four inch high storage area where you could slide in your books and pencils. The desks were progressively bigger to accommodate students in the higher grades. You could tell who had sat in a particular desk in previous years because of the names etched into the top with a jackknife.

At the front of the room was the blackboard and that is where Mr.

MacKay presided over the process of enlightening our little agrarian minds. Mr. MacKay was my teacher for most of my elementary schooling. He was a retired drill sergeant, a veteran of World War II, and he taught us more about life than he did the three Rs. He wasn't shy about using his drill sergeant's demeanor to restore order when things got out of hand, though I don't ever recall him using profanity.

When Mr. MacKay gave the math assignments, he wrote down five columns of figures for us to add with four numbers in each. The top four numbers were always six, four, seven and three. He would write down six, four, seven, and three and then write down other numbers below them. I used to watch that in amazement. It must have held some meaning for him. Above the blackboard stretching all the way across the front was the alphabet: big A, small a, big B, small b, in cursive script.

Between the fourth and fifth rows of desks was where the furnace register kept the place warm in winter. We used to break the erasers off our pencils and throw them down the register and soon the smell of burning rubber would fill the room much to our delight and Mr. MacKay's irritation.

A low stage ran across the front and on the right hand side was a piano turned at an angle. The stage was used during our Christmas concerts. We had a wonderful time at Christmas. A music teacher came in once a week to teach us music and singing. Beginning in November, we would prepare for that year's Christmas concert. There were plays, Christmas carols, skits and recitations. One year, I had a two-word part in the play, though I always sang in the choir as well. We hung burgundy curtains across the stage using wire and brass rings, and two students would open them simultaneously to reveal the entire student body singing or performing a Christmas play for the entertainment of our parents. The grand finale would be the arrival of Santa, one of the neighbors familiar to us all from his stance and gait, but also the whiskey on his breath.

On the left hand side of the classroom was a big wooden box. It held maps of the world that Mr. MacKay used for geography and history lessons. Each was on a spring loaded coil. There were maps of Canada, North America, Europe and other places and he used a black rubber tipped pointer to indicate whatever he was talking about at the time.

In the back of the room, four steps went up to a door which opened into the library and the shelves that held all our books. I wish I had some of them today. There were old readers from 1914 and others that the school board thought were beneficial. There were three little rooms in the library that could be divided off. There weren't any books on the top shelves because nobody could reach them. That's not to say the space wasn't used. We would climb the shelves and hide on top hugging our knees in a fetal position. When Mr. MacKay looked for missing kids, the library was where he checked first.

One time, my friend Freddie Hoogenboom and I were up there on the shelf, me next to the wall and Freddie in front. We were small enough for both of us to fit up there. Mr. MacKay came into the room asking who all was in the library. I was in a mischievous mood so I gave Freddie a little shove and he fell down past the four or five shelves of books and landed on the floor right in front of Mr. MacKay which took the attention away from me. I liked being under the radar.

In the middle of winter one year there was a terrible storm. The storms in that area were horrific some days because we were only ten miles from the lake and, though we didn't know it then, we were under the lake effect. When cold winds blow across the relatively warmer water, huge amounts of water vapor are picked up and deposited on the leeward shores. To us it was just a snow storm. I remember snow banks so high we could touch the phone lines that ran along the highway.

I trudged off to school one morning with my parka, big boots and toque. I arrived about ten till nine and, hearing the door slam, one of the kids came downstairs. It was Mr. MacKay's son, John, who said, "Oh, I'm so sorry you came. My dad said if no one else shows up we're canceling school today."

John ran back upstairs and I stood by the door passing the message to other students who were coming in late. A conspiracy formed with unanimous agreement to take a school day off, so we hid. A couple went under the stairs leading into the basement. Others hid in the hot water room beside the girls' washroom. There were other little rooms in the basement and several more hid in there. We had a big snow fort in one corner of the schoolyard and I hid in there where it was freezing. Funny, it was always too cold to walk to school but it was never too cold when there was a school day off to go outside and play.

School was dismissed about ten o'clock and we came out of our hiding places. We went home and played outside and had a great day. Unfortunately, some of the students went to the general store in the village and the old storekeeper, Mr. Phillips, asked, "How come you're home from school? It's not lunchtime."

One student bragged about how they had fooled Mr. MacKay. Well, when Mr. MacKay came to the store to buy his pipe tobacco, he got a lot more than his pipe filled because the next day, when we went to school thinking we had pulled the wool over his eyes, we didn't see recess for at least a month. "Put that in your pipe and smoke it, kids," I am sure he was thinking.

Hanging above the blackboard where the maps were kept, Mr. MacKay kept his strap, a menacing 15 inch strip of wire-reinforced leather. Mr. MacKay may not have used profanity but he did use the strap. Many of us used to get the strap. I never did. I should have but I always got away with stuff. I like to think it was because I was smarter than the other kids or sneakier, but for whatever reason I avoided it. Whenever Mr. MacKay was upset with us or wanted to get our attention, he would take it over to the piano and whack it so hard the strings reverberated loudly. Mr. MacKay also hollered a lot. My parents would be working out in the garden when I came home from school and they would say, "Mr. MacKay was very upset today."

"Why? How do you know?" I would ask.

"We could hear him all the way up here."

A regularly scheduled school day off happened each spring on Arbor Day, which we all looked forward to because it was a day off from school. That's the day we went out and cleaned up the school yard and washed the windows. We would finish by noon and after lunch, go on a hike through the forest, or bush as we called it, down by the river or to a farm to learn something. It was a great day, Arbor Day.

That's a snapshot of that wonderful one room school. It's still standing today. The school closed due to urbanization but it is still used today for other purposes. Every time I go back to my village I think of it fondly. That goes to show that pleasant memories never seem to dull even as the painful ones fade from memory or become buried. Though I had fun in that school and even made some lifelong friends there, there was the teasing and the bullying and my indifference to my studies.

But above all, there was Oral Composition Day.

BREAKING THROUGH

CHAPTER 4

SHAKING LIKE A LEAF

All experience is an arch to build on.
–HENRY BROOKS ADAMS

OF THE MANY UNPLEASANT ASPECTS TO SCHOOL, and there were many, the worst by far was Oral Composition Day. It was the main reason I hated Labor Day because its arrival signaled the end of summer, the beginning of school and six weeks of dread leading up to my annual humiliation.

Oral composition was the simple exercise of teaching students to address a group, which while uncomfortable for many, was terrifying for me, year after year. Each student had to prepare a short talk on a subject of their choosing, learn it and then recite it in front of the class.

Each year, I had my topic memorized, and went over it with my mother a week before the appointed day. It was the biography of Abraham Lincoln. Why I chose that, I don't know but I would swear to her that I would do it, that I'd finish it and make her and Dad proud.

To this day, I still think about Oral Composition Day and can still smell the school. I can smell the chalkboard. I can smell the dust bane and see the sun rays spilling across the desks through the big old windows. I was convinced that the eyes of 51 other students were boring straight through me as I made my way to the front of the class. I was so fearful. When I stuttered, I could hear two or three people laugh, but it

45

sounded like the whole school was roaring hysterically at my expense.

Knees shaking, stomach in a knot, I would begin, "M--M--Mr. McK--K--K--Kay and f--f--f--fellow s--s--s--students, the t--t--t--topic I have ch--ch--ch--ch--chosen i--i--i--i--is . . ." followed by my tears. I would stand in front of the class, the entire school, and cry. Finally, Mr. MacKay would tell me to sit down and I would slink back to my desk, humiliated, the other kids' laughter burning my ears.

Each year after my mortifying day had ended, I would dawdle home dragging my feet, kicking stones along the shoulder of the road, because I knew I had disappointed not only Mom and Dad but also myself.

I would think about Oral Composition Day for weeks leading up to it, that day of fear and humiliation bearing inexorably down on me to further flatten the image I had of myself. As a result, I hated school, just detested being there. I saw no value in it whatsoever.

Fast-forward to 2005 and the homecoming we had for the centennial of our village. I was sitting in the Auburn Hall at a reunion for students of USS #5. I was in a much different place than many years ago. One of my fellow alumni came over and said, "You know, Allan, we want to do a trivia contest. One of the questions is 'Who used to stand up at the front of the school and cry every time he gave his oral composition? Who in this last year just graduated with a Master of Science of Labor Administration degree from the University of Massachusetts? And who, more importantly, teaches public speaking seminars across North America?' We wanted to have that as a trivia question."

Judy, who was a year ahead of me, then added, "You know, Allan, I just want you to know when you got up to speak those many years ago, we were all hoping inside that you would do it. Our hearts would stop. There were always one or two of the bullies who used to laugh at you, however. We always wanted you to finish your speech."

What a wonderful healing of those moments 40 years before when I would stand there hating life, hating myself and hating everything around me in that one-room school. From crying in front of everybody as an underweight, asthmatic, ringworm-infested kid to where I am today teaching public speaking around North America has been an incredible journey.

I remember another time on the school grounds. The three or four bullies who made my life miserable were away on a bus trip. I was playing soccer at lunchtime and scored a goal. That was unheard of. Afterwards, as we climbed the stairs back to class after recess, the kids were saying, "Oh my goodness, Allan, you really played well today. What a great game you had."

I had never heard those words of encouragement in my life before, either at home or in school. I remember that day. Those positive episodes, unfortunately, were rare.

In Grade 1, the depth of my anxiety was such that when I put my assignment book on top of the pile at the end of the school day, if it wasn't on top the next morning I would panic and begin to cry. Bernice would dig my book out of the pile and I would calm down, but never all the way. Some level of apprehension was my constant companion.

Breaking Through

CHAPTER 5

DEALING WITH IT

Three grand essentials to happiness in this life are something to do,
something to love, and something to hope for.
–JOSEPH ADDISON

GROWING UP ON A FARM IN THOSE DAYS was tough because all the farm boys worked on the farm with their fathers and established some measure of recognition and self-worth. With my asthma, I was more or less housebound and therefore was always looked on as a wimpish boy. I know today that there are books and movies out called, "Diary of a Wimpy Kid." They came about 50 years too late for me because that was my nickname at school, courtesy of the kids who bullied me. They called me "Wimpy." My dad tried to ease the sting by saying that it was because of a baseball player of the day named Wimpy Stephenson and that it was a good nickname to have. That's not how the kids at school meant it.

Yet, even the tiniest seed will somehow find its way through a crack in the concrete. Even the most windblown spore will cling to a rock and make the best of it.

Out of my very, very humble beginnings I developed my own coping skills.

My first, perhaps, was imagination. I used it as an escape hatch into a world of my own creation. School was terrible and home was worse. The universe of thought afforded me a measure of real, if temporary, relief. We didn't have television at the time, which I viewed was one more curse upon me. Today, I see it was a blessing because I used my imagination, and I was forced to read and spell and do the Three Rs. I received all of that from reading books. I escaped by reading cowboy and western books and any other books that I could obtain from the county library. I have heard that most kids who do badly in school do not read well and even in that I was different. I loved reading, yet the constant threatening environment of the school ground and classroom virtually guaranteed that I would detest anything to do with either. So, reading became a light that I hid under a bushel.

Life at home was still not good, but there were occasional moments of enjoyment.

On winter nights, the family would sit around the kitchen table and play cards or board games after dinner. I looked forward to those, in spite of my fear of my mother's anger, which was never far off. Mom and Bernice would be partners against Dad and me and we would play Rummy or Lost Heir, which was an old card game that may not even be around anymore. At some point, Dad would have to leave for chores in the barn. I always felt guilty that I was never able to help him very much because of my asthma.

When I was about 7, I got a miniature hockey rink with players that spun around when you turned handles. Every Sunday afternoon after church, the farmer from across the road, Everett Taylor, came over and he and I would test our hockey skills on the kitchen table. He would be the Montreal Canadiens and I was the Toronto Maple Leafs and we had many a fun afternoon playing that hockey game.

We didn't have a TV until I was about 14, hence the after-dinner card games. My grandmother and grandfather did have TV, however. We would visit them in the village on Sunday nights to watch the *Ed Sullivan Show* at 8:00 p.m. and then *Bonanza* at 9:00. I remember my grandfather watching *Don Messer's Jubilee* show starring the famous Canadian Maritime fiddle player.

Another escape was hot rods, and my passion for them has stuck with me throughout all the years of my life. The county highway ran past our farm into the little village of Auburn. In the village was a garage with a body shop. One of the local boys worked in the body shop, and he had built a hot rod from a 1932 Ford. I could hear him driving from the village down the road that ran past our farm. When I heard that hot rod bombing our way, I would run as fast as my little legs and shortness of breath could carry me down to our roadside gate. He would turn his hot rod around on the first stretch of level road outside of Auburn that, luckily for me, ran right in front of our farm. He'd pause for a moment gunning the engine, give me, ME!, a thumbs up and then take off like a rocket back toward town and do the quarter mile in this old car. Someone, probably him, had painted lines across the road to mark the distance.

I stood at the gate, my hands white-knuckling the wires with excitement, mesmerized by the noise, the power and the speed as he vanished into the distance. I wished with everything I could muster that someday I could be like him. In later years, I would repaint those same lines and burn down the track in my dad's car. Something about the experience seemed so out of the ordinary in this poor farming community. This man and his hot rod seemed, like me, different from everything around. Whereas I viewed my differences as purely negative, I saw the contrast he presented as absolutely positive. It was as if he were trying to shatter the dull monotony of farm life, shake the cows and the people out of the somnambulant condition of their lives. I don't know about anyone else, but it sure woke me up.

It gave me a sense of rebelliousness. He was Auburn's version of the Fonz from *Happy Days*. He represented something that I had never experienced in my short, unhappy life. I fell in love with the automobile. I fell in love with hot rods. I fell in love with speed, adventure, and from then on I lived vicariously through his actions.

The kindling of this flame took me into the world of soapbox racers. We used our imaginations to build our toys. I had this old flour bin out of a cupboard from our pantry. It was shaped so that I could put my legs in. I nailed it to a plank six feet long and two feet wide and affixed a movable cross member to the front. I put a set of wagon wheels on the front and back, affixed a length of twine to the front to steer with and I was set to go. I tore down the hills on the farm on the front lawn with my little race car. It was heavy, slow, cumbersome and ugly, but to me it was a sleek Indy racer.

One year for Christmas, my parents gave me a plastic football helmet, green with number 31 on the sides. From then on, my cars always had 31 scrawled in paint or crayon somewhere on the car. Again and again, I would fly down the hill, pulling on the front axle to steer the car. Since I didn't have brakes, I usually ended up tangled in the fence or hitting a post. More often than not a wheel would fall off on a run and I would have to find a rusty nail to put the wheel back on the little axle.

Amidst all the rocks and shoals of my life, here was a taste of freedom. Speed, daring and heading down the hill. For many years that was a metaphor for my life.

Eventually, my flour bin and little wheels no longer furnished the adrenaline rush I needed. I became accustomed to the speed and tired of putting the wheels back on. One night, Dad said, "I'm going to help you build a better soapbox." That was a great night for me. I spent the entire evening in the garage with my dad, who usually occupied most of his hours in the barn where I could not go. He spent much of his time there just to be away from the house and the anger of my mother.

Our garage was a big old drive-in shed. It housed the tractor and the farm implements, and the dirt floor smelled of oil, grease and brake fluid. I still love that smell when I go into old garages or service stations on the county highways off the interstate.

Dad found some different wheels and we put together a nice looking soap box racer. Then he said, "How would you like to have an actual steering wheel?" Nobody in those days had a steering wheel on their soapbox racers.

We drove to the next village where my dad's cousin lived. His cousin was a mechanical genius. He was great at souping up engines, motorcycles and hot rods. Sadly though, he had an alcohol problem and his drinking eventually cost him not only his job but his family as well. That night though, everything was wonderful.

"Sure," he said, "I can help the young lad," and he put a steering wheel on my cart. It was just like the steering wheel of a 1923 Ford Model T Bucket hot rod, which runs straight up and down. Then he welded some plates underneath and installed cables running to the axle. It was a lovely, lovely soapbox. Of course, I painted number 31 on the side as well as my new car's name, "The Flaming Coffin." Still, in the larger reality of farm life, my new racer was little more than a diversion.

Because we always struggled financially, Dad had to take other jobs to supplement our income. One of these was driving other farmers' pigs to market every Wednesday afternoon. When he returned home at supper time, he would have a 10 cent bag of Hostess potato chips for me. Inside, the bag included a plastic prize the size of a silver dollar that had a picture of a classic car in the center. I was so excited to rip that bag open and dig out the prize. I still have a couple of these tokens of my childhood and even today when I open a bag of chips I revisit those wonderful memories.

Generally, it was a lonelier existence out on the farm than in the village. Kids from the village would come down to play sometimes but I always thought they had a much better time of it in Auburn. They had friends nearby and more things to do such as swimming or fishing. In the village, a neighbor would be 100 feet away. On the farm, it was a bike ride away.

A hay loft though, was not something they had, so when kids came down we often played there. We built tunnels in the haymow and picked up bales and laid them cross ways over the tunnel. These tunnels were maybe two feet wide and eighteen inches high and we ran them all over the hay loft. We had little forts at either end of the barn, carved ourselves wooden guns and indulged our fantasies. Those were fun battles.

One time, we built a monstrous hay silo. It was 12 feet deep and 6 feet on each side. We broke open some bales and put loose hay in the bottom. We had a knotted inch-thick rope running down into this big hole. We covered the top with old boards and pieces of rotten wood and put loose hay over that. Then we built tunnels entering the silo at different levels from different sides. The kids from the village and I really enjoyed it.

One night soon afterwards, I was going to bed and my mother came for me, saying, "Your dad wants to talk to you."

I went out to the kitchen and Dad was standing there covered with hay all over his head and clothes with dust on his glasses. He had climbed into the mow to get hay to feed the cattle and stepped on these rotten barn boards. He fell straight down about twelve feet in the dark, probably thinking he was in a hole 500 feet deep. He was scared to light a match to find out where the hell he was with all that dry hay around. He finally found the rope and climbed out, and told me in no uncertain terms that I was never again to build a hut in the barn upstairs for the rest of my natural life.

Another time my friend Wayne Arthur came down to the farm to play. Dad was sweating over the barn chores when Wayne came up to him and asked shyly, "Mr. McDougall, how do you train all these cows to poop in one big pile outside the barn? We have been trying to train our dog."

My dad grinned and said, "I have asked the same question over and over myself. Perhaps when you get your dog trained you can come back here and tell me your secret. In the meantime, I will continue to shovel the manure behind each cow, put it into a wheelbarrow and haul it outside."

"Wow," said Wayne, "that is a lot of work, Mr. McDougall."

"Yes, it certainly is," said my dad.

BREAKING THROUGH

CHAPTER 6

BOY IN A BUBBLE

A thousand eyes, but none with correct vision.
—ISACHER HURWITZ

AT PLANTING AND HARVEST TIMES, farmers are chained to their land. The rest of the year they have some freedom from the demands of the land. On the other hand, a dairy farmer is chained to his cows who must be milked twice a day, every day all year long. My dad's dairy had 43 cows and at any one time 35 or so were being milked. The others were calving or nursing their newborns.

Sometimes, with the help of my dad or our dog Lucky, I would take the tractor to round them up and head them back at milking time. When Dad wasn't with me, I would make a figure 8 racetrack in the fields to race the tractor around.

Back at the barn, Dad squatted on his stool, grabbed a pair of teats, squeezed and pulled, emptying another udder into the bucket. He emptied the bucket into a milk can that weighed 80 pounds when full. He hammered a lid on the can and moved to the next cow. Squat, grab, pull, empty, squat, grab, pull, empty, 35 cows, twice a day, every day, year after year. We didn't have a milking machine; he did it all by hand. If you didn't milk them they dumped their milk in the fields and that meant less money, which was already scarce.

After milking was done, Dad hefted each can outside to a trough near the lane that was filled with cold water. The next morning at 7:00

Bernice and me with one of the calves in front of the barn.

a.m., the milk truck drove through the gate and the burly driver lifted the cans into the back like they were so many baskets of flowers. That milk was our primary source of income. Years later, Dad purchased two automatic milking machines, which helped ease his workload.

Dad also raised pigs and sold them at the market every second week. Every so often when a sow was coming in, that is, giving birth, he would spend the night delivering piglets. Boars or sows will eat their young, so Dad would have to get the newborns safely into another pen.

For our own consumption, we had chickens that gave us eggs and I remember Dad winding up on the chicken house roof one day when our bull got out of his pen and chased him. We always had large vegetable gardens where I snacked on raw onions, tomatoes and lettuce seasoned with dirt. Even today, I sometimes make a lettuce leaf sandwich—lettuce, butter and salt on bread. They are still tasty, however, the memories sprinkled on them are even more delicious to my palate.

We also had a big pony named Hazy that a neighbor bought for his daughter but gave to us when the animal would not take a saddle. Dad tried, too, but with similar results; we rode him bareback. Hazy was ornery so he was outfitted with a special bit with wire wound around it that jabbed the inside of his mouth when we needed to rein him in, which was often. Once, when I was about 12, Hazy stopped but I didn't and ended up in a thistle bush. Dad made me dust myself off and get back on.

Unfortunately, that was about the extent of my participation around the farm. My asthma prevented me from helping out in the barn. Dust from crops or animals would trigger an attack. I could never work in the barn where he really needed me to do the milking and chores. I wanted to help and always regretted that I couldn't.

Dad would be milking the cows, but I had to be inside the house reading or listening to the Lone Ranger on our old radio that sat on a table near the stove.

The stirring sounds of the William Tell Overture, the galloping hoofs thundering ever nearer and the powerful voice, "A fiery horse with a speed of light, a cloud of dust, and a hearty 'Hi-Ho, Silver!'" set the stage for me to experience the power of words decades later.

At that age though, I had to content myself to peering out the window wistfully, watching Dad, wanting to be out helping him but knowing that it would trigger an asthma attack. It was a life and death conflict playing out in a little boy's mind. Life was being in the barn helping my dad, being a man. Death was struggling to get air into my lungs. Panic, fear, suffocating—death won out as it so often did in those days.

There was another village about six miles down the road from Auburn called Blyth. It had a population of around 800-900, a few little restaurants and some shopping. It was a big night to go to Blyth on a Friday or Saturday to pick up things we couldn't buy in Auburn. Auburn had a general store where rubber boots and overalls shared shelf space with the groceries. It also had dry goods and a few kids' toys all under the one roof.

One thing that Auburn had that Blyth didn't was its own weather station. At the entrance to the village, a board stood in a flower bed from which hung a rock at the end of a string. Lettered on the board was the following: "If the rock is warm, it's a hot day. If the rock is wet, it's raining. If the rock is white, it's snowing. If the rock is waving, it's windy. And if the rock is missing, run like hell, there's a tornado!"

Something more common in the 1950s and 60s that we don't often see today is community cooperation of work. Along the Auburn/Blyth road, it was all farmers. Every summer we would do our own haying individually. Then Dad bought a hay baler in partnership with one of the neighbors, and farmers would help each other with their haying.

Threshing the grain was done very differently in those days. There weren't any combines for the threshing machine. So, the dozen or so farmers along that Auburn/Blyth road would work together to bring in the harvest. My brother-in-law's family owned a threshing machine and they would charge so much a day to come in and do the threshing on each farm. All the farmers helping out would come in for lunch and when they were at our place, my mother would have the kitchen table piled with food. Her neighbors would help and my grandmother would come down to help cook. They would make six or seven fruit pies and big roasts of beef and pork, chickens, vegetables and potatoes. There were mounds and mounds of food for the farmers at their noontime meal.

To improve his barn, my dad installed an eight foot high stone and cement foundation. This was another instance of the community pulling together for a neighbor's benefit. For the barn raising, all the farmers in the community came to pitch in.

Sometimes hay would spontaneously catch fire in a barn from the dampness and the heat. Layering salt on the bales would help if the

The entire community came to help my dad raise the barn and install a new foundation. Dad is fourth from the right in the front row, with the bill of his cap raised. My Uncle Aubrey is just to the left of Dad. At the far left is my youthful-looking grandfather, Fred Toll.

hay was "heating." When a fire did start, if you could remove the bales quickly enough you could prevent it from spreading. Everyone came during emergencies like that to help whoever needed it. We don't see that anymore. We see a lot more corporate farms. The days of the small farmer are fading fast into history.

My condition prevented participation as much as I would have liked. Fortunately, hay did not trigger asthma attacks, so I was able to help somewhat in the fields at haying and harvest time. One of the few times I would feel some self-worth was when my dad would come to school and take me from class to help him hay or help with the harvest or to spread manure. On those days I really felt like a man. I felt proud, like I belonged. I felt some positive reinforcement when Dad would come to school and say, "Allan, I need you for the rest of the day to work on the farm."

To me, this pathetic little boy, it was an amazing vote of confidence. Any time I got to go home and miss half a day of school, I felt important. Dad would usually have me spread manure from the piles outside of the barn. I especially enjoyed the times when I had to spread manure on the five-acre field that was directly across from the school on a hot day when the wind was blowing in that direction. As I spread the waste matter, I could look over to the place that I hated and see Mr. MacKay closing the windows because I was disrupting class with the smell of fresh manure.

My mother used to come and take me out of school occasionally at the end of the month. Grandfather had 100 acres of wild bush called the Wild Hundred. It was majorly swampland, and it is still not settled today. It was just a 100 acres of swamps and quicksand.

Davy Gwyn was a tenant on my grandfather's Wild Hundred. An old shack stood there where Davy and his family lived. Davy had a couple of daughters and a couple of older boys. They were dirt poor. Davy was a veteran from World War II and they came from England after the war.

Davy, like so many others around Auburn, had an issue with drinking. He was a bootlegger and he never wanted to pay my grandfather the $35 a month rent because he was always broke. My grandfather was a soft soul and he'd take my mother with him to collect the rent because Mom was a very businesslike, no nonsense person with a flamethrower temper. Anytime Mom was nervous about collecting the rent money from Davy, she'd bring me. She was afraid that Davy would shoot her and bury her in the swamp, but that if I came along he might not.

The three of us used to trek back to Davy Gwyn's. I would be sitting in the backseat terrified of these hill people. I got to know them later in life and they were great folks. I am not sure he was a good businessman though. He would tell Dad, "I sell my beer three for a dollar, but my friends can buy it for 35 cents apiece." It didn't pay to be a friend.

Imagine driving up this big old gravel road through the swamps. People had gone missing in Grandpa's Wild Hundred. Over the years, folks had gotten lost in there and never came out. Stories and stereotypes of a swampland person abounded, and to me, they were frightening.

Davy used to kill skunks, skin them and hang them on the walls to dry. He was also a raccoon hunter. He'd skin the coons and sell the hides to make coonskin caps.

His boys were always there wearing nothing but T-shirts and underwear. They were around 12 or 13, scrawny kids, and smoking cigarettes. My mother said it was like traveling back into time even at that period.

Mom would begin screaming at Davy for the rent and Davy would scream back. It was quite unnerving for me. I was always scared that he would grab his gun and shoot my mother, my grandpa and then me, in that order. Truth be told, the one day I preferred to be in school was rent collection day.

I was always glad to get out of there and back to our farm. Although I couldn't be in the lower part of the barn, I could work upstairs in the haymow and could help with harvesting and taking in the hay. I always went overboard to do as much as I could to make my father proud. I know he was proud of me, even though we never expressed much in terms of endearment.

One day I was up in the hayloft and hay bales started coming in. I was hauling the hay in—85, 90 pound bales. It would be 100, 105 degrees up in the haymow. The bales came in off the elevator, situated beside the hay wagon, which lifted them up to the door in the hayloft. The door would be removed and the bales would tumble through the opening. Then, using big steel hooks with handles we would drag the bales across the floor and stack them in rows.

Some barns are 18 to 20 feet high and the haymows are 100 feet long by 60 feet wide, so we could stack lots hay in there, enough to feed the livestock for the whole winter.

As I continued to work this one hot day, I wanted to show my dad and neighbors, but moreso myself, that I could be of value around the farm. I jammed my hook into this bale and started to drag it across the loft. Halfway over, my leg slipped into a hole between four bales. I lost my balance and fell. My head jerked forward and I hit my mouth on the steel hook and broke a chip off my front tooth.

As I went up to the house to show my mother what had happened, the pain in my mouth paled in comparison to the prospect of what her reaction would be. Dad did not accompany me, since he was as afraid of Mom as I was. She was in the kitchen preparing meals for the other farmers who were helping us with the hay. Her basic coping mechanism was to let forth with a piercing scream whenever she was hit with something stressful. I'm not sure what it did for her but for me, it certainly made me think that I had done something terribly wrong.

This was before healthcare came to Canada and we had no dental coverage. So, we went to a dentist in a little town about ten miles away, which normally we could never afford. He squeezed a silver cap on my tooth and we went home. We couldn't afford anything more.

Behind our church in the village, there was a large old livery barn that once housed horses and buggies for the congregation during church services years before.

Of course, it wasn't being used anymore. There was a young minister at our church who brought in new ideas. He formed a Boy Scout troop and then decided to flood this old barn floor and make it our skating rink for the winter.

There were two holes in the back end of the barn that had been used to shovel out manure. Both were 4' x 4,' and at floor level.

The speed skaters and hockey players would impress us by starting off at the front of the ice, skate down as fast as they could, dive through the holes and land in a snow bank outside. It looked like fun but it was probably a good thing I couldn't do it physically; chances are I probably would have hit my head. No helmets in those days. It was called the old church shed and that's where we spent time on weekends skating.

My sister bought a pair of Bauer ice skates for me at Christmas when I was in seventh grade. I thought I had the world by the tail even though I couldn't skate well. The cold would affect my asthma. I had weak ankles and they turned in constantly. Still, it was nice to have new skates; they helped me feel that I belonged.

Another year, my dad bought a hockey stick for me. I think he wanted me to be more athletically inclined and I feel sometimes that I probably disappointed him because of my inability at sports. We bought a black and white television set when I was 14 and he and I would watch Hockey Night in Canada together on Saturday evenings. With the original six hockey teams, the Toronto and Montreal rivalry was exciting.

It wasn't until the mid-1960s that universal health care came to all Canadians. Before then, folk remedies played their part in rural communities like ours, for example, the sliced potato remedy used on my ringworm.

One of the old remedies for whooping cough and pneumonia, both of which I had at one time or another, was the mustard plaster. You mixed dry mustard and flour with water to make a paste. You put the paste on a piece of flannel, folded it about a foot square and put in the oven to heat it up. Then you placed it on your chest when you went to bed at night.

I asked Bernice what was the magic of that and she said the fumes from the mustard would get into your chest and loosen up the mucus in your lungs. I said to myself, "No wonder I didn't have that many boyhood friends—I probably smelled like an old hot dog in school with mustard aroma all around me."

Another remedy was goose grease. My mother would get it from the neighbors who raised geese that were slaughtered around Thanksgiving and Christmas. We would smear goose grease on our feet and then pull on a pair of socks at night and this was supposed to keep us from catching a cold. With the mustard plaster on my chest and the goose grease on my feet, I looked and smelled like a shish kabob.

Onions by themselves would help with a cold. The remedy made use of a Spanish onion, or a white onion. A big onion from the garden, not a scallion but a good sized onion, was heated in the oven and then put into a pouch and placed onto the chest. The juices would soak into the skin and help relieve the cold and congestion. It really worked.

My dad would go to the store and pick up a little box of sulphur. When he threw a few particles of sulphur on the hot stove, a sea of blue flames would shoot across the stove and that was supposed to take the germs out of the air in our old farm house.

Bernice used to get earaches often, and what Dad would do is take a cigarette, inhale a mouthful of tobacco smoke and then gently blow it into her ear. It seemed to soothe the earache. I don't know if it was the heat or the chemicals in the smoke.

If I had a splinter in my finger and couldn't get it out, my mother would make a bread and milk poultice. She'd cut a piece off an old flannelette blanket and then put a mixture of milk and bread on it, heat it up in the oven and put that on my finger. The next morning, or within a very few hours, the splinter would be out of my finger. The finger would be all wrinkly like a prune but the splinter and the blood poison were gone.

Door to door salesmen would come around, from the Watkins company or the Raleigh company, peddling salves, herbs and medicines to farmers. I still buy Watkins pepper today.

We couldn't afford most things other kids had such as bicycles and skates. I remember collection agencies coming out to the farm to make Dad pay our medical bills. Mom had been hospitalized numerous times due to emotional issues. It's amazing to me that people fight the idea of having universal healthcare. I'd fight tooth and nail to keep the healthcare system we have in Canada. It was a godsend to our family.

It was about this time that I developed another method of coping with my own stresses—cigarettes.

I was in Grade 7 when I smoked my first cigarette. It doesn't make any sense to have asthma and start smoking, but I did. Maybe I was rebelling in my own way. I just wanted to try something different and I loved it.

My best friend at the time was Freddie Hoogenboom and he lived on the next farm. One day, Freddie and I discovered the magic of smoking. His family had come over from Holland. He had three brothers, John, Leo and Benny, and a sister named Joanne. Freddie was the youngest and I was the youngest in my family.

All Freddie's brothers and his parents smoked, so the accessibility to cigarettes was there for us. He gave me a cigarette, and I remember holding that long white tube with the colored stripes running the length of it. It was a Peter Jackson cigarette, a Canadian brand. I carefully stashed it in a safe place for later use.

Back home, I went into our big garage and climbed into the rafters and sat on a big 12" x 12" beam where I could look out a crack and see the house and the barn. Sitting up on that beam in that dusty old garage with those wonderful smells of oil and grease and brake fluid, I lit up my first cigarette. A little boy with asthma, feet dangling over the beam smoking his first Peter Jackson cigarette. It took three matches to light it, and when I sucked in my first drag of nicotine, I was so dizzy that I thought I would fall off that beam, but it became a milestone for me. I had moved onto another level.

As I reflect back, smoking my first cigarette indicated how my coping skills were beginning to lead me down the wrong path. Who would imagine that a boy who had asthma, who had even died once and had to be brought back by a doctor with a shot of adrenaline to the heart with a 50/50 chance of making it, would sit there and smoke a cigarette. Maybe I was acting out some sort of death wish. Maybe I just unconsciously didn't want to live anymore.

Maybe, just maybe, this was a way out of the bubble of my small, sickly, suffocating, cowed life.

CHAPTER 7

ONE DEMON FINALLY SLAIN

When you say yes to a risk and you go to the edge of a cliff and jump off,
you may not know where you're going to land,
but you grow wings on the way down.
–ANONYMOUS

IN MY LAST YEAR OF ELEMENTARY SCHOOL, we all had bicycles. Mine, of course, was an old wreck with balloon tires, handlebars like a longhorn steer and a rock hard seat. My parents bought it at an auction. The other kids had three-speed racers with narrow racing wheels and tires. Theirs were lovely bicycles but I had this big old clunker, which was another example of being poor in a community that was finally beginning to see more money coming in from the postwar industrial boom. I had fun clothespinning a piece of cardboard to the rear fender, which made an "engine" sound as it "thwapped" the spokes as I pedaled.

With their lighter bikes, the other kids could pop wheelies. Of course, I thought I could, too. One day, riding into the village I practiced heaving back on the handlebars and physically lifting the front wheel off the ground, hence a wheelie. On one such occasion, actually, the final time I ever tried it, the wheel came out of the forks and when the forks hit the pavement the bike stopped dead. As the pain settled in, my passion for wheelies left, never to return.

In Grade 8, my last year before high school, I still had asthma. I still stuttered, but less often, usually only when I was nervous or scared. The ringworm, at least, had cleared up and I could grow my hair longer to hide the scars. I still had the silver cap on my tooth which marred my smile but in some way my self-image had grown in some small measure. Perhaps it was what smoking represented for me.

Another one of my escapes as a young boy was drawing. I drew cars all the time, wishing for hot rods and motorcycles and to be like that Fonzi-type guy who roared his '32 Ford up and down the highway. His hot rod had no doors, just had a floor and half a body with a big motor that created much noise and scared people. That machine drew me into living on the edge and aspiring to a different life than I had known. Smoking became a token of an image that I longed for. I was dizzy and coughing, my eyes watered, but for the first time I was living a dream of my own making.

Smoking didn't help me, however, with the yearly torture of oral composition. When I entered Grade 8, Mr. MacKay had decided to teach for a few years at another school in a city several hours north of Auburn.

Our new teacher was Mrs. Bishop. She came in from a city east of us, and on the first day of school she said that she didn't believe in giving the strap to students who misbehaved. She believed in talking problems out and that was music to the ears of us dairy farm and village kids. That gave us all a little feeling of hope. We thought she would to be a new teacher with innovative ideas.

About two or three weeks into the school year, I was slouched down at my desk and Mrs. Bishop told me to sit up straight. I complied but after a while slouched down again. Mrs. Bishop noticed and evidently thought her point needed to be made a little more firmly. She came up behind me with one of those old 12-inch rulers that had a steel strip along the edge for cutting paper. She took that ruler and, without my suspecting it, gave me a hard whack across the side of my neck. The steel strip cut into my skin and it started to bleed quite heavily. She looked at it and ordered me downstairs to the restroom to clean up. I did so, but instead of returning to class, I hopped on my bicycle and rode home.

The prospect of facing my mother gave me second thoughts as I peddled up our lane. She likely would blame me. I heard her voice in my head, "It must have been your fault. You didn't have your homework done. What did you do to deserve it?!" I considered turning the bike around and pedaling back to school.

Dad came to my defense though. He saw me riding home early and knew that wasn't like me. I always stuck it out from the beginning to the end of the day despite my distaste for the place. He came up to the house from the barn and saw that my neck was bleeding.

I didn't get stitches, though I probably should have had some; as I said, we didn't go to the doctor unless we were at death's door. We stopped the bleeding, and I was told to stay home from school for a couple of days, and I loved that. I had my parents' permission and I wasn't sick, so I thought I was on vacation.

Dad was on the school board at the time and, unbeknownst to me, he had meetings with the other board members. They went to the school and discharged Mrs. Bishop, sending her and her innovative ideas on their way.

Of course, they now had to find another teacher. They selected my great aunt who was a retired teacher and lived in the village. She agreed to come back to work and fill in for the year until they hired someone new.

"My God," I thought, "I've got it made now." How wrong I was and yet how fortunate I was.

October came, which was the time for the oral compositions. As the day drew closer, I still experienced the same dread. Even though I was in Grade 8, I was still small in stature, had asthma and even though the bully boys were gone, I still had my own fear. I had to get up and speak.

Now, there's one fortunate aspect of having a speech memorized in Grade 3 right up to Grade 8 and never giving the speech—I never had to learn a new one. For 5 years I had never delivered my speech on Abraham Lincoln. As in years past, I memorized it and went over it with my mother the week before.

Oral Composition Day came with our new teacher, my great-aunt, Mrs. Munroe, presiding. "Okay, Allan, give us your speech."

"Mrs. Munroe and fellow students, the topic I have chosen for my oral composition is . . ." and I began to stutter and broke into tears. So, I stood there and cried at the front of the class as I had done for, by now, half my life.

"Allan," she said, "you can go sit down."

I sat down at my desk totally embarrassed. Before recess, she came over and said, "I want you to stay behind at recess, Allan. I need to talk to you."

The class rushed downstairs to romp in the afternoon autumn air and I stayed at my desk, apprehensive about what was coming next. Mrs. Munroe sat down in the seat in front of me.

"Allan, you're a big boy. You'll be in high school next year where there are 700 students. It's going to be a big change for you, and you cannot go to high school if you cannot get up and give a speech without crying."

She continued to talk to me and for the first time I could remember, someone took time to show me some compassion, demonstrate some love and impart some wisdom.

I sat there and when she finished I told her, "I can do it," and I meant it.

After recess, she announced to the class, "Anybody else want to give an oral composition?"

I put my hand up and stood up again. Yes, I was scared. Yes, I was shaking inside. Yes, my voice was quivering. Yes, I was stuttering, but I got the speech out. I made many mistakes, but I didn't care because I was floating on air. I finished and stood there for a moment. The class applauded me. I'll never forget that sound and maybe that's why I'm a public speaker today. I loved that applause. I loved the fact that I did it. I saw the smiles on my friends' faces.

Five years of suffering ended. There are lot of days that I hated in my young life, but the one I had always hated most was Oral Composition Day.

When I walked home that afternoon, I wasn't kicking stones along the side of the highway. I was walking as straight as my little frame could carry me. I went in and told my mom and dad I did it. I did it! I made it through my oral composition and from that day on, I felt a little more confident.

Breaking Through

CHAPTER 8

THE ONLY ONE FOR ME

*I wonder why love is so often equated with joy when it is everything else
as well: devastation, balm, obsession, granting and
receiving excessive value, and losing it again.*
—FLORIDA SCOTT MAXWELL

IN SEPTEMBER 1964, I MOVED ONTO HIGH SCHOOL, still carrying all my
baggage and my coping mechanisms such as cigarette smoking. Early
on in high school though, I began a long love affair which ultimately
proved tragic for me but which, for a long time, became a great equalizer
in my life.

It's pleasant to think back about those days with the camaraderie
and the helping hand that neighbors lent each other.

We worked very hard on the farm especially in the summer during
harvest time. Farm kids grow up faster than their city peers. At the
ages of eight or nine, kids in farming communities are driving tractors
even along the side of county roads. The police understood and never
bothered them. It's a hard life and the help of sons and daughters made
it at little easier.

It was an everyday occurrence that when workers came in after
working hard all day, they had a beer. Even with children, twelve,
thirteen, fourteen years old, it was quite common to have a beer when
the work was done.

After hours of dragging and stacking hay bales in a sweltering barn,
we would usually drive down to the river to cool off. Someone who was

old enough to drive would pack everyone in a car along with a 12 pack of beer and we would spend some time relaxing in the late afternoon. My dad always had the cows to milk in the evening and other chores, so he would keep on working. No one gave any thought to a 12 year old having a beer. It was like having a Coke. I liked the taste immediately.

Most farmers also planted grains, winter wheat, summer wheat, barley and rye, and October was harvest time. A machine, called a binder, cut and tied the grain into sheaves and Dad stacked them in three foot high teepee shapes called stooks with about 12 sheaves to each "teepee." That was so the grain would dry out if it rained, something it wouldn't do if left on the ground. Neat stooks dotting the fields was an iconic image of autumn in our parts.

One family along the Auburn/Blyth line had a threshing machine, and the farmers pitched in to help each other bring in their grain. Two men would pitchfork sheaves into the thresher. Serrated bars separated the grain from the stalks. The grain was then blown through a big pipe into the upstairs in the barn in a small area called the granary. Boards could be added to raise the walls of the granary as more grain was blown in.

The cows grazed in the pasture all summer, but were in the barn all winter and lived on a diet of hay with some grain. Grain was mixed with the hay and made the milk taste better. Hay-fed beef tends to be dry. Grain fed beef is much tastier, in my opinion.

The straw had its uses too, as bedding for the animals and to keep the barn clean. Manure-laden straw was swept out and replaced with fresh.

Oftentimes, those of us working in the lofts had to wait for the thresher to return with another load of grain and straw. Sometimes during a break beers were handed out to the workers, even us kids. One day, during a particularly long break, I drank three beers.

It changed my life.

Something magical happened to me that day. For many years

thereafter, when I took a swig of beer or a sip of whiskey I felt my body relax the instant the alcohol slid down my throat. In time, it became instantaneous, Pavlovian. Suddenly, I could live inside the same skin with that small, painfully shy, stuttering boy. Alcohol buried the separation anxieties of my childhood. It soothed the sting of my mother's anger when she had commanded me not to be sick. It submerged the mocking I suffered from the bullies at school. The effect alcohol had on me was completely unexpected, but believe me, I quickly grew to welcome the way it could dull the slings and arrows of outrageous fortune, of which I had my share.

I should state right here that by the time I was 18, alcohol had become the love of my life. Drinking was better than romantic love, it was better than sex. It was better than hotrodding around the countryside, though the two experiences were often recklessly joined. In time, alcohol became the best thing in my life. That should tell you what the rest of my existence was like.

Those who drink alcohol normally do so for pleasure. I never did. I drank for its transformative effect because it allowed me to live with myself.

BREAKING THROUGH

CHAPTER 9

Off the Farm

Life is 10 percent what happens to us and
90 percent how we respond to it.
−Charles R. Swindoll

To make extra money, not only did Dad deliver pigs to market on Wednesday afternoons but for a summer or two, he worked in a saw mill. He also drove a water truck for the road construction crews in late summer when things were slow on the farm after harvest time.

My dad may never have made much money, but he sure could work. That is something I picked up from him and later would prove to be my saving grace. At any rate, he overslept one morning while working road construction, probably the only time in his life he did so. Panicked, he threw on a pair of hush puppies instead of lacing up his steel-toed boots and raced to work.

Summer is the time for thunderstorms in Ontario, and that morning there was a big one. Wind blew the rain horizontally. Dad couldn't see in front of him and parked his truck on a village street and rolled down the window to look out. His elbow was out the window just as lightning hit the transformer on a nearby utility pole and shot down to his elbow. My dad recalled feeling only a little tingle in his arm before he slumped over onto the seat, unconscious.

The bolt created a vacuum so strong that it sucked in the windshield and the glass blasted his chest. It took some time for others to find him because he was across the seat out of view. When they did find him, the seat of his pants had been blown out. As fate would have it, had he been wearing his usual work boots he would have been killed instantly. It makes me wonder sometimes.

He regained consciousness about 20 minutes later and was dizzy and shook up. Our farm was close to the river and since thunderstorms follow water, after that day, whenever a storm came through, Dad would go down to the basement and sweat. Years later though, I also got a job at the same construction company and my boss said my dad was able to joke about the incident.

"Marjorie and me, we had sex last night, and boy, let me tell you, she lit up like a Christmas tree!" he would joke.

He never missed a day of work because of the accident. Later, however, he developed serious problems. His sense of balance left him and he would stumble over a dirt clod or long grass and fall. He began having blackouts. The lightning had compromised his central nervous system. Finally, the doctor told him, "Ken, if you don't get off the farm, you're going to die."

So, in 1965 we sold the farm and moved into Auburn. We moved into a house that was built the same year I was born, 1950. Bernice and I each had our own bedrooms upstairs. For the first time in my life, we had indoor amenities. We didn't have to walk forty paces through waist-high snow to use an outhouse. We no longer had to bathe in a tub on the lawn or go to my grandmother's to take a shower once a week. Above all, we had a furnace and during the long cold winters, we no longer had to huddle around a stove to feel some warmth.

Dad, God bless him, returned to school, a rare achievement in the 1960s for a man 50 years old. He completed a three-year university program by correspondence coupled with some residential study and became a certified tax assessor. He had already been conducting tax assessments for the township and the county on occasion, but after obtaining his degree, it became a full time position, which enabled him to secure a pension.

Dad was very good with people, always laughing and joking with them. When doing a tax assessment, he was supposed to find out how old the people were. Instead of saying, "I need to ask how old you are," he would say, "Listen, I'm supposed to ask how old you are but I won't do that because I respect you. I'll just ask what year you were born." The majority of those people willingly gave the year they were born.

Living at home still, my drinking was limited to weekends. Even while we were still on the farm, I drank beer only during harvest time. My parents were only occasional drinkers, and while they did keep some booze in the house, I never thought to sneak any. The memory of that three-beer work break that one afternoon, however, lay dormant, waiting for the opportunity to take over my life.

Compared to the farm, Auburn was a beautiful place to grow up because we could stay out until the street lights went on. We had the whole village in which to play. We played hide and seek, kick the can and other childhood games. The Maitland River ran next to the village where we could swim, have picnics and camp out. We were known to peek in people's windows from time to time to see what was playing on their televisions. There were some farm kids who used to come to the village and bully us once in a while, but as sad as my life was on the farm and as nervous and scared as I was, when I got to Auburn I began to grow into my adolescence. I formed friendships in that little village that have become as strong and binding as a friendship can be. The experiences we shared brought us together in a special way.

I built a tree house in the village with two or three other guys in a huge beechnut tree. The branches were a foot in diameter, at least. We had room for three or four people to sleep in there. We insulated the walls with cardboard and went there to smoke and hide from our parents.

My parents bought me a mini-bike that I rode for endless hours over the gravel roads in the area. The same cousin who had helped me with my soap box racer souped up my mini-bike so it would go faster. I rode that thing for three years.

We had loads of fun in Auburn, mostly harmless mischief, and of all the nights of the year, Halloween night was our favorite. Halloween is much different today. We didn't have to check our candies for poison or apples for razor blades. We knew all the houses to go to that had homemade candies. Mrs. Molden, the woman who my mother always threatened to drop me off with, lived with her son who was a cobbler. He handed out nickels and we all made sure to go to their house. The fear that I had about his mother suddenly dissipated with the prospect of getting a nickel or two in my little bag.

Five cents would buy a soda pop in those days or a bag of potato chips or a chocolate bar. If you bought a bottle of pop and drank it inside the store, it was five cents. If you took the bottle out it was seven cents for the pop and two cents for the bottle deposit. When you returned the bottle, we'd get our two cents back, which were promptly spent on jawbreakers. A nickel had some value back in the 1960s. We also went to the local butcher on Halloween because he also gave out something different: a raw wiener to each kid.

If, as the saying goes, preparation and opportunity leads to success, well, we had our greatest success on Halloween. We spent significant time conniving and planning for the big night. A month before, we started pilfering small amounts of gasoline from a neighbor who sold gasoline in a big delivery truck, which we stored it in little containers.

There was a vacant house right next door to my parents'. People in Toronto owned it but rarely came by. They hired someone to maintain the property and look after the grass, but no one had lived there for longer than I can remember. Next to it was a very steep incline, a 20 or 30 percent grade, that sloped down the hill towards the river and into a T at the bottom. It was the end of Main Street in Auburn and where I raced my soapbox racers as a kid.

We would take our stolen gasoline and pour it down the middle of the hill. We let it run down the hill and when we saw a car turn to come up the hill, we'd light it on fire. Drivers would see the flames coming down the hill towards them, and you could hear the gears grinding as they tried to get into reverse in a panic. Then as they hurriedly backed down the hill, we'd throw rotten eggs and tomatoes at them. There were never any accidents or damage to a car, though there could have been. We never thought of that; for us, it was just great fun.

During the year, some people in the village always squealed on us for our antics. My mother always knew about it when I got home, whether it was throwing a bottle out on a lawn, or screeching our tires at 2:00 a.m.

So, Halloween was the time for payback. We got together and talked about who had squealed on us during the year. We went out and put junk on their doorsteps and soaped their windows. That was a big payback, soaping the windows of their cars and houses.

Main Street was maybe half a mile long. If people were silly enough to leave furniture out on their stoops on Halloween, they were likely to find it the next morning out in the middle of the road.

I think my father lived vicariously through me to a degree. On Halloween nights, he always took a drive through the village after we had gone to bed to investigate what kind of nonsense had occurred. We'd take farmer's gates off and leave them in the middle of the road. We'd swap people's mailboxes around. We would put lawn furniture up on the roof of a shed. Nothing malicious, just old-fashioned fun. It was our way of rebelling against the soul-numbing status quo of a poor farming community.

One of the farmers in the village was a chicken broker. He sold chickens by the truckload. Truckers would haul in a load of chickens and he would take an inventory of how many chickens were on the truck. He would sign off and they would deliver the load to some processing plant. One year, they made the fatal mistake of bringing the chickens into Auburn on Halloween night.

Chicken trucks are much different today. Back then, there were simply wooden crates stacked five or six high on the truck bed, maybe 60 crates of live chickens. Each one was maybe 5 feet x 4 feet x 18 inches high with little bars just like a jail cell holding 20 or 25 chickens. Their heads would stick through the cracks. I felt sorry for them, knowing their fate.

This night, there was no cover on the truck. The drivers parked and went inside, probably had a drink or did whatever business they had with the broker. Even though I was shy and scared, I always wanted to be a ringleader. Here I saw an opportunity for Allan McDougall to shine.

I ran home as fast as I could to my dad's garage, picked up a pair of pliers and ran back. The crates had sliding openings on top that were wired shut. I climbed on the truck and cut all the wires to the cage doors. We opened up the doors and liberated the chickens, so to speak. It made me feel good to do something that everybody else was afraid to do.

I opened five or six crates, the whole top row and let out maybe 100 chickens. I clambered down and the 10 or 15 of us scurried off to a ditch some distance away to watch the show. The drivers came out to find all these chickens scrambling around the village taking advantage of their newfound freedom. The drivers were responsible for them so they had to catch them.

My dad made his customary inspection through the village that midnight to see the results of the night's festivities. He was always a kid at heart. The next morning at breakfast, he was laughing so hard. He said, very nonchalantly, "How were things last night?"

"Oh, very quiet. Didn't do much. Got a bunch of candy and saw some people."

"Wow, there was a lot of excitement in the village when I went up. There were three or four men chasing chickens. Do you know anything about that?" He had a big grin on his face.

"No. Absolutely not," I lied. "I wonder what happened there."

One of our schoolmates in Auburn was very smart and so, sad to say, we didn't associate with him much. He was what you would term today a geek. He loved school and wanted to be a teacher. He was goal oriented, while my friends and I were not. He had a Volkswagen and one Halloween night, we turned the car sideways in his driveway. His father worked with my dad at the tax assessor's office and he was very upset because our prank made it impossible for him to get out of the driveway the next morning.

Next year on Halloween night, my dad said, "Allan, I don't think you should go out tonight." I was 17 and got very upset. I listened to him and didn't go out, even though I was extremely pissed off.

The next morning when Dad went to work with that young man's father, the kids had picked up the Volkswagen and turned it upside down and broke the windows and damaged it. The father blamed it on me and the kids I hung around with.

"Allan must have been part of that," he insisted.

Dad said, "No, he was home all night." The father never believed him, of course, because I was always out there having fun. I was guilty by association even though I wasn't there.

My dad was so controlled by my mom and the intractable routine of the dairy farm that he never developed any real pastime or hobby. He was easygoing and avoided a confrontation if he could help it. Truth be told, he was miserable with my mom and she was miserable with him. Late in his life, Dad once told me that he felt more comfortable sleeping out in the barn on straw, wrapped in a blanket with the dog for company than in the house with my mom.

He didn't encourage my antics but he protected me when he could, especially from Mom. If a neighbor told him about some stunt I pulled, he would withhold it from Mom because he knew she would go ballistic.

Practical jokes were not completely foreign to him, either. On

Halloween nights he sometimes played tricks on the neighbors, harmless stuff such as moving a wagon from a neighbor's backyard to his front yard or moving a manure spreader from another farmer's 50 acre field to his front lawn so that people driving by the next morning would see it on their front lawn.

My dad loved to tell jokes and have fun. One night when we were still on the farm, my sister was dating her future husband and they went out on a double date with another couple. Gordon, her boyfriend, drove his car into our driveway up to the farmhouse and left it there, jumped in with their friends and off they went.

Afterwards, my dad got an idea and enlisted my support. We grabbed some baler twine from the barn, which is a strong but very thin and pliable twine that holds hay bales and sheaves of grain together. We interwove the twine around the car's horn on the steering wheel and then tied all the doors shut in such a way that when Gordon tried to open a car door the horn would blow.

My mother was against any sort of dating and laid down a very rigid curfew. Whenever my sister came home from a date, my mother would hear the car pull in, wait about three seconds after the motor shut off and start flicking our yard light on and off repeatedly to signal my sister to leave the car and get in the house. Gordon tried to follow the rules because he knew about my mother's temper. So, he was very thoughtful and tried to keep things on an even keel with her.

This particular night, however, they came home late and tried to be extra quiet so as not to wake Mom. Well, every time he opened the car door the horn blew. Needless to say, there was considerable conversation the next morning about all that noise from the night before.

The summer after we moved to the village, I decided I wanted to have some extra money, so I worked at a gas station while school was out. People would pull up to the pump and I would come out. They would ask for $2.00 worth of gas, which half-filled their tank, while I checked the oil, tire pressure and washed the windshield.

The station owner was an alcoholic. Every Monday morning he'd be hung over, bitchy, pissed-off and broke from having spent all his money over the weekend. He would fire me on some cooked-up pretense, and I would drag myself back home, my ego bruised and once again, terrified of having to go home and explain to my mom why I had been fired. By noon, however, he would need to leave the station to pick up a car part, so he'd hire me back again. By the end of summer, I had been fired seven times and rehired eight. As you can imagine, the whole experience was another blow, proving clearly that I couldn't keep a job, even in a gas station.

Regardless, I loved the smell of that old gas station, the old oil-soaked floor, the smell of fuel and gas and exhaust. It permeates the walls of these old garages. It soaked right in and to me it was beautiful, and still is to this day.

I haven't had the opportunity to attend too many car races in my life, but I'm sure it's the same when you're down on pit row. They have that smell. The sense of smell is one of the strongest triggers of memories. When I go looking at antique cars or hot rods or visit my friends who have these old garages and go inside, it takes me back to a wonderful place. I've always had this connection with power, whether it's horsepower or the power to create or the power of love.

BREAKING THROUGH

CHAPTER 10

GROWING BUT NOT GROWING UP

One comes, finally, to believe whatever one repeats to one's self,
whether the statement is true or false.
–NAPOLEON HILL

THOUGH MY LIFE IMPROVED SOMEWHAT after our move to Auburn, it contained one especially dark episode. It was about 2:00 a.m. on a March night when my parents returned from a social function. They found me in the kitchen doubled over rocking back and forth clutching my sides.

"Mom! Dad!" I screamed. "My stomach hurts bad. Really bad!"

"What did you have to eat?" Dad asked.

"Mark came over and we ate a pizza. Owwww! I haven't been able to sleep at all. It really hurts."

"It's probably something in the pizza. Let's see how it is in the morning," Mom said.

With that, they shut the door to their room. I had been so relieved when I saw the car come into the yard. I had waited for hours while they were out and desperately needed their help. I was crestfallen. Bernice was away at teacher's college and I felt utterly lost, alone and in severe pain.

I went back to bed and screamed and sweated for what seemed to be the next hundred years but no one came to ask how I was. It was the most lonely feeling in the world.

By morning I was almost delirious, exhausted by the pain. In a childhood filled with painful moments, this was the most intense.

"Before we do anything with Allan, I'm taking him up to the chiropractor and get a diagnosis," Mom said.

It wasn't so much that my mother put her faith in chiropractors as much as she did not trust medical doctors. Worst of all, she didn't believe me! So, she and Dad drove me ten miles in the opposite direction of the hospital, which is where I should have been taken hours earlier.

The chiropractor took one look at me and said, "He needs to be in the hospital hours ago. He's suffering with a severe appendicitis attack."

Just the fact that someone was going to help me was a relief. We raced to the hospital in another small town, and as they were giving me anaesthesia before the surgery, I remember feeling so relieved that something was being done and that someone finally listened. The ordeal of the past 12 hours was finally ending.

Afterwards, the surgeons told my parents that my appendix would have ruptured in 20 minutes and they were not sure if my health would have been able to withstand all those toxins coursing through my system.

An appendectomy typically lasts 30 to 45 minutes. I was on the operating table for more than 4 hours. During the surgery they found that my appendix had a growth on it that was wrapped around my bowels and literally strangling my intestines, and they had to remove that growth as well.

I was in the hospital for five or six days and lying there I began to feel better. I had been smoking for two or three years by then and decided to quit. It seemed like a good time but it took another 27 years to finally act on my decision.

With my rotten appendix gone and my insides no longer knotted, I sprouted like corn in the summer sun. In the next 10 months I grew an entire foot and gained 25 pounds. The next year, I was as big as the other kids in class. I went from being the scrawny little kid in Grade 9

My class picture from Grade 10. I am the shrimp at the far right in the middle row. A year after my appendectomy, I was as big as any of the other kids.

who had to jump to reach the high bar to simply reaching up to grab it like everyone else.

The additional height and weight didn't change the fact that I still hated school. I still never fit in. Mr. MacKay always wrote on my report cards in elementary school, "Allan has the ability but is extremely careless." He was right. I had been a good reader all my life but refused to squander my aptitude in the institution I detested so deeply.

My dream life during those years was to quit school, get a job in a factory, smoke, race hot rods and motorcycles and live my own life.

Because I missed so much school—my appendicitis attack occurred during Easter exams—my grades, which were never good, sank to abysmal depths and I flunked Grade 10. The newspaper in Goderich listed all students who had passed onto the next grade. My name was missing. That was a huge embarrassment to my mother but no real concern for me. I simply returned for my second year of Grade 10, this time at the age of 16. I attended physical education class, but was still limited in any sporting activities.

I now know that I always had the ability but never believed in myself. As a result, I didn't have the ambition or motivation until I was much older, when I discovered I could do things that I thought I could never do. Today, I'm living my life beyond my wildest dreams. Coming from very humble beginnings, I was petrified of my own shadow and scared to try new things. Filling a hole in my soul and trying to relieve the fear that was always present deep in the pit of my stomach was something I could never manage. In that diaphragm of mine was a fear so pervasive that I was always afraid.

My second shot at Grade 10 was better in some respects. I took woodworking and welding shop and those were great. I was better there than in the academic subjects. Regardless, I didn't have any social skills as far as relationships or dating. My stuttering began to abate somewhat, but returned with gusto any time I became nervous or anxious. Approaching a girl for a date was always nerve-wracking and my stutter did little for my success in that field.

During high school, I belonged to the Boy Scout troop we had in the village. We met every Tuesday night at 8:00 o'clock. Walking home from Boy Scouts, I would encounter the farm bullies. Another boy who belonged to the troop had two older brothers who picked him up after the meetings. Because I was still the stuttering, wimpy, sensitive, undersized kid who wouldn't fight back, there was many a fearful night walking home down a lonely street in the village. Invariably, their car would pull up beside me, lights off, slowly keeping pace as I kept placing one foot ahead of the other, looking straight ahead. The wind would be blowing on these evenings and I felt so threatened and alone. Then the three brothers would hop out and begin teasing me. They would beat me up and throw me in the ditch or leave me on the sidewalk, climb back in their car and laugh. I thoroughly enjoyed the camaraderie of the Boy Scouts but I was always terrified to walk home late at night knowing I would be teased and pushed around by that set of brothers.

Turning 16 though, enabled me to apply for a driver's license. Even that was a severe test of my nervousness and insecurity. I didn't have any trouble passing the written exam but the driving test was another matter. My sister had a standard transmission car that I used in the driving exam and I'm still embarrassed to say that I had to take it five times before I was successful.

Part of the reason had to do with a growing rebellious streak. It was a small town, so I was forced to go to the same license examiner every time. There were only two people who did the testing. Every time I left the parking lot after failing, I would angrily spin the tires and spray him with gravel. I'd tear off down the road squealing the tries and then come back a week or two later hoping that he would not remember and try again. My dad finally had to write a Member of Parliament, and the next time I took the test after that, I passed.

Driving gave me a measure of independence from my parents and I began to delve increasingly into alcohol. The memory of that day in the hay loft began to stir. On weekends, I would meet my friends, someone would buy us beer, I would drink and each time, magically, I could live with myself. After 16 years of never feeling that way, this sensation was one I began to look forward to more and more. My weekdays were still the same painful routine—my mother's anger, my dislike for school, my parent's arguments—but I found relief on weekends in a can of beer and soon, a bottle of whiskey.

Socially, I was still a failure. Just as she drilled it into my head as a sickly child to stay healthy, my mother would bore into my soul with those eyes of anger when giving advice on the subject of dating. It wasn't really advice so much as imperious commands.

"Don't you take anybody out." "Don't you date anybody." "Don't get anybody pregnant." "You will be strapped for life." "I'm not happily married, so you won't be happily married." It went on and on and on and on, so much so that I was scared to date anyone even though I wanted to.

A young girl came along one day and told my cousin that she liked me. I've always tended to wait for girls to make the first move and, as a result, I've had many missed opportunities in my life, to be sure. Even when I did date during those years, it wasn't magical because my love affairs were with cars and alcohol. I always took my first love, alcohol, with me when I began dating.

After I finally graduated Grade 10, I participated more in school the next two years and I have to give my mother credit for that. Without her prodding I wouldn't have finished high school.

For some strange reason, throughout my last two years of high school I wanted to join the Ontario Provincial Police. I was probably the last person they would have ever considered because of the drinking and driving that I engaged in during high school. My life then was a little like the Dukes of Hazzard, with fast cars careening down gravel roads and roaring through corn fields.

The only difference between their life and mine was that mine was spiced up with alcohol. Every time the police stopped me, which was often, because I'm sure they knew I wanted to become a police officer, they thoroughly searched the car. Sometimes they were successful in finding alcohol and sometimes they weren't.

Back in the 60s in Canada, alcohol and young drivers weren't the concern they are today. Their main focus was that we didn't litter the countryside with empty bottles. Certainly, drunk drivers were dealt with differently then.

The police would bust us and we would receive a small fine of $27.50 or, if they were really upset with us, $52.50, and they would confiscate the alcohol. If there were three of us driving around on a Saturday afternoon and were pulled over, they would ask whose turn it was this time and charge one of us with underage possession. We would each chip in eight or nine dollars if the fine was $27.50 and that was it. Nothing ever went on our record. It was a different time, a different era. Growing up on a farm, we had an adage that if you worked like a man and worked long hours, then you played like a man. Alcohol and smoking were more accepted back in those days by everyone, including some parents.

Grade 12 was the last year of my science, technology and trades program. I really did apply myself to school because the finish line was in sight and I wanted to be out of there. I played hooky one day in my life in Grade 12 and I got caught. There was a bus that took us to our high school in Goderich and then another bus went on to another high school ten miles down the road, and that's where a girl that I liked went to school.

A school chum of mine decided that we would pretend to be new students in that high school. We jumped on the second bus. The only problem was that the Vice Principal, Mr. Boyce, spotted us boarding the wrong bus. Mr. Boyce knew me all too well, having assigned me regular detentions to walk the school grounds picking up cigarette butts, often my own, for one infraction or another.

We had fun at the other school and returned to our regular high school at the end of the day. We boarded our usual bus laughing about the whole experience. It was a different story at home. I faced my mother's anger again and saw that look in her eyes.

"I know you weren't at school today," she yelled.

"Yes, I was at school today," I shouted back, covering up.

"No, you weren't!"

"Yes, I was."

"No! Mr. Boyce called me and said he saw you leaving school."

"You're right," I argued, "but I went to another school. So you can't chastise me for being in another school even though it wasn't mine."

At age 17 I was finally beginning to stand up to my mother's anger, even if I knew I was wrong. I was grounded for it though.

In June 1969, I graduated with the highest marks I ever received in my entire my life. I'm sure I know why—the fear of failure and having to spend another year in high school at the age of 19 instead of 18. Here is a snapshot of my life as I graduated high school: I didn't have any real goals. I was just glad to be out of that place. My mother was finally off my back as far as studying went. In honor of my achievement, I took my schoolbooks and notes down to the Maitland River, and in a self-fantasized rite of passage, I threw them in, solemnly swearing to the river gods that I would never open another textbook for the rest of my life. The value of education and the power of books were utterly lost on me in those days. Some say that a person's greatest weapon against the vicissitudes of life is one's ability to reason. My lifelong resistance to developing that faculty left me with no way to inspect my life analytically, to look at the decisions I made or chart a life of which I could feel proud.

Without realizing it, I locked myself into a pattern that would cost me dearly over the next 20 years.

CHAPTER 11

YOUNG AND ROOTLESS

It takes more courage to reveal insecurities than to hide them, more strength to relate to people than to dominate them, more "manhood" to abide by thought-out principles rather than blind reflex. Toughness is in the soul and spirit, not in muscles and an immature mind.

–ALEX KARRAS

RATHER THAN FACE MY FEARS, rather than take any positive step to fill the hole in my soul, in my heart I remained the frightened asthmatic little boy who had never felt the security of a stable place in the world.

My high school behavior aped role models who lived out on the margins, the hot rodders, smokers, Fonzi-type rebels. Increasingly, the fuel I relied on to see me through my teenage years was alcohol.

Underage drinking was a rarely questioned part of life where I came from. Enablers were everywhere. It was never a problem to accost someone walking into a store and give them money for beer. Mr. MacKay's house became a good place to visit after we moved to the village and I was hanging out with his son, John. Mr. MacKay had relocated but always returned to Auburn for the summer. I would sit in his house listening to Roy Orbison records over and over and found a soulful connection in his music that I loved then and still do today.

As long as I could remember, I carried a vague uneasiness that I did not belong. Drinking had the effect on my eggshell psyche of making these feelings go away temporarily. My driver's license gave me a slight status with my peers. Dad had a 1966 Ford Meteor, a secondhand car that he let me take out on weekends, and he made sure it was full of gas. Ford only sold the Meteor in Canada and when they retired the make there they put the name on a Mercury and sold it in the U.S.

My father loved cars but never had money for a new one, so had to be satisfied with older secondhand models. He had a friend who worked at a dealership in Goderich and would sneak a visit to the lot now and again when my mother wasn't with him. He would tell his friend, "Next time you've got a good used car on the lot that you think I might like, why don't you just happen to drive by the farm so I can see it. But don't tell Marjorie I said so."

Every so often, the man would bring by another car, which pleased Dad but upset Mom to no end. She couldn't pin it on Dad though, and he was able to keep his dream alive of one day having a nice car.

Now that I was licensed, I became very much in demand; the village kids were still getting their dollar or two a week allowance while I was getting the use of my dad's car. Most of the time, we would go to the drive-in and then drive around afterwards. I managed to get a girlfriend and would take her and my drinking buddy to the drive-in. After dropping her off at home, my buddy and I would drive around drinking beer all night, see what kind of action there was and whether we could get away with some mischief.

I looked forward to Fridays and being free from school for the weekend. The unofficial official announcement that the weekend was here was the distinctive four note call sign on radio station CKLW, a 50,000 watt blowtorch in Windsor. They'd play their four notes at 5:00 p.m. followed by a factory whistle, and that signified the start of the weekend.

At one point I developed a crush on another girl who had a really slick car, a '68 Malibu. We met at a dance one night and both were drinking. Of course, the only topic that I was comfortable discussing was cars. We hit it off because she was into cars as well. I had my Dad's '66 Meteor and when the dance was over she wanted to race me to Blyth. (I thought that was a sign of true love.)

I agreed immediately. I had consumed a fifth of whiskey, no exaggeration, and during our 20 mile race home along the deserted country roads, I never once took the car's automatic transmission out of second gear. I'm not even sure who won, but as I got closer to home, I noticed that the transmission was slipping. I had to pull over and wait for the transmission to cool down. Then the bands would grab again and I'd drive another two miles. The transmission would heat up again and I wouldn't be able to move until they cooled off.

I stopped about four times in the last four miles on my ride home. I parked the car and never said a word to my dad. The next morning he said to my mother and me, "I'm heading into Blyth to pick up something for the garage. I'll be back in about 15 minutes."

Silently, I thought to myself, "No, you won't."

Being the good son, I stood by the telephone because I knew he would be calling. He broke down halfway to the village and called from a neighboring farmhouse. When he got back, he said, "Allan, did you have any trouble with that car last night?"

"Absolutely not."

"Well," he said, "I don't know what's wrong with this transmission but it certainly isn't working right." He had to take it to the garage for repairs.

Years later, he said to me, "My cars have never worked better since the day you got your own."

He could have presented the following as evidence. One Sunday morning, I woke up and out my bedroom window I saw Mom in the passenger seat and Dad with his head under the hood. They were on their way to church but obviously something was wrong with the car. Dad was frantically pulling corn stalks and leaves out from the grille, fan belt and radiator.

The night before, the police had been chasing me and I drove through a corn field to lose them. The evidence came with me, however, which Dad discovered on the way to church. I am glad that CSI was not around then. Dad never let Mom know the real reason he had to fiddle with the car that morning.

We had a favorite spot for parties—a six mile U-shaped gravel road, along which there were very few homes, called the Maitland Block. We would stash our beer and whiskey the morning of the party in a spring where the fresh water kept our treasure cold and then pick it up as we headed to the night's festivities.

One evening, 15 people from high school delegated my girlfriend and me to pick up the alcohol for the party. What a mistake that was. We picked up the alcohol at 2:00 in the afternoon on a Saturday and the party started at 8:00 that night in some gravel pit in a farmer's field. There were about 12 people waiting for us when we showed up.

There was a God looking after me that day because when we got there and I stopped the car, we both opened our doors and fell out. Most of the booze that was commissioned for the party had been consumed.

My friends and I spent a huge portion of our free time driving: drive-ins, the car wash or just aimlessly driving around and drinking, gravel-running we called it. Those were our three main destinations. I would be headed out and Mom and Dad would ask, "Where are you going?"

"Oh, just driving around, driving around." For the most part, that was the case.

One night my dad gave me a limitation of 50 miles on the car. "You're only allowed to put 50 miles on the car tonight, Allan."

"Okay."

I ended up driving 92 miles. There were three of us in the car and of course, we were all drinking. At the end of the night, I realized I had put 92 miles on the car.

In those days, you could jack up the car, put it in reverse and run the engine to take miles off the odometer. However, I didn't know any better at the time and the alcohol didn't help my decision-making. My two friends, John and Mark, and I ended up driving 40 miles in reverse up and down the gravel roads for the better part of three or four hours, doing 15 miles an hour trying to get those miles off the odometer.

I backed into my cousin's farm about six in the morning to get gas because we were running out. All the farmers had gas tanks. They were just headed out to do the morning chores so my cousins and my uncle saw me backing in up to their gas tank. I had money so I asked them to fill up my tank. Then I turned around and backed out of their lane and we continued on our way backwards down the road. I'm sure they were scratching their heads about that but then thought, "Well, that's just Cousin Allan."

Another time, my friend and I were driving down the road having a few beers, and we wanted to see how fast that old car would go. We had all four windows down, making like we were in a two-door hardtop, even though it was a four-door sedan. We had the heater on because it was early spring and still cold, but we thought we were pretty cool.

When we got over onto the main road, we opened it up. There was a tear in the headliner in the interior of the car right beside the passenger window. The wind got into the tear and suddenly, there was a pop and a big bang. The headliner snapped loose from the supporting ribs and came down around our heads, blinding us.

I was probably doing 90 miles an hour and I couldn't see. I lifted my arm and got the fabric off my head and eventually pulled over. We re-bowed the frames into the ceiling so that the headliner was back in place again.

Another time, friends and I went to the drive-in with two bottles of homemade wine. It was a hot summer night and we didn't know much about homemade wine. The bottles got jostled and the corks were not in the necks sufficiently far. Long story short, both bottles blew up in the backseat. I couldn't believe it. Wine sprayed all over the interior of the car, and we spent most of the night making trips to the concession stand for napkins and water to clean Dad's formerly white interior.

It smelled like a winery. If a police officer had been within a mile, he would have been over like a bee to honey.

My dad got up in the morning and went for a ride in his car and it was still sticky. "What the hell have you guys been doing?" he asked.

"Oh, we had a bottle of Coca-Cola last night and I guess it blew up. You know, the heat, Dad, and it was sticky. I said I'll clean it up. Not to worry."

My family could never afford 8-tracks or stereos for the car, so my friends and I left the drive-in one time with two extra speakers for my parent's car. My mom and dad's car radio only had one speaker in the dash, and I wanted two speakers for the back window. We successfully installed these speakers in the back.

However, I also wanted some sexy little lights on the floor up by the clutch and brake pedals. We bought these cheap small red lights and wired them to the battery. We didn't do such a good job because every time anybody used the right turn signal the horn would blow. Mom and Dad discovered this one day driving down the road and they had to take it to the garage to be repaired.

That ended my modifications to the Meteor. For a while back on the farm, Dad had a '57 Dodge that had a bulb by the brake pedal that you pumped two or three times to force washing fluid onto the windshield. This was before mechanical windshield washers. That bulb spurred me on to the only thing I took from high school chemistry, an extra container to hold whiskey. I adapted that mechanism to Dad's Meteor.

I went to the scrap yard and picked up a bulb similar to the one attached to the firewall inside the engine compartment of a '57 Dodge where the windshield washer was. I hacksawed out a piece of the fender well of the Meteor in a location that was difficult to see. I installed the other container, bolted it to the firewall and filled it full of whiskey. I drilled a hole through the firewall, ran the hose into the interior and secured the hose with some pilfered alligator clips from chemistry class.

Thereafter, every time I hit this bulb, which no one could see, it would pump an ounce of whiskey into this hose. I could release the alligator clip and have instant alcohol in my glass. I thought that was clever.

This was during the time I had submitted my name to become a police officer. Naturally, the police were watching me. I always thought they were picking on me but of course, if you had your name in to be a police officer they wanted to make sure you were living a respectable life, which I wasn't.

The cops stopped me a lot in those days for speeding or just to check if they could smell the alcohol. They tore that car apart but they could never find the source. My high school chemistry finally paid off!

One day the Ontario Provincial Police came to see my dad. The officer walked in and said, "Ken McDougall?"

"Yes, what can I do for you?"

"We have a message for your son Allan. You can tell Allan that someday we will catch him."

Those words came true 18 years later. Just as my dad lived somewhat vicariously through me, I lived vicariously through that guy in the hot rod so many years earlier. To me, he represented another way, an avenue of escape. Even as a little boy I was looking for something different, something more "normal," though I didn't know it then. I see that I was looking outwards for my escape but now, in my sixties, I can tell you that my freedom is found on the inside.

Although I'm not sure why all of this happened to me, I can attest to the fact of my fears and my insecurities, not believing in myself and not seeing any potential in myself or having any hopes or dreams.

The stage was set for me to develop a serious drinking problem.

BREAKING THROUGH

CHAPTER 12

Not Comfortable in My Own Skin

We have within us a limitless supply of new beginnings.
—Joan Fitzgerald

For two summers, I worked on road construction. The work was exciting, with heavy equipment everywhere and I made good wages. A great deal of drinking went on and I was dating the boss' niece. The men used to tease that I was pouring all my money back into the company, but it was good times. I felt freer then than at any time in my life.

The boss would leave at noon on Fridays, which more or less signaled the end of the work week. The foreman would go to his truck and bring out five cases of beer and we started the weekend right then. The boss did not drink but he knew what was happening and it would continue on into the night. I would come home and my mother would smell the alcohol on my breath. "Oh, we just had a beer on the way home," was my standard lie.

I also drove tractors for farmers who needed help with the farm work. I was paid $2.00 an hour, which was a decent wage in those days. At the end of the day, I would pick up a case of beer, which was inexpensive. It all seemed harmless at the time but it was very hard on my mother, knowing that I was into alcohol. I would often come home sick, but I always worked hard.

When I first started drinking, I must admit that I would come home and lie on the bed with one leg on the floor because the room was spinning. I was not a natural alcoholic, if there is such a thing. In the beginning, I would become violently ill after three or four bottles of beer or a Mickey of whiskey (13 ounces). I didn't earn the disease of alcoholism or the reputation as a prodigious drinker the easy way. I had to fight through the sickness and the dizziness and make a serious commitment to drink. Considering what I was running from, it was a price I was willing to pay.

After each bout of sickness, I would go right back drinking again, forgetting about the dizziness and the embarrassment of it all. My reaction to alcohol subsided in a year's time. I kept at it weekend after weekend. There came a time when my body built up such a tolerance that I began getting recognition for the amount of alcohol that I could hold and still function at a somewhat manageable level.

If those two paragraphs do not reflect the depths of my desperation or the size of the hole in my soul, then the words don't exist.

By 18 years of age, I could not do without the effect that alcohol provided me. I had become an alcoholic.

After graduating high school, I found work in a saw mill making pool cues and bowling alley floors. I was making $2.50 an hour for working a 40 hour week. I rode to work every day with one of the men from the village who also worked there. It was my first employment other than road construction or farming. My life as an adult began that July.

In December, I bought myself a brand new 1969 Camaro, blue with a white vinyl roof and a 327 engine. I really, really loved that car. Before I bought it I went to Human Resources and asked if my job was secure and was told, "Absolutely." Absolutely lasted until March when I was handed a layoff slip.

On that night at the dealership though, life was grand. I stopped by to get my drinking buddy and he and I drove home in my brand new car. We were drinking whiskey on the way and both of us got sick in the car even before I reached my own driveway.

I truly enjoyed drinking and all that came with it. It made me feel magical. It allowed me to feel everything that I didn't otherwise feel. It took away at least 70% of my shyness around girls. When I drank alcohol, my nerves calmed. There was a feeling of well being that went through me. My stuttering went away and I felt comfortable within my skin. I knew things would be okay, not that I became Superman, but simply being Al was more than good enough.

Looking back after more than 20 years of sobriety, I now know that drinking was **not** my problem. Drinking was the **solution** to my problems.

My Camaro had to be purchased through a finance company and my dad had to cosign for it because I didn't have the money for a down payment. He agreed, and I was to make payments of $107.00 a month to Household Finance Company.

Then, about nine weeks after I bought my car and had the insurance, I was laid off from my job.

This was the first difficult time of my post high school life, but it wouldn't be the last.

Unemployment insurance at the time was $35.00 a week. With my $107.00 car payment plus insurance and gas there was not enough money at the end of the month. I was grateful that my parents did not charge me room and board.

Clearly, I needed to find another job. In the morning my drinking buddy and I would go job hunting and our first stop was the beer store for a case of twelve. We would drive around and drink beer all day with our resumes, two knuckleheads job hunting with alcohol on their breath. We did not get too many takers with that kind of job search.

Mom and Dad would ask me every night when I got home how our job search went and I would answer, "Well, we went to five or six places but haven't heard anything back."

Me as a young man, in a car with my first love cradled in my jacket pocket. Sadly, this picture says it all—cars and alcohol.

My dad was getting worried because he had his name on the car loan ahead of mine. One Saturday morning, I was lying upstairs in bed and he came in and woke me up. It was rare for him to do that.

"Allan," he began, "what do you think of becoming a miner. I think you would make a good one."

"Yes," I said, "I think I would too. Whereabouts?"

"I found an ad in the paper for miners in Sudbury. It's eight hours north. Come on downstairs and I'll give you all the information."

The prospect excited me, really excited me. It was a chance to get away from the house, get away from the fighting between Mom and Dad, allow me to continue on with my drinking without any interference and probably mean more money. As a kid of 19 it was a good opportunity to simply get away.

My social life with girls remained null and void. I always wanted to be able to talk to girls; I could carry on dialogues with men, but never could fit into the conversations women were having. I felt I didn't have anything to contribute. The only time I felt like talking was when I had a twelve pack of beer inside of me. Of course, then my conversation probably wasn't even on the same topic, but I felt comfortable. As I said earlier, I never drank for pleasure. I always drank for the effect. Many people who drink alcohol do so as part of social gatherings. It is part of the entertainment. I drank for the "therapeutic" effect it had on my personality.

The one girl that I had been dating had been seeing another guy and I couldn't handle that. I automatically assumed that when I was dating someone, we should be going steady. I never talked to her about whether we should exclusively be dating only each other. I thought of it but I never brought it up because I didn't have the confidence. I would take her out on Friday and she would date another guy on Saturday and that hurt me deeply.

One night I went to pick her up. I didn't realize it was the wrong night and when I arrived at her house, her mother answered the door and said, "I'm sorry, she's gone out with the other guy."

I looked at her and she looked at me.

"Well, perhaps you could tell her that unless she wants to go steady with me, I won't be back."

"It's about time you said that," the girl's mother replied.

I left there brokenhearted, really sad. I really did like this girl. She drank as much as I did. It might not have become a wonderful relationship later on, but it sure was fun at the time. Driving down the road with a case of beer in the back seat, we shared many laughs.

I really enjoyed her company but I wanted "more." However, I was afraid of "more" and was also scared by my mother's constant harping, "Don't date." "Don't have sexual relations." "You're going to get a girl pregnant, and you will be trapped like I am."

I was more scared of my mother's anger than I was of anything else.

Any relationships I had with the opposite sex were overshadowed by my mother's warnings.

Later on, I met a new girl in church. She participated in the program for young Christian people when I met her. She was about three years younger than I and a very beautiful young woman. She was a farmer's daughter and I would take her to meetings at church or to dances. We had many good times.

I thought that I was fooling everybody. I was drinking wine at the time and I would put it in a can of grape soda pop. Visualize me coming around to see your daughter wearing jeans, a T-shirt, cigarettes rolled up in the sleeve a la James Dean, a case of beer in the back seat hidden under a blanket and a half a bottle of wine in a soft drink can, drinking it in your living room as though it were grape soda.

My Camaro had shackles on the back end to jack up the profile and glass pack mufflers, surely something every parent wants to see their daughter in as she drives off. I was portraying an image that was so unlike the real me. We dated for several months, and I was really fond of her but then came this offer of a job eight hours north. I went there to work and we saw each other infrequently after that because I came home only every three weeks. As much as I wanted a steady relationship, I never expressed those feelings and she began dating someone else. Once that happened, I walked away and never looked back.

CHAPTER 13

They Call it the Geographical Cure

"The secret, kid," said the seal, bending toward him and speaking behind
his flipper, "is to have a good compass and a following wind."
—Will Watkins – Sid Seal, Houseman

I was excited about becoming a miner even though the job was far
away and I knew nothing about mining. Here I was, on the verge of
turning 20, no job, but still had my car and was paying on it as best I
could. To interview for the job and get my physical, I had to drive to
an arena in London, Ontario, about an hour away.

The company was called International Nickel Company of Ontario,
INCO, and they were traveling from city to city hiring young miners.
The demand for nickel had skyrocketed. This was during the height
of the Vietnam War and miners were needed to pull nickel out of the
ground.

The company was hiring 250 miners a week on average but also
losing 250 a week. Many miners were itinerants, pack sack miners they
are called, who drifted from job site to job site scraping up enough
money to get to the next pile of gold. Many were simply trying to
make money as fast as their alcoholism or gambling or other personal
demons could steal it away from them.

I drove to London, found the arena and went inside. There were
probably 600 young men and a few women standing around and the
company had twelve booths set up. I had never seen anything like it.

I had their ad from the newspaper, and they gave me a number and a place to stand in line at one of the tables. They arranged the crowd into lines and then the announcements started.

"Anybody here on probation can leave."

"Anybody here who is a member of a biker gang, anybody here who does not want to get their hair cut, anybody who doesn't want to shave off their beard because it will interfere with respirators can leave now."

Many people left, but I stayed in line. When my turn came they asked me, "Your name, age and what work have you done?"

I told them I had just graduated high school but had worked in road construction and in a sawmill.

"Well, you don't have much of a work record."

"You're right," I said, "but I lived on a farm for 15 years."

Their response was immediate: "Oh, a farmer. Sign here."

They knew that farmers were probably ignorant of the labor movement and unions but were used to hard work, all of which was good from a management perspective. They sent me to receive a short physical and then gave me the information I needed for a back X-ray.

I passed my requirements and was on my way north to become a miner. You had three days to get there to keep your job once you passed a back X-ray showing that your spinal column was okay.

My dad had an engineer friend who had worked at INCO for 25 years, and he called him saying, "Allan's moving to Sudbury for a job. Is there anywhere that he should stay away from or a place where he should go? He's looking for a place to live."

The man said, "Yes. He should go to Levack. That's where they have bunkhouses. It's a good mine and about 30 miles from the city. There is good hunting and fishing and a nice town of 3,000."

The night before leaving, I borrowed $200 from my brother-in-law for expenses. I was pretty excited, but also scared. I had never been away from home before. That night the phone rang.

The start of a new life. Dave and me in front of my Camaro, about to leave for the drive north to Sudbury on Easter Sunday, 1970.

A young man at the other end said, "Hi, my name is Dave. I went to school with you. I heard from a friend of a friend that you got a job in Sudbury. I got one too. I'd like to travel with you."

On Easter Sunday in 1970, we jumped into my Camaro and drove eight hours to Sudbury, rented a hotel room for $8 apiece, spent the night and next day proceeded to the hiring office.

I'd never been in a big city like Sudbury before. It was a mining town. Numerous young men were around and INCO was hiring like crazy. There were more than 20,000 men working at INCO in the Sudbury Basin at the time.

More than 1.8 billion years ago, a meteor eight miles in diameter crashed into northern Ontario and left a crater 150 miles wide. It is the second largest impact crater on earth. Today it is called the Sudbury Basin, an oval shaped depression 40 miles long, 20 miles wide and 10 miles deep just north of Georgian Bay in Lake Huron. The meteor created one of the world's richest mineral deposits.

It was exciting to be there. I felt alive and vibrant. All of a sudden I felt a willingness to make wholesale changes in my life. I was in a brand new community. I didn't know a soul except Dave, who I had met a day before. I hadn't known him in high school because he had been in the academic crowd, a place I surely was not. I said to myself, "Maybe I can quit my drinking and get my life in order." I had not yet discovered the old adage, "No matter where you go, there you are."

I was hired on April Fool's Day 1970, beginning the better part of two decades of fooling myself.

CHAPTER 14

New Life, Same Problems

It is clear the future holds opportunities—it also holds pitfalls.
The trick will be to seize the opportunities, avoid the pitfalls,
and get back home by 6:00.
–Woody Allen

After spending the night in Sudbury, Dave and I drove to the main office in town and met with the Human Resources person. He gave us each a badge, told us we had passed our back X-rays and that we would be starting work the next morning.

Next, we drove about 30 miles northwest to Levack, a much smaller town than Sudbury. That's where bunkhouses for the single miners were. Levack was a company town. INCO had company stores, company houses that they rented to mining families for $15 a month plus $6 for the hydro (electricity), a company police force, even a company jail.

Eight three-story bluish-gray stucco bunkhouses were home to some 300 miners, about 44 to a bunkhouse. On the long side of the ground floor was the entrance, and to the left as you came in were quarters for the manager. In our bunkhouse the manager was Tammi Jokennin, a large Finnish woman. To the right was the kitchen and dining hall. Then, running down the corridor on either side were 10' X 12' rooms with the showers and toilets at the end of the hall. Payday was Tuesday and Tammi knew that if she didn't sit out front of the bunkhouse with her hand out when the men came back, she was not likely to be paid that week.

Rent was $22.50 each a week for room, board and maid service. They changed our bedding every day, served us breakfast and made lunches we could take to work. Some men wanted single rooms and paid more for the privilege. The accommodations were spartan: two army cots and two little dressers was about it. I didn't care; it was the beginning of a whole new life for this little farm boy who didn't have any confidence, who was easily influenced and manipulated but who desperately wanted to feel like he belonged somewhere, anywhere.

There were men working on the afternoon, or swing, shift at 4:00 p.m., so Tammi would have a big dinner for them at noon and lunch for the day shift. Crews who worked on the night shift had a breakfast when they came home the morning and another one before they went to work at midnight.

My first job was above ground in the nickel mill a mile and a half away from the bunkhouse. I weighed under 150 pounds, heavy enough to work in the mill, but too light to work underground. For the first year, I worked in the mill where heat and chemicals extracted minerals from the ore. I was hired at $2.71 an hour in 1970 and cleared $107 a week.

That first week consisted of training for our jobs and I met other young guys like myself who had been newly hired. I was so excited because of the independence and freedom. I could do the things I wanted without having to answer to anyone, especially my parents. I spent the majority of my time in the mill working on the "bull gang," which meant shoveling ore that had fallen off the conveyor belt and other general labor duties. We loaded the giant mills with heavy steel rods or steel pellets that rotated or shook, thereby grinding the chunks of ore into a fine slurry.

It was hard work, especially when we came in hung over from a night of drinking and partying. I learned how to take naps resting on my shovel. By propping the shovel at an angle against a wall, I could sit in the shovel head, rest my head in the D-ring handle and catch 40 winks. If I was fortunate to be working with a wheelbarrow, that was the nickel mill equivalent of napping in a king-sized sleep number bed.

Some people wanted to keep working in the mill and moved up to become mill operators or other specialties. My sights were set on working underground, so I purposely did not advance my job skills. I was warned that if I became a mill operator, I would make more money, sure, but the company would not let me leave to work underground because mill operators were needed on the surface. I stayed on the bull gang until I gained enough weight to be allowed underground. For me, that was where the action was. It also became a metaphor for where my life would soon be headed.

Drinking was quite prevalent in the bunkhouse and acceptable so long as we didn't cause too much trouble or make too much noise. Miners were working seven days a week, 24 hours a day on shift work so there were people sleeping at all hours. If I entertained thoughts of curbing my drinking, I had come to the wrong place. The culture of a bunkhouse full of hard rock miners practically mandated excessive drinking and, because it was the 1970s, a bit of marijuana and other recreational drugs. The latter, I made clear, I was not interested in, but I certainly was interested in the drinking. It wasn't long before I was drinking every day. At first, I didn't drink as much as I did on the weekends back home because I knew I would be able to drink the next and the day after that. As long as we kept the noise to a minimum, it was okay. I was 19 years old but it was accepted, and anybody there would always buy us beer, even though the legal drinking age in Ontario was 21.

I became popular in the bunkhouse because I had a car and it was 30 miles to Sudbury. Sometimes people would ask me to drive to a bar or a movie. Just as at home, because of my car, I fit in.

I joined a gym to gain weight so I could work underground. The gym was in a hotel basement. I would work out and then go upstairs and drink. Sometimes I would drink before my workout and wind up puking. The money underground was better and I thought there was prestige with being a miner. Once I began working underground, I was proud to be a miner. It counterbalanced all my wimpy days at school and my frightened upbringing. The world of a hard rock miner is the exact opposite of a timid little boy who was scared of his shadow. There were plenty of other things besides one's shadow to be scared of underground. (With the success of the Diary of a Wimpy Kid series, perhaps I should have called this book Diary of a Wimpy Miner.)

After months in the gym, I gained enough weight to go underground. I was exhilarated because, in my own mind, by going underground I was confronting the elements and fighting every one of my childhood fears. I would do a day's work, come up at the end of the shift and go home with good money. There was a certain macho appeal to being a hard rock miner, in my view at least. Driving back home from far away and seeing the people who used to beat me up walking home from Boy Scouts, or seeing my mother who used to scream at me, or the schoolyard bullies, ceased to bother me. I had made a break with my past, at least geographically.

I will always remember my first trip underground. We each had a hard hat with a light on top and a battery pack attached to our belts. We wore coveralls over long underwear and had rubber boots with steel toes. Frankly, I was terrified. I was packed into an elevator with 43 other men. We called it the cage. Space was so tight you had to hold your lunch pail between your knees. Everyone's clothes smelled of the day before, sweat and oil and the mustiness of the mine. Even if the clothes were brand new at the beginning of our shift, one day underground and everything became a dingy gray color that was indelible. No matter if we washed them, the smell never left. What's more, there was a chemical used in the mines during fire drills that smelled a lot like rotten eggs. Each mine I have ever been in had a distinct smell of must and mold and old timbers. Mines smell dank. It's a smell that is hard to describe but it has an odor of its own.

That is the kind of place that I went down into and worked for many years. The cage descended 3000 feet to my level and dropped very quickly, about 22 miles per hour, which isn't that fast when you are in a car, but equates to 32 feet per second. We reached our level in a minute and a half. As I would learn, time is money underground. Management tried to increase the speed to 30 mph, but between the speed, the smells and the hangovers, too many guys were throwing up. Also, it was hard on the men's knees when the cage jerked to a halt at each level.

The different levels were 200 feet apart and each had a number attached to it: 2600, 2800, 3000, 3200, etc. The cagetender pulled a short bell cord that sent a signal to the hoistman to raise or lower the cage. The call sign for 3000 was eight fast rings followed by a pause, then five fast rings, another pause then one ring for raising the cage or two rings for lowering it.

The cage was controlled by the hoistman who was in the hoist room, on surface an eighth of a mile away from the cage itself. The cagetender was the only person in the cage who was allowed to touch the signal system. The hoistman moved the cage up and down the shaft according to the bell signal. It took up to six months to become qualified to run the hoist. If anyone besides the cagetender or the hoistman so much as touched the bell signals for any reason, he or she was fired. That is how vital that communication system was to the lives of the men underground.

Out of my lifelong respect for miners, every time I am waiting for an elevator I press the signal button eight times, then five and then two. People may assume that I'm being impatient, but really I do it in memory of the friends I made and then lost in the mine over the years.

As I descended that first morning, water from somewhere

dripped down my neck. In such close quarters I could smell what each man near me had for breakfast that morning or what he drank the night before. I could smell the oil on their clothes. Some hadn't changed their clothes or washed them for weeks at a time. It was a very unpleasant place to be. No matter, I felt like I fit right in. I really felt that I fit in.

Before long, the cage stopped, bounced a couple of feet and settled. We stepped out at the 3000 foot level and walked a quarter mile along railroad tracks through a tunnel, or drift, braced with big timbers to the lunchroom. The lunchroom in a mine is simply two long, long benches against the edge of the drift. Everybody had his own spot on the lunch bench and Lord help you if you sat in someone's place.

It was a whole new world. The blackness at 3000 feet is absolute and miners are utterly reliant on their cap lamps for illumination. When digging for the ore in their individual excavations, camp lamps were all they had. If a miner's light went out, he could hold his hand two inches from his face and see nothing. A blackness that is infinite and becomes disorienting, and a miner in the dark is wise to sit still until help arrives. A mine shaft may be only a stumble away. The mine became a fitting metaphor for my life up to that time and would remain so for many years.

The environment underground was truly dangerous and I felt real fear, but the apprehension blended with a surging excitement and a myriad of feelings that I had never experienced before. Fear was there the first couple of times I went underground, but the older men were always watching the new guys to see how they would take it. If they discovered that someone had an anxiety about him, they would take him under their wings to help him deal with it. I've never seen a level of trust as I have among miners because we worked together underground in dangerous situations and because of the unforgivable accidents that occur.

We had to trust each other to do the job safely so that when we went down the next day, the ground was protected and safely secured. We had to trust that the blasting was done properly. We developed a great, great, great solidarity. For the first time in my life, I truly felt that I belonged. I didn't belong in grade school. I didn't belong in high school. I didn't belong in Boy Scouts. I didn't belong on sports teams, but I belonged with my fellow miners, men sharing the same dangers, living on the edge every day.

Deep inside Mother Earth, half a mile beneath her skin, among rough, hardworking men, that is where I first tasted a sense of security and where I learned to live one day at a time.

BREAKING THROUGH

CHAPTER 15

LIFE UNDERGROUND

God creates. People rearrange.
—JOSEPH CASEY

MEN HAVE BEEN DIGGING MINERALS out of the earth for more than 40,000 years, so I had become a member in one of mankind's oldest fraternities. In the beginning, Neanderthal tribes mined flint for tools and weapons. Later, the Egyptians mined gold and green copper ore for ornamental purposes. At one time miners set fires to heat the rock face and then doused the rock with water to fracture and release the ore. Three thousand years later, we used dynamite.

Before mining begins, geologists map the potential mine site and know where the ore is by taking core samples throughout the area. Many core holes are drilled and tubular samples a few feet long and a few inches wide are gathered, carefully marked and analyzed. From these a picture of the ore body begins to appear. After having a picture of the size and value of the ore body, a mine shaft is sunk vertically in hard, stable rock next to the deposit. Tunnels, or drifts, are then blasted horizontally 200 feet apart to reach the ore. Perpendicular to these drifts are excavations into the ore, called stopes. It's a physically demanding process, first getting down to the ore, and then extracting it.

We worked with 110 pound pneumatic jackleg drills that turned six foot shanks tipped with industrial diamond bits. The jackleg supported the drill body and could be positioned to maximize the operator's leverage against the rock face. Pneumatics inside the jackleg that I regulated with a trigger kept forcing the drill shaft into the face. Water was misted into the bore hole to cool the bit and hold down dust. At the end of a shift, we hammered off the bits and sent them out to be re-sharpened. Earplugs and headphone-like ear muffs protected our ears from the deafening racket. Besides the drills, there were trains, equipment, ventilation fans which brought fresh air in and cleared out the smoke and fumes, as well as the blasts of explosives for our ears to contend with.

For the first six months, the drill worked me rather than the other way around. If a shank was even the slightest bit bent, there were big problems, especially in the beginning. Imagine a warped pool cue rolling on a table and visualize that in a 110 pound drill boring through rock at several hundred revolutions per minute. After wrestling with my drill for half a year, I got stronger and more savvy and learned how to position the jackleg and control it to my advantage. There was no apprenticeship or training; it was all on-the-job and quite frankly, no other way to learn.

The basic mining procedure went like this: Drill holes in the ore face, fill the holes with dynamite, blast the face to pieces, muck the ore down a chute to a train waiting below. The train took the ore to an ore pass which bottomed out at the 4800 foot level where it was crushed and removed to the surface. We then shored up the excavation with timbers and repeated these actions the next day. One complete cycle was a productive day's work; my partner and I would earn a bonus equal to our wages. At the end of a shift, it always felt good to tell the next guys coming in, "We cycled today!"

A typical stope was nine feet high, seven feet wide and as deep as there was ore to be recovered, sometimes a hundred feet long. Two men worked a stope at a time. We would drill 35 holes six feet into the rock face, each one about an inch and a quarter in size. The holes had to

Miners operating jackleg drills. Pneumatic pressure in the jackleg keeps the drill boring into the rock face.

be drilled in a certain pattern. Six holes in the center were surrounded by the remainder fanning out across the face. If we were drilling in rich ore, the bits would cut through easily. If it was mostly rock, it was much harder.

Once drilling was done, we packed the holes with dynamite or, later, a blasting agent called Amex. This was a mixture of ammonium nitrate fertilizer and fuel oil and was more convenient to use than dynamite because it was in a powder form that was easier to handle and more stable than dynamite.

Three of the six holes in the center we left empty. The other three, we packed with a blasting cap that was rammed to the end of the bore hole that had a fuse attached to it that was long enough to stick out of the hole a foot. We packed the rest of the hole with sticks of dynamite and repeated the procedure with the rest of the holes in the face. Dynamite has to blast into something to break up the rock. If it was just solid rock, nothing happened and the blast would freeze. The three center charges would break open the center of the face and the next ring of charges would blast into that and so on. The result of a properly done blast was six more feet of ore removed from the face.

Fuses were installed in each hole in such a way that the center charges went off first followed closely by the remaining blasts. A fuse burned at a rate of one foot every two minutes so seven foot fuses meant we had 14 minutes after lighting to get out of the stope. As I said, time is money underground so there was no sense waiting 14 minutes when fewer minutes would do, and we sometimes cut the fuses short, lit them and got the hell out.

Once safely away from the blast, we both waited by a timber, first making sure that no one else came near the blast area and then counting the shots as we heard them go off. We marked them with chalk on the timber, and when everything settled down, compared notes. If we put 32 shots in a face, we made sure we heard 32 shots and that our partner heard the same. We were supposed to wait 30 minutes before reentering the stope in case there was a slow burning fuse. Of course some miners considered that a waste of time. They would miscount—the shots go off rapidly—and go back in before the fog and smoke cleared. The missed shot would go off and kill them.

After the blast, we headed back into the stope. Each time we reentered a newly blasted stope, we stood in a space that no man had ever seen or occupied before. Were we further violating the integrity of Mother Earth? The thought never crossed our minds. We were hot, tired, and usually hung over. Our first action inside the stope was to install timbers to shore up the roof. Then the slusher, which was a big scraper, mucked out the ore and dragged it into the chute near the entrance to the stope.

The chute in the stope was essentially a 200 foot shaft from one level to another with a big hopper and a hydraulic gate at the bottom. Five ton battery powered train cars moved under the gate and filled them with ore when the gate was opened. The ore train moved to another opening, the ore pass, where hydraulics tipped the car and emptied it, dumping it to the 4800 foot level, which was the bottom of the mine. There, a massive crusher broke the rocks into five-inch pieces for transport to the rock house above ground. An open steel container, called a skip, that held 22 tons brought it to surface in 90 seconds. It was counterbalanced by another skip that was headed back down at the same time. At the surface, the skip unloaded onto a conveyor belt and through another crusher that reduced it to one-and-a-half-inch rocks.

The cage and the skip ran in the same shaft only feet apart, separated by a wooden wall. While riding in the cage you could hear the skip and feel it whizzing up and down, making it seem that the cage was moving in slow motion.

From the rock house the ore was transported to the mill on long conveyor belts. In the mill it was ground into powder and chemically processed to extract 14 different minerals, primarily nickel but also copper, gold, platinum and others. The chemicals used in processing had long-term effects on mill employees' health. For example, men who worked in the silver smelting plant developed breath that smelled like garlic because of the processing. Even years after they left, they still had garlic breath. Down in the mine, we had to wear long johns, coveralls and gloves to guard against nickel rash from ore dust, which is carcinogenic. In the sintering plant, which was on surface, the dust was so

Miners in a card game in the lunch room during break.

thick that it was hard to see your coworkers and the carcinogens in the dust made it a cancer-causing killing field.

Two shifts worked the same stope and shared production bonuses. At shift's end we walked back to the cage and met the other shift coming down. We had two minutes to discuss what happened on our shift with the next crew before we turned it over to them. I worked in stope 228. Our pay was determined by how far we broke ground in a month. An engineer would come in and count the number of timbers erected since the last month's inspection and that's how we got paid. Timbers had to be erected every six feet.

Every so often, management staff would come down to conduct time motion studies and when this happened, we used the dullest bits we could find to draw out the study, which meant higher production incentives, since drilling in harder rock takes longer. There was an expected time frame for every action: drilling, blasting, mucking, installing timbers, wedges, everything, and you were paid accordingly. So, if we could extend the time motion studies we stood to make a bigger bonus. That mentality also led to cutting corners. Shorten the fuses. Make do with 30 holes instead of 35.

Of course, sometimes fewer holes in the face resulted in a chunk of rock so large that it jammed the gate in our chute, and we didn't want to anger the guys running the ore trains. If they wouldn't load our ore, we were in trouble. Miners could only work as fast as the motor crew would empty their chutes. If they didn't like us, they could make excuses such as saying that the batteries on the train were down. Delays hurt our pay, so we wanted to treat the guys below decently.

I worked on a motor crew for a year or two and sometimes when guys above were cutting corners we would get a huge chunk that jammed the gate. That would really cause us problems. We would have to break it up, and the only way was to blast it. To make our displeasure apparent to the crew above, we would fill a plastic gallon bottle with drilling oil and then tape old rubber gloves to the container. We would set this on top of the blast, which made a stink bomb that filled the chute with stinky smoke and the miners above would have to evacuate. The smarter guys working above would curry favor with the motor crews by giving them a bottle of whiskey every so often. When I worked in the stope, you can be sure that the motor crew was "well oiled" with free booze.

Releasing a jam in a chute could be very dangerous. It might be 20 or more feet above the gate and a miner would have to climb a ladder up the chute and place a bomb to dislodge the jam. Any movement could bring it down on top of him. Crazy business, mining.

The "break men," as they were called because they measured the amount of ground broken since their last visit, recorded all their data in log books and this documentation was the heart of their jobs and also the prime determinant of our bonuses. That was unfortunate for one break man who always tried to give the impression that he owned the company and was a real bastard about his measurements. My partner at the time was a real bad-tempered Dutchman named Pete.

"McDougall," Pete told me one day, "when Joe the Break Man comes in today, you just walk away for a while. He's been screwing us on our bonuses and I'm tired of it."

Joe came in with his pompous airs and I grabbed a scaling bar and meandered away from the scene. A minute or so later, I heard hollering and screaming and then Joe came hurrying out of the stope looking much the worse for wear.

"Jesus, Pete, what'd you do to him?"

"I ripped the sonofabitch's log book out of his pocket, chopped it up with my axe and threw the goddamn thing down the chute. Then I told 'im, 'Next time, it won't be your log book! Now, get the fuck out of here!'"

We got called behind the green door for that one. The general foreman asked us what happened.

"I dunno," I said. "I was at the face scaling."

"Joe dropped his book down the chute and blamed me," said Pete.

We had the foreman by the short hairs. He knew that if you pissed off the miners they would purposely slow down, production would drop and he would catch it from up top. The miners ran the mine and we knew it and all the smart supervisors underground knew it. Antics like these went on all the time but hardly ever reached the ears of management above ground. Solidarity among miners was nearly absolute.

Payday was Tuesday, and company payroll men spent the day outside the Toronto Dominion Banks in mining towns that ringed the Sudbury Basin. Everybody had a numbered silver badge that we were supposed to carry all the time and show to be allowed past security at the mine and to receive pay. Sometimes we'd forget our badges at home and guys would flash a Zippo lighter or a spoon with the handle hidden in their hand. My first badge number was 11355. Later, I had to get a new badge, No. 10320. The payroll officer knew me by my badge number, not my name. "Oh, hiya, 10320," is how he would greet me.

He'd mark his log, slide my check off the stack with the rubber thimble on his finger and I'd take it inside to the window and cash it. Then, like most of the other men, I headed straight to a hotel bar.

Breaking Through

CHAPTER 16

LIFE ABOVE GROUND

Contentment makes poor men rich.
Discontent makes rich men poor.
—BENJAMIN FRANKLIN

I ALWAYS TOLD MY MOTHER that everybody who lived in the bunkhouse had demons chasing them, but I never really looked at my own until much later. So, for me it was a great life. Lots of drinking and partying.

In the beginning, I missed my girlfriend. I drove home every three weeks and it was an eight hour drive down to Auburn. I know that there was someone or something looking after me because I never drove home unless I was under the influence. Usually, I worked overtime on the night shift and then drove all day to go home. Back home, I was always drinking and spending money. I never saw my parents when I was totally sober. My mother and dad never had more than the occasional drink, but I was always significantly intoxicated.

In those early days, I weighed 155 pounds and was 6'2" tall. I was rugged and had grown physically since my asthmatic childhood. I was still smoking a pack a day though, and drinking as much as I could, which fit me perfectly into the lifestyle of hard rock miners. Some people in the bunkhouse you would befriend and they'd leave in a week or sometimes we'd have friends for six months and they'd leave. Sometimes, the police came into the bunkhouse to arrest someone on an outstanding warrant.

Even though the company had strict hiring policies, some employees never owned up to their past transgressions.

I was having fun in my life. The food was good. There was an abundance of money, much different from the $35 a week unemployment I had been receiving only months earlier. To me, $107 a week was good money and I had plans to save it and live a somewhat normal life in Sudbury.

I never personally heard from any of the plants or companies where I had submitted my resume when I was out looking for work before I moved to Sudbury. Later though, I found out that two weeks after I'd been hired at the mine, my dad received a call from the plant in Goderich that made road graders. "We're hiring right now and we'd like you to bring in your son, Allan," they told him. "We'd like to have him interview with us and we'll hire him if things work out."

Dad told them I already had a job and had moved away. He knew that I would get in trouble living back home. He knew there was better money in the mine. He knew that I would not be laid off in the mine but would be from time to time at the grader plant. Most important, he also knew that I'd be away from Mom and him and their constant bickering and that I could start a new life.

He finally told me ten years after the fact that he had received that phone call, and that every time that he heard of a mining accident or someone being killed in a mine whether it was in Sudbury or anywhere, it drove him crazy with worry. "What happens if Allan gets hurt or he got killed and I knew that he didn't have to work there?" he would think to himself.

I empathized with his concerns and guilt, but in the long run it was the best thing for me. I have been afforded opportunities in Sudbury that otherwise, would never been opened to me. Yet, what a burden for him to carry. He knew that I didn't get along with my mother and what life would be like there with all my drinking friends. Little did he realize that I was developing a close circle of drinking friends in Sudbury.

One of the things that bothered me the most at that time, was that all my life Mom had said to me over and over, "You're the reason, Allan, that I am so unhappy. I wouldn't be married to your father if you hadn't been born and I would be happy."

What a burden of guilt to place onto a young lad of 5 or 6 years old and then to reinforce it for the next 12 or 14 years. One of the main reasons I went north was so she could leave my father, get a divorce and be happy at the relatively young age of 57.

I would return home every two or three weeks, always disappointed to find them still together. They were miserable with each other, but they refused to separate. I said to them every so often, under the influence, of course, "I'm so disappointed that you never loved each other. You have nothing to live for together. Why would you want to stay together? You used to blame me for your difficulties but now I'm out of the picture. Why don't you leave?"

Their excuse was that they came from a small village. What would the neighbors think? What would the relatives think? They had been together so long that it was too late to have any happiness. These are the circumstances I was driving back to all the time. So, I went home less and less and stayed in Sudbury more and more. When I did visit, I stayed with my partying friends.

Their decision upset me because I knew it was just an excuse. It was like the traveling salesman who becomes lost one day in rural Texas. He drives up to a rancher's house and asks for directions. The rancher invites him to rest a spell and gives him a soft drink. There is a hound dog lying in a corner and every so often he yelps out in pain and shifts a little.

Finally, the visitor asks, "What's wrong with your dog?"

"Oh," the rancher says, "he's lying on a nail."

"Why doesn't he just move?" the salesman asks.

"He's not hurting bad enough yet."

That was my parents! As Abraham Lincoln said, "Most folks are as happy as they make up their minds to be."

Sudbury is a mining town with no shortage of establishments to help a man whose throat felt a little parched. To say there was a bar on every corner would be to exaggerate, but barely. If hockey is Canada's national religion, drinking was Sudbury's favorite pastime. I made good money but never saved as I envisioned. I just lived and drank heavily. I never missed any time on the job though, because right from the beginning I knew that if I wanted to play hard, I'd have to work hard.

Besides the company bunkhouse, store and jail, there was also a company recreational hall, complete with televisions and pool tables, where the single men could go. Every night we'd drop in, sit in easy chairs and watch television. Every Tuesday night, a little club opened up just down the street. There was card playing and drinking in a little bar. They closed the bar early because they didn't want men drinking until 2:00 in the morning and then going into the mine hung over the following day. So, they kept as tight a rein on the drinking as they could, but they couldn't control it in the bunkhouse and that's where we did most of it. That also opened up the entrepreneurship of bootlegging.

I was developing a high tolerance for alcohol. My tactic for controlling the sickness by putting my foot on the floor to stop the room from spinning began to pay off in spades. I overcame my nausea and became, if such a thing is possible, a competent drinker.

For our first three months, we were in a probationary period and we all worked hard. At the end of the three months, I qualified to join a trade union. Growing up on a farm, I had never heard of a union except on TV newsreels showing the United Mine Workers going on strike. Looking back, those newsreels always excited me. Now that we were in a union, we had protection. We were members of the United Steel Workers of America (USWA) and we paid union dues in exchange for which they looked after our health and safety plus other benefits. This was important, because there were an average of 15 to 18 fatalities a year and the company did nothing about it.

Mining methods were very different from today, it was much more dangerous and miners were ruthlessly exploited. I have to thank the Steel Workers Union, the Mine Workers Union and other unions that brought better laws to the mining industry and better OSHA (Occupational Safety and Health Act) laws. We have a law in Canada today that if there's a fatality and someone in management knew about the hazard but didn't fix it, they can be charged with manslaughter under the criminal code. It took the USW more than 10 years of diligent persistence to bring that law through Parliament.

That's quite a change from 1970 when, if someone was killed next to me, the boss would say, "Listen, McDougall. This is where you work. This is not a candy factory. You knew this going in and if you need a day off as a little wimp, that's fine. Take a day off. We may or may not pay you. You can drink yourself to death, or you can do whatever you need to do to get rid of that stress but then come on back and just get back to work and forget about it."

So, as miners, we developed ways to forget about it.

Breaking Through

CHAPTER 17

THINGS MINERS NEVER TALKED ABOUT

The best things in life are appreciated most after they have been lost.
–ROY L. SMITH

EVERY MONTH, QUALIFIED RIGGERS, called shaft inspectors, examined the shaft down into the mine. They rode on top of the cage all the way down inspecting to make sure everything was safe. The mining industry, reacting to union demands and public opinion, had become more safety-conscious over the years, and shaft inspections became a regular procedure.

One day in 1984, four men were riding on top of the cage with an aluminum cover overhead to keep water from dripping on them from exposed fissures in the shaft. Two thousand feet above them and a quarter of a mile down a tunnel, a miner was working in his stope. He shut off his air line to lubricate his drill. Earlier, someone had completed a band-aid repair job on a piece of equipment somewhere else on the level. When the miner cut off his air, it opened a gate and dumped 13 tons of ore into the shaft.

Standing on top of the cage 2,000 feet below, the four men could feel the air pressure in the shaft suddenly shift and they could hear the load hurtling down. For probably 30 seconds, the men must have stood there listening to the sound of approaching doom. They were on top of the cage with nowhere to go. Imagine what those 30 seconds must have been like. The regrets, the things they never told their loved ones, the dreams they'd had for their lives. Were they able to make their peace in so short a time? The only way the bodies were identified was from the numbers on the battery packs that were issued to each man to keep their cap lights working.

The entire mine was shut down for two weeks while an investigation took place. The miner who shut down his air line did nothing wrong. The tragedy was a culmination of several omissions for which no one could be faulted, but which caused four fatalities.

That one affected me profoundly. I had worked underground for years and professed to know what I was doing, though I never had total confidence to do things myself. That tragedy shook my confidence to the core. How could I survive in such an unforgiving environment when these guys, who were more experienced miners, had their lives snuffed out in an instant? Moreover, who could I share those feelings with? Nobody. I felt very vulnerable, so I retreated into my familiar refuge, the bottle.

We always knew when there was an accident because all hoisting ceased. The cage would be brought to the level where the accident occurred. The lunch room attendant would receive a call from surface on the antiquated phone system with instructions to spread the word there had been an accident. Lunchroom attendants were usually old miners or guys who had been disabled. They kept the lunchroom as clean and orderly as can be expected in a mine and relayed communications from up top. Whenever we got word, we put down our tools and gathered in the lunchroom to await further news.

Throughout the mine in each stope there were shafts 16 inches square, called a steel box, running vertically for hoisting tools and equipment. If someone was hurt in the stope, a wire stretcher basket was hooked to a tugger hoist that hauled the victim to where he could be transported to the cage and up to surface.

Meanwhile, the rest of us would sit in the lunchroom on our

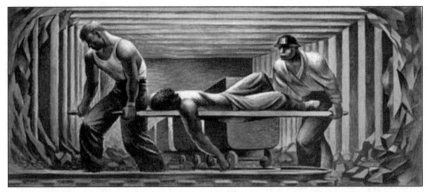

This Depression Era painting depicts the all-too-frequent accidents that occurred underground. Note the timbers holding up the ground. Today, these have mostly been replaced by mechanized bolts and heavy screening.

benches, isolated from each other by our thoughts. We wouldn't know what happened or what level or to whom. The cagetender and the hoistman on surface would send word once they knew. Both shifts of the miners who worked on the victim's level would attend the funeral at their own expense, that is, losing that day's wages. INCO, the heartless bastards, wouldn't reimburse them for missing their shift.

Tragic episodes like these were filtered through miners' egos, which suppressed them, forcing men to believe that they could deal with anything. Considering the environment, it was one of the only coping mechanisms they had.

The human body has been called "the soft machine," and it never appears more fragile than when standing beneath 3,000 feet of solid rock. Displaying any sort of mental or emotional weakness was totally out of character, and miners kept up a very false front. Alcohol helped fortify the artificial bravado we exhibited while being up against Death or the Devil each day of our lives.

One thing that worked in our favor, I have come to realize, was the darkness itself. Our vision was limited by whatever we could see within the range of our cap lamps. The lunchroom and shaft stations were lit, but inside a stope, it was you and your cap lamp. For the most part, the roof bolts coming loose, the wowing timbers, the thousand foot shafts five feet behind you remained hidden in darkness and the old saying, "Out of sight, out of mind" worked to our benefit. I sometimes wonder how many men would work in the mines if they could see everything around them all the time. It's not as scary when you can see only what is directly in front of you. If you were working by yourself and the light went out, you'd sit there until someone came to get you. There were no telephones. There was no radio contact because the ground would interrupt radio signals.

Because miners wouldn't or couldn't express their feelings about the things that happened underground, they developed other ways of releasing the tension. Of course, alcohol was a primary means above

That's me on the right with two other miners at Christmastime when the prohibition against bringing alcohol underground was relaxed somewhat.

ground but wasn't allowed in the mine except on special occasions like Christmas, when we would sneak it in. Underground, the socially accepted outlet was humor, of a coarse and at times, brutal nature.

Guys would often bring their jackets down the shaft with them because, even though the mine was hot, it might be 30 degrees below on surface. They would hang their jackets on a timber and sometimes we would nail a guy's sleeve to it. At the end of the shift, a guy would be racing to make the cage for the trip up and grab his jacket as he raced by. The sleeve would rip off and we'd think that was hilarious.

For years, all we had for toilets underground was a six hole platform, three holes on each side, that emptied into a container that was mounted on wheels. Every week the train crew would haul it to surface in the cage, clean it out and roll it back into place at the end of a drift. That was our restroom. A rod between the rows of holes held the rolls of toilet paper.

One day, a miner named John was sitting there minding his own business while taking care of business. I had been sitting at the opposite end on the other row. Before I finished, I unrolled a big wad of toilet paper and threw it behind where he was sitting. After I pulled up my pants, I lit the paper on fire and verified that I could run a lot faster with my pants up than John could with his pants down.

We used to play a lot in the cage. We'd have our stinking old clothes on. Some miners didn't wash their clothes very regularly. Coming up on Friday night, the smell would be so bad from the oil and the sweat and the urine and everything else that was in the mine that we couldn't stand it.

Riding up in the cage, three or four of us would grab a guy's coveralls that were particularly rank and rip them off him. We would then rip off his long underwear, because these were also rotten and stunk. We threw them on the floor of the cage and everybody got into the act. We took his socks off and his underwear, too. When we got to surface, he was standing there with his helmet, his light, his belt, his battery, his boots, but was otherwise stark naked. He had to walk out of the cage that way. It was maybe a hundred degrees underground but he had to walk out of the cage and to the change room naked. He held his hat over his genitals and his lunch pail over his rear, and it was a funny sight.

I always threw my long rubber gloves away at the end of the week because they were full of nickel and I didn't want to get nickel rash on my skin. There might be a hole in one of the gloves where I held the drill all day. The other glove would be like new.

Some older miners would ransack the garbage cans to retrieve a glove that was good, and they'd use it. That was an amazing culture shock when I first went underground. Someone else would throw his boots away because there would be a hole in one, and some of these older guys would take the other boot and use it because it was still good.

We often hid behind timbers when we saw a light approaching, and then jump out to scare a guy. Once we knew someone was nervous, we would do it more and more and more. It broke the tension of living that life underground. If he was skittish about mining, we helped him, but if we found out he scared easily, he was fair game.

In 1976, INCO opened a new mine two miles from Levack called Levack West Mine. The company transferred some men over there and I was one who went. At first, I hated all the differences. There was no cage. A mile long 20 degree ramp ran down to 1500 feet. There were no 9' X 7' stopes. In this mine, the drifts were giant, 16' X 16,' to accommodate large mechanized low profile diesel equipment. The ground was secured by mechanical bolts drilled upwards into the rock, not timbers.

Another miner who had worked his entire life in the mine, named George, was transferred over to Levack West with me. George was a great guy, always laughing. He was afraid of snakes and other guys were fond of putting rubber snakes in his lunch pail. They would be sure to watch when George sat down for lunch and roared when his lunch pail and sandwiches went flying after another rubber reptile launched itself out.

One day before we were transferred, I got an idea to give George a scare. Planks ran above the tunnels, which created a storage gangway that held supplies. We used tons of burlap in the mines to hold back the cement that was shot into an excavation to fill it and shore up the ground. I knew George would be coming up after lunch to get some rolls so I snuck up there and hid inside a roll of burlap, planning to scare him. As I waited with my cap light off, it began to dawn on me that he would be coming up there with an axe to cut the ties on the rolls and that this might go badly for me if he freaked out and began swinging.

Finally, my realization got the better of me and as I heard him coming, I called out, "George! George! It's me up here. It's McDougall. Don't be scared."

Just the sound of a voice scared the devil out of him and he started running the other way.

For all his jumpiness, George had an impeccable safety record. He was a miner who had worked his entire career without a single serious mishap. Six months from retirement, he was working on a front end loader and stepped out the cab while others were finishing a loading job. He lit a cigarette and waited, thinking perhaps of how in six months he could sleep late and enjoy time with the grandkids. Suddenly, with no warning, a wall-sized, foot thick slab of rock cleaved off and crushed him. In less time than it took you to read that sentence, George's life was snuffed out. The only sign that he had been standing there was his rubber boot and his hand, cigarette still burning, sticking out from opposite sides of the slab. It was gruesome.

It happened on a Friday, and I don't know if I used George's death as an excuse, but I stayed blind drunk the whole weekend. His death shook my confidence to the core.

Standing there looking at the grisly sight cast me straight back into the dark pit of my childhood fears. Here was a miner with an impeccable safety record, who had never been seriously injured in his entire career underground. I was 27 at the time and an alcoholic who went underground hung over on most days. "I'll never make it," I said to myself. "If that happened to George, what will happen to me?"

Of course, there was no one I could confide in, so I buried these thoughts deep within myself and then flooded that part of my psyche with booze.

It's not hard to understand why miners become excessively jumpy, much like soldiers who hit the ground reflexively at the sound of a door slamming or a car backfire once they return to civilian life. Underground, rocks fall, cables snap, strange noises occur and a split second can make all the difference.

We developed a grim philosophical outlook: "If it's your time, it's your time and nothing can be done about it." It was a viewpoint that management reinforced, too, probably to justify why they usually came down on the profit side of the profit/safety equation.

I was sitting in a stope one day in Levack Mine with two other miners and the timbers began to do something I had never seen before, called wowing. All I had a chance to spit out to the others was, "Look!" and I was headed down the ladder out of the stope. The other two didn't even bother with the ladder as I felt them jumping past me. A second later everything caved in. We made it out just in time.

So, yes, miners are a skittish lot. Of course, we played on that to humorous advantage. One guy, Frenchy, was so nervous that if you came up behind him and scared him, his instant reaction was to yell, "Fuck, fuck, fuck, fuck, fuck!" We would wait until he was in front of the bank teller on pay day, then someone would sneak up and kick him in the ankle. That was always good for a laugh.

Another miner would reflexively swing his arms wildly whenever he was startled. We would be in a store picking up cigarettes or snacks for our lunch pails and wait until he was reaching for a can of soup on the shelf. Someone would hit him and he would start swinging and knock all the cans off the shelf. One time, he pulled a bottle of pop from the cooler, opened it and was rummaging through the little bin beneath the bottle opener to retrieve his cap and see if he had won a prize. We jumped up behind him and hundreds of bottle caps flew into the air and soda pop sprayed all over the shelves and floor when the bottle hit the floor and exploded.

I was involved in another episode that is funny now but wasn't at the time. The Levack West Mine was situated directly under the town of Levack. One day, a blast was planned only 250 feet below surface. The rock there was notorious for never breaking right. Some rock is soft and some is hard. This area was hard, unyielding rock, so I loaded the stope heavy with "Amex." As I finished, I began to have second thoughts that maybe I overloaded it and went to the foreman to voice my concern.

"Jesus Christ, do what I tell you! Light the goddamn fuses!" he yelled at me.

"Tony," I said, "we should be careful with this blast. We're only down 250 feet."

"Fuck! Light the fucking thing! Do what I tell you. It's Friday night and let's get the fuck home!"

Less than a football field directly above, there was a social event at the Levack Community Hall with drinking and dancing, probably a wedding reception.

The blast rocked the entire town. Dishes came crashing down. Cabinets toppled as they would in a big earthquake. The miners attending the event flipped out and began swinging on each other and diving for cover.

Lawsuits were filed after that one and I got called in during the investigation.

"Who lit the fuse?" the investigators wanted to know.

"I did," I said.

"Who told you to light it? Did Tony tell you?" they asked.

"Well, it was the end of the shift and I had to do it," I replied.

"Who told you to light it? Was it Tony?" they persisted.

"That's for Tony to answer. It's not for me to answer," I said. I wasn't about to rat Tony out.

Being a foreman, Tony was not a union member but part of management and was fired. I felt bad for him.

We had many close calls, but at the end of the day, we always went back up top and every single day, the first thing we did was head to the bar or the beer store or go back to the bunkhouse where we would continue to drink until it was time to go to bed or until we passed out.

Every day you carried a lunch bag down with you but you never really knew whether you would go up in a body bag. There were enough accidents and fatalities that the thought was never far from our minds.

Because Levack was a company town, the men who lived in the bunkhouses or company houses paid minimal rent. Much money was spent on toys such as cars or motorcycles or hunting and fishing and of course, drinking. That's the kind of lifestyle that I grew into, and I acclimated to it very quickly.

Social skills though, were severely limited. We had eight bunkhouses in a town of 3,000 people. The men were between the ages of 18 and 50, mostly single. If I had daughters in my family at the time, I certainly wouldn't want them exposed to the men living in a miner's bunkhouse. Dating skills were totally absent.

Occasionally, we would drive into Sudbury to the hotels to drink and listen to country and western bands. That is the other environment where I felt totally comfortable. I loved the atmosphere of the bar scene, the drinking, the music, the dim lights. It was the siren's call pulling me in. I just loved it. You can imagine the amount of money being blown on payday in the hotels and bars all over the Sudbury Basin. Some country and western songs have been written about the area. "Sudbury Saturday Night," written by Stompin' Tom Conners captures the scene perfectly:

The girls are out to Bingo and the boys are gettin' stinko,
And we think no more of Inco on a Sudbury Saturday night.
The glasses they will tinkle when our eyes begin to twinkle,
And we'll think no more of Inco on a Sudbury Saturday night.

With Irish Jim O'Connel there and Scotty Jack MacDonald,
There's honky Fredrick Hurchell gettin' tight, but that's alright,
There's happy German Fritzy there with Frenchy getting tipsy,
And even Joe the Gypsy knows it's Saturday tonight.

Now when Mary Ann and Mabel come to join us at the table,
And tell us how the Bingo went tonight, we'll look a fright.
But if they won the money, we'll be lappin' up the honey, boys,
'Cause everything is funny, for it's Saturday tonight

The girls are out to Bingo and the boys are gettin' stinko,
And we think no more of Inco on a Sudbury Saturday night.
The glasses they will tinkle when our eyes begin to twinkle,
And we'll think no more of Inco on a Sudbury Saturday night.

We'll drink the loot we borrowed and recuperate tomorrow,
'Cause everything is wonderful tonight, we had a good fight,
We ate the Dilly Pickle and we forgot about the Nickel,
And everybody's tickled, for it's Saturday tonight

The songs that we'll be singing,
they might be wrong but they'll be ringing,
When the lights of town are shining bright, and we're all tight,
We'll get to work on Monday, but tomorrow's only Sunday,
And we're out to have a fun day for it's Saturday tonight. Yeah

The girls are out to Bingo and the boys are gettin' stinko,
And we think no more of Inco on a Sudbury Saturday night.
The glasses they will tinkle when our eyes begin to twinkle,
And we'll think no more of Inco on a Sudbury Saturday night.

We'll think no more of Inco on a Sudbury Saturday night.

I hated fighting and detested violence. I became very much a pacifist alcoholic. I never wanted to get into fights or arguments. I had seen too many arguments in my life and I avoided them and still do.

I'd be sitting at a table with two or three young guys and having a drink with them and then they would get rowdy. There was always testosterone flowing freely in the bars and a fight would break out over a pool game or a shuffleboard game or an argument with the guys at the next table. I would get up and leave, saying, "I'm going to the washroom and I'll be right back," and I would be gone to the next bar.

The bars were so busy that sometimes you'd go the bathroom and the guys at your table would sell your chair for $5 to another table. I only wanted peace and quiet, to be alone with my own dreams and my own thoughts. I could not relate to the emotionally charged conversations taking place at other tables. I never wanted violence. More importantly, I never wanted the party to end. The party was my escape.

The daily life of a single miner was to go to work everyday and work eight hours on the day or swing shift, make good money and do the best you could. We had to have complete faith in our fellow miners underground. We also had the same level of faith and respect in the recreational world of drinking.

As I said, alcohol was never permitted underground, even though many of us brought it down daily coursing through our bloodstream. To be under the effects of alcohol in the morning with a hangover was acceptable. One thing for certain though, underground in the 70s,

Me, wearing my drinking hat.

there was no place for anybody doing any sort of recreational drugs. It seemed that there was a sharp divide between us and the people who worked above ground in the smelter with their marijuana and hash. The coping skills of miners were strictly limited to alcohol.

I had many issues that required coping skills. I had to deal with my wimpiness, my childhood, my being bullied. I drank and smoked as a means of dealing with my parental issues, feelings of rejection and lack of self-worth. My ways of coping were drinking and smoking, fast cars, dangerous work and living on the edge, which I think helped me develop a sense that I was a man and worthy of being called a man instead of a kid.

I resented the whole hippie movement. They replaced the music I liked with their psychedelic crap. Underground, we wouldn't trust anybody who used drugs. We all thought that drugs put your mind off in fantasyland and we couldn't tolerate that underground. We certainly would not let them drive any equipment or do any blasting.

I guess one would characterize me as a redneck. Some say the term originated from Southern farmers whose necks became red from the sun. While that may be true, "redneck" also referred to a union miner. Labor organizers in the coal fields of West Virginia, Kentucky and Pennsylvania tried to build coalitions of miners across geographical lines by having union supporters wear red bandanas around their necks. Whatever the origin, I preferred the Dukes of Hazzard lifestyle over what came out of San Francisco.

CHAPTER 18

The Family Man

If you go around thinking you are being cheated,
life becomes very unpleasant.
—Felix Salten

I lived in the bunkhouse for two years and during that period I kept going back home. Six months after Dave and I were hired, he quit while I was away for a couple days. He wanted to continue his education and get a degree. When I came back, I found out and really missed him because he was my backup guy.

Our first week at the mine, a teenage girl was walking past the bunkhouse on her way home from school. Her boyfriend lived in our bunkhouse along with his brother. I was driving back from my shift in my Camaro. When I pulled into the parking lot, her boyfriend confronted me about trying to take his girlfriend away from him while his older brother stood behind me in case I decided to fight, in which case he would be able to take me from behind. What I didn't realize at that moment is that Dave was there backing me up in case there was trouble.

When the boyfriend approached, I just said, "Hey, I'm not interested in anybody. I have a girlfriend down home and I just want to be left alone." That was the only confrontation I ever had in all my years working as a miner. I later found out that the guy and his brother were fighters and just wanted a fight that day. Dave backed me up and became a good friend. He was much more interested in continuing his education where I certainly wasn't. I was just happy to have a job and a paycheck and to be far away from the people in the small village where I grew up.

If you worked hard underground and took chances and worked at the face, that is, the wall where advancement into the ore body is being made, or did the dynamiting and blasting, you could make really good money. With incentives, you could double your wages, depending on how much you produced. Because I grew up on a farm, even though I couldn't work in the barn, I adopted the good work habits of my dad, which I carry on to this day. When you first went underground, you had to gain seniority as a laborer, usually shoveling, before you could go into stopes. Whatever failings I had, working hard was not one of them.

The routine of my life consisted of drinking, working, sleeping, hanging around the bunkhouse, driving home to Auburn, partying and coming back to work. Still, nothing was able to fill that gaping hole in my soul. From the outside, it may have looked like a good life. Inside, I still didn't really know my place in the world. I still had no place to sink my roots and the unforgiving rock where I struggled for my daily bread and booze allowed me to forget the life I had come from and nothing more.

My mom and dad drove up every six months to visit. For eight years, I never told mom that I worked underground. She thought I worked on surface. One day during their visit, I took them out to the mine site.

We were standing in the parking lot and my mother asked, "What building do you work in, again?"

I couldn't lie to her anymore and I said, "Well, actually, it's 3,000 feet right below where we're standing. I've been working underground for quite some time."

"How long?" she asked in surprise.

"Eight years."

"Well," she said, "you must know what you're doing because you're still here."

That was the extent of my involvement with my parents. They had their lives to live and I had mine, such as these were.

One day about a year and a half into my career, I was sitting in a restaurant in Levack and a man came in who knew me from town. He was the son of a local miner and asked me if I had any plans for Friday. No, I said, and he went on, "Well, my girlfriend has a cousin that I'd like you to meet." So, we went on a blind date and hit it off okay. We began dating in Sudbury; it was nice to have a date now and then.

My sister Bernice, meanwhile, had married a farmer. She still lived in Auburn, worked as a teacher and to this day has lived a wonderful life. By contrast, I was just kind of floating around, which was fine by me at the time.

I wasn't really too interested in her in the beginning, but later we became involved, and within nine months we were engaged. Here is a snapshot of the support that my mother gave me when I proudly called my parents to share the news.

"Guess what I bought today, Mom?"

"Probably a diamond ring," came the deadpan reply.

"That's right, a diamond ring." I was so excited.

"Don't get it thrown back in your face," she said and disconnected the line. That was the level of emotional support that I received from my mother at home.

My future wife's father worked at INCO, and she loved him dearly. Like me, he had a problem with alcohol. As with many mining families, alcohol was an accepted part of the life and he liked his booze.

She was a very beautiful young woman and could easily have been a model. She dropped out of school after Grade 9 and worked behind the lunch counter at S.S. Kresge, which later became K-Mart. When

I was on swing shift, I would often visit her at work. She was a hard worker and loved fishing and in time, we developed feelings for each other. In reality, however, she turned out to be the first girl who came along, and perhaps, because of my addiction to alcohol, I became the embodiment of the father she loved.

I wouldn't have to educate her to the reality that I wouldn't be home every night after work. It was quite acceptable in her family that her father would go to work, then go to the bar afterwards and sit there drinking and rehashing the day. In the years to follow, it was common for me to come home at 8:00, even though my shift ended at 4:00, find dinner sitting on the table, cold, slug down a few more beers and go to bed. That was the ritual of the average person who worked in a mine. Not all mining families lived this way, but many of them did, and I certainly gravitated to those.

Her mother also had an alcohol addiction, which deepened when her husband passed away six months before our wedding. He was only 51 when he died of a heart attack, way too young. After that, her mother became a much heavier drinker. She had a very difficult time holding her liquor.

Working underground, I always imagined that I would simply freeze if something dangerous happened, but every time a rock fell or a post cracked or a dynamite shot went off too closely, I always reacted very quickly. One time though, I did not, but it didn't occur in the mine.

One night before we were married, I was sleeping on the couch in their living room. Something woke me in the middle of the night. Standing above me, I saw a figure illuminated by the streetlight coming through the picture window. Eight inches from my chest I could see the blade of a butcher knife.

I tried to move, but I was frozen. I just froze. She stood there with that knife…I don't know if she'd been there for three hours or three seconds, but even today it still gives me goose bumps. Finally, the most mournful sound came out of the pit of my stomach and woke my fiancé. Later, she said it was the most frightful sound she'd ever heard. She came running out of her bedroom and grabbed her mother who was in the middle of the DTs with a butcher knife in her hand.

We got her into a detox center, which she signed herself out of immediately afterwards. Later, she told me, "Allan, I wasn't about to hurt you. I was going to stab the man in the plaid shirt who was under the couch."

The only problem I had with that was I was between her and him. That was my first experience seeing someone with the DTs. Delirium tremens are the hallucinations and convulsions stemming from the overuse or chronic abuse of alcohol on the body's central nervous system.

I still think about that night and how frozen I was. When someone tells me that they freeze or that time stops, I can really relate. In short, I really fit into the dynamics of that family. I enjoyed the partying, the alcohol, the music and the conversation.

A year and a half after we met, we were married and moved into a small apartment in Sudbury. We didn't have any children yet and we lived there for about a year. She got another job and we enjoyed each other's company; however, I was drinking more and more.

When we were married, I thought my life would improve. We had our good times, and although we had disagreements, I always thought that things would somehow get better.

About a year into our marriage, we received a phone call about 11:30 on a Saturday night. It was from one of the detectives at the police station. He asked to speak to my wife. I handed her the phone and he gave her a message, not like they do on television when they go to your front door and talk to you in person, but impersonally over the telephone. The detective said that her mother had died and they suspected foul play.

That was a terrible night for us. We drove over to the house and met with the detectives. We learned a bit about what they found. Yes, it was foul play. At the end of the investigation a man was found guilty of manslaughter after a domestic dispute, and did time in jail.

After that, we moved into her mother's house, a duplex; we lived upstairs in the apartment while we renovated the downstairs with the help of some of my wife's cousins.

Now, I was not a carpenter or skilled at renovations. I was a drinker, but I could plan things. So, everything that we planned, every remodeling job or paint job or wallpaper job revolved around how much beer we bought. That was always the first thing we did. Instead of heading to the local lumber yard for the renovation materials we needed, our first stop was invariably the liquor store to pick up our "tools" of choice. Only then did we drive for the paint, wallpaper, hammers, nails, power saws, etc. One time we did some work on our low pitched roof. We brought up a cooler of wine and pulled up the ladder as well so my wife couldn't climb up to check on us.

By now, everything in my life revolved around alcohol. Alcohol dictated my life. I had long since conquered the feeling of nausea when I drank too much as well as the physical hangovers. My hangovers were never so much physical as they were emotional. I would tell my wife that I would be attending a union meeting or going out for a few drinks or driving downtown to pay some bills and that I'd be back in two hours. I sincerely meant it, but once I had one or two drinks, that intention left my mind. She used to say that the union hall bar was a 10 minute walk there but a 4 day walk home. Kind of funny but kind of sad.

I would be sitting at a bar having promised my wife earlier, "I'll be home at 10:00." If I looked up and saw that it was five minutes to 10:00 and I knew that I couldn't get home until five after 10:00, I said, "Well, I'll be late and catch hell anyway. I might as well be good and late and make it worth my while." I would stay there for several more hours. That's the kind of attitude I had. Alcohol was still the best love affair I'd ever had, even though I was now married.

Our marriage was not what I expected it to be. I didn't know what a marriage would or could be. I certainly didn't have the example of a good marriage to follow, whatever that is. Every time my wife and I got into an argument, I would shut down, retreat into a shell and walk away. I didn't want to argue, and soon I developed into a great avoider. It was either avoidance by retreating to the basement and occupying myself down there or going into the backyard or heading to a hotel bar in town to drink.

As I said earlier, drinking was not my problem, but drinking was the solution to my problems. Every time we had another child, I always thought things would get better. I'm an eternal optimist and I don't like to lose. I never liked being viewed as a failure of any kind, and even though we stayed married for 15 years, I was terribly unhappy, as was my wife. I thought we could stick it out, but I eventually got to the point where I couldn't do that anymore.

One day, soon after we were married, I walked into my living room, and tried to describe something to my wife that I was feeling. I forget what it was now, but I felt so deeply about it at that moment. I was so full of emotion, something which I had probably never touched in my life. My eyes were red and I had tears in them.

We weren't in an argument. It was just something that I believed in very strongly and wanted to communicate. Her response was to laugh at me.

"What are you trying to do, bring tears to your eyes and cry?" she asked sarcastically. "What kind of a man are you? Are you a wimp?"

What a name to call me, the very name I had suffered under all through my school days.

Her words split the last wowing timber holding up my emotional life. I could feel it coming down as I stood there, just like those timbers I saw wowing in the stope, my face reddening from the sting of her sarcasm.

All the deficiencies of my childhood, everything I felt I had gone through had left me in the position where anything could have brought the whole mess down. This episode carried just enough weight to cave me in. I made a conscious decision right then.

"From this moment forward," I said to myself, "you will never, ever see me like that again. Never. You will never see me cry," and she never did. I shut down emotionally from then on and bottled everything up. I felt it was no longer safe to reveal things to her. From that night onwards, and for many years, my heart lay buried under the rubble I was making of my life, and I lived totally in my head.

I realized that I didn't love my wife. I didn't dislike her. I didn't hate her, but I was living in a world of indifference even though I stayed with the marriage. I remained with her for 15 years. Perhaps that was a benefit of the alcohol, indifference to everything. It shut off the pain but it shut off caring, affection and joy as well. That was a big price to pay but I was too numb to know it at the time.

My disinterest in my marriage did not diminish my interest in cars during this time, and one weekend, I went home to Auburn with her cousin and we picked up a 1932 Ford Roadster. A friend of a friend learned that it was for sale. When I opened the door of an old barn where it was stored, the sun filtered through the darkness and I laid eyes onto a beautiful 1932 Ford Roadster. It was chopped and channeled. No top and no hood. The rumble seat had been taken out. The motor was all chrome. Three speed standard transmission. My heart began to race! I can still see it in my mind's eye, more clearly than I can see my wife.

Needless to say, I was smitten, so I bought it and drove it back to Sudbury. I spent time and money on that car and really enjoyed it. I had that hot rod, we had our own home and were living well. We both worked and the income we got from renting the upstairs was paying the mortgage.

Then one Christmas, she gave me a card saying, "You are going to be a father in June." That was a real moment of joy for me. I was overwhelmed. I told myself that I needed to change my life and get my drinking under control. I was about to be a father and I wanted to be a good one.

Still, I was spending a good deal of time working on the car with friends and of course, drinking, which didn't sit well with her. One day during the pregnancy, she came to me with an ultimatum, "Allan, either the car goes or I go."

I don't do well with ultimatums. I didn't want to let either go, but eventually I made the decision to let the car go. That became another source of resentment against her. I never said a word. I sold the car and buried my feelings.

I wasn't thinking about that on June 22, 1975, at 8:15 p.m., though, because that is when our first daughter, Angie, was born, weighing 8 pounds. I had a bottle of whiskey in my car and as my wife was in the delivery room giving birth, I was in the waiting room drinking.

We named her after the actress Angie Dickinson, who was popular at the time, and I adored my little girl. Now that I was a father, I was sure that things would get better. We had great times together, buying things for her.

Over time, I became more emotionally attached to Angie than to my wife. She had beautiful blond straight hair and people would see her on the street and comment on it often. As a joke, I taught Angie to say, "Bullshit," the next time someone remarked how beautiful her hair was. One day, I came home from work and the wife was shooting daggers at me. It turns out she had taken Angie to the mall and someone complimented her on her hair.

Two years later, my wife was pregnant again but we didn't know it. I was in the mine one day and received a message that I was needed on surface right away. All they told me was that I was needed at home. It was policy never to tell someone what the problem was so I was left in a mystery. Another miner drove me home and I learned that she was in the hospital and had had a tubular pregnancy and the embryo had been aborted. The doctors told us not to have another child for at least a couple more years.

Six years after Angie, my son Shane was born and we named him after the famous western movie. I had two bottles of whiskey in the waiting room hidden behind a curtain and drank them with Pepsi to help mask the smell, at least somewhat, and to give the impression I was drinking soda.

That night, while my wife recuperated, I went out and celebrated. I was so happy to have a son. I called my longest-time drinking buddy, Crusher, and we closed the bar. He ordered me a quadruple shot of rye. I had drunk doubles before but never a quadruple. After closing time, I went home and invited the neighbors over. This was in 1979 during a strike at the mine, which lasted the better part of a year, and many people didn't have money for booze, but I did, and they were glad to come over.

We drank until 7:00 the next morning. I went to bed for a few hours and then headed back to the bar when it opened at noon. I sat by myself at a table and ordered two drafts to settle my nerves. When I tried to raise the first, my hand was shaking so that I could not hold it. Luckily, no one else was in the bar or I would have been mortified. I was embarrassed enough as it was when I got two straws and drank my beers through them, at which point my nerves began to settle down. That was the first time in all my years of drinking that I ever had the shakes.

We were now a family of four, and again, I thought things would begin to get better. At the time, there was a wives' tale that a woman cannot get pregnant if she is breast-feeding. Don't believe it. When Shane was six months old, my wife got pregnant again and 15 months after the birth of our son, our second daughter, Marcie, was born.

We knew that we wouldn't have any more, so I went into the delivery room and witnessed Marcie's birth. What an incredible experience.

I am sorry today that I didn't do that with my other two children.

Standing in the delivery room, watching the miracle of a new life, I was full of wonderment and overcome by elation and curiosity. The fact I had been drinking could not dull the feeling of joy I felt at the birth of my child. I remember hoping with everything I could muster that the feelings of the moment would carry over into the rest of my family life.

It was not to be.

BREAKING THROUGH

CHAPTER 19

Life with an Alcoholic

The chains of habit are too weak to be felt
until they are too strong to be broken.
–Samuel Johnson

We had three beautiful children and I have always loved them dearly, but I was never really there for them though I recall us having some great times together.

I played with my kids, but my wife is the one who raised them. It wasn't out of the ordinary, really, for a husband to be the breadwinner and the wife to look after the house and the children. I worked hard in the mines. I went to union meetings. I brought home a paycheck. We made good money and from the outside looking in, we appeared to be the model family, but I was never emotionally there for them. Or myself. I was always under the influence.

The subject of alcoholism and my drinking never surfaced directly. My wife said to me once, "Allan, we really have to look at your drinking. From now on, I don't want you drinking at the bar. I want you to drink at home."

I said, "Okay." So, I drank at home. I drank in the house. I drank in the backyard. I had lots of neighbor friends. As you can well imagine, since I made good money, I always had alcohol in the house. We had barbecues and lawn parties, and people would come over and we just drank and drank.

One day, my wife counted up the number of empty bottles lying around and realized that I drank 69 beers in a single day. There had been a sale of Miller Lite in the store and I bought three cases of tall neck bottles on a Friday night and put them in my cooler. On Saturday morning I got up at 6:00, went out to my backyard to enjoy the morning and started drinking. Miller Lite is weak; the alcohol content is half that of Canadian beer. After breakfast, I went back out and continued drinking on a hot Ontario summer day. A friend came over and had one beer and then had to leave to do something. I cut the lawn, cooked a barbecue dinner for the family and continued drinking until 3:00 a.m.

The next morning, she said there were two beers left in the cooler. Minus the one my friend had, that meant I drank 69 bottles of beer in one day. I did a good job mowing the lawn in spite of it. Another time, I was not so successful; I attempted to cut the lawn while drinking moonshine and 7UP and the lines were weaving all over the place so I had to redo it.

Some friends and I made our own moonshine. The local whiskey distillery sold us old whiskey barrels. We would pour 5 or 10 gallons of boiling water into a barrel along with some sugar, put the bungs back in and let it sit out in the sun. I would rotate the barrel every so often. This process would extract the whiskey that had soaked into the wood. In about five weeks, I would have 10 gallons of rotgut. I'd pour the stuff into gallon jugs and then cut the barrels in half to make flower beds for the backyard.

Most of my friends doing the same thing used hot water in their barrels. I wanted mine stronger so I used 2/3 water and 1/3 moonshine which I bought from a bootlegger. More potent was good! You could determine the alcohol content by taking a spoonful of it and lighting it on fire. All that would remain when the flame extinguished was a single drop of water. That moonshine was pure! My wife saw me pouring myself a glass one day and just shook her head and walked away.

For many years, the biggest problem I had with drinking was with others. Most people would drink till 9:00 or midnight or 2:00 in the morning, but I never wanted the party to end. I would go to bed at 2:00 under the influence and get up at 6:30 and have two or three more drinks because I had discovered that this was a magical way to avoid a hangover.

Another two or three beers or another shot of whiskey would clear my mind, straighten out my emotions and settle me down. After that, I could continue to drink the next day.

Drinking at home went on for a couple more years when again, my wife said, "Okay, Allan. We have to look at your drinking. You're drinking way too much, so from now on, I don't want you drinking at home anymore. If you're going to drink, go downtown and drink."

That was the last time I heard her say, "We have to look at your drinking," though I was scared she would bring it up again.

One night, however, she did threaten me with, "You know, I'm going to start drinking with you."

"You can't do that," I replied, "because we can't afford it. This family only has one alcoholic and only one of us can afford to drink."

I meant the word "alcoholic" in a humorous vein to defuse the tension of the moment. The truth was however, that I was trapped deep in a world of addiction.

I would look at my friends and think that they had good marriages because they always seemed to get along. I'm sure that was not the reality, but that was my perception. I always thought that I was so unfortunate to be in an unhappy marriage. I didn't want to tell anybody. My wife was extremely good looking; people would not have understood why I wasn't happy, even early on in my marriage. Being the eternal optimist, I always thought that things would get better with time, but of course, they deteriorated. The truth is that a happy marriage is based more on communication than physical attraction. She and I never really connected on the first level and eventually ceased connecting on the second.

As I shut down emotionally, my wife became more vocal. I would sit there and take it. She was the talker and the screamer. She turned into my mother, and I turned into my dad. My wife used to tell me when I took a drag off a cigarette or took a sip of whiskey, "Allan, I wish that you would have that same look of desire in your eyes for me as you do for your cigarettes and alcohol. I wish you would look at me like that."

What a sad statement on her part, and what a sad commentary on me, but it just wasn't there.

Meanwhile, my life underground was going well. There were occasional layoffs at the mine but I was never laid off. I never lost any pay. I always worked every day even though I was hung over, and I developed a reputation not only as a hardworking miner, but also as a prodigious drinker. One of my remarkable negative attributes was the amount I could drink. I would stop at the bar with some fellow miners on the way home. Quarter to 6:00 would arrive and some men would get up from the table saying, "I'm heading home for dinner." I couldn't understand that. I couldn't relate to going home for dinner even though I had a wife and children waiting.

Around 6:00 or 6:30, another friend or two would come in and I would sit and drink with them until midnight. They would get up to head home, and I'd say, "What are you going home for?" I did not want to leave the security of the bar and all that it represented to me.

Then, at midnight, some other guy just getting in off his shift would come in and we would drink till 4:00 in the morning. I never wanted to go home. Drinking was my escape. It dulled the pain inside of me. I didn't want any of that pain to escape, to touch me, and for years it worked.

As my drinking skyrocketed out of control and my consumption increased, so did my tolerance. I drank at home and away. My wife never knew how much I drank. I hid alcohol in the ceiling tiles of the basement. I would leave a little bit of alcohol half-visible behind some shelf in a bookcase that she would find in the morning after a weekend of drinking and she would be happy to find that, completely unaware that I had a full bottle of whiskey in a ceiling tile or behind my work bench.

I had beer hidden in snowbanks. I would come home from work in the winter and the driveway had to be shoveled before I could drive in. We had a 120-foot driveway and I stuck a full beer in the snowbank every 25 or 50 feet, so when I shoveled the snowbank I could stop and have a beer before more shoveling.

I also hid the amount of money I spent on alcohol and cigarettes. I was so disappointed when INCO decided to make direct deposits on payday. They did it to end the long lines at the bank and they could cut back on the accounting department. Unfortunately for many of us, it also ended the practice of receiving our incentive bonus checks separate from our regular paychecks.

When the company announced the switch, I was so upset that I called the payroll office to see if I could get my money differently from the rest of the men. He said, "No, Al. You're probably the 35th person that called in today to see if you can get your paychecks hidden so that your family doesn't know how much you make."

It was all a game. My life was a sad game, but it was a game that I played very well. I lied to my family. I lied to myself. As my drinking escalated and my tolerance grew, I drank with people who had the same craving for alcohol and who had the same problems as I did. We could all sit around the table in a bar and complain about our families and our wives and how the people who loved us didn't really understand.

I could never sit and drink with someone who was having only one beer an hour. I would cringe because it took so long for them to drink and I wouldn't want to drink that much faster because it made me look as though I had a problem with alcohol. So, I drank with people who had the same drinking tolerance and capacity.

As I've mentioned, I would go out drinking and tell my wife that I would be home by 10:00 but not return until 1:00 or 2:00 in the morning and then go to sleep. I'd wake up at 5:00 a.m. to go to work and realize how much money I had spent the night before. My hangovers were not so much physical as they were emotional and filled with remorse because I had told her with absolute sincerity that I would be home by 10:00.

Back in the late 70s and early 80s, Sudbury had what they called Country Jamborees. They would bring in local country and western singers and bands, and we'd have a weekend or three or four days at a park or out in the wilderness somewhere.

They brought in some fairly big names in those days such as John Conlee from Nashville and other singers and performers. I like country music and I actively looked for excuses to be away from home.

People set up their trailers three or four days in advance and loaded them with beer and whiskey along with their families and had a great time in their lawn chairs. A temporary city of four or five thousand people might spring up with camper trailers, people sleeping out of their trucks, sort of a country and western Woodstock.

This one particular jamboree was about 30 miles from Sudbury, so a bus left downtown every so often to drop people off, which saved traffic as well as drinking and driving problems, and brought people back at night.

One year, a neighbor, who was one of my drinking buddies, headed down with his family. I gave him money to buy beer and whiskey for me so I wouldn't need to transport it. My booze was already at his trailer, and I planned to go down and spend a couple days.

I got on the bus at seven in the morning and had already been drinking whiskey most of the previous night just to get ready for the performances that evening. I had to be prepared.

The bus made two or three stops and by the time I got down there, I was well on the way. I met my buddy and got further on the way. It had been raining off and on for the last couple weeks and the fields were muddy.

They had a hot air balloon and were giving rides. I do not like heights but, as a result of my alcoholic thinking, decided to go up anyway. The balloon was tethered to the ground but riders went up a couple hundred feet to view the jamboree, the people on stage and the surrounding landscape. To this day, when I walk to the edge of a building I have to step back because a sensation of fear comes over me. It's called acrophobia. I tell people that I worked underground because I was scared of heights.

In my wisdom, I decided to carry two fifths of whiskey, one in each back pocket, to bolster my courage. There was a long line ahead of me and I kept drinking to get my nerve up. About eight o'clock, darkness fell and at 9:00 they said, "Sorry, folks. We've run out of helium, so there aren't any more balloon rides."

I looked around. It was dark. I was three sheets to the wind and couldn't find my neighbor's trailer, so I just of wandered around. The fields were in terrible shape but I sat down anyway to rest because I was tired.

I decided to lie down on a muddy patch of grass. As I lay there with my arm supporting my head, I swear that I heard Tammy Wynette's voice. I think it was coming from an eight track player in someone's truck. I don't think it was Tammy Wynette in person.

About 10:30, I decided it was time to head back to Sudbury. I wanted to go to a bar and dance and drink. That was my pattern: stay and drink for so long at a bar or party and then move to someplace else.

I had been drinking now for nearly 15 hours and still had one bottle of whiskey left. I hadn't gotten sick. There was a makeshift police station set up in a trailer with police and first aid attendants. I walked in, and you can imagine my state of mind, let alone my physical appearance.

"Excuse me," I asked, "can you tell me where the bus is and what time it's coming to go back to town?"

"One o'clock," the officer said, never looking up. I am sure he was tired of dealing with inebriated people.

"Oh," I said, "it's imperative that I get back sooner than that. I need a ride back quicker. Can you give me a ride back?"

"Absolutely not," he snorted.

I had an idea, and said in all earnestness, "Why don't you arrest me for being drunk in a public place. Take me back to Sudbury and that way I'll get a ride back."

He said, "Why don't you get the hell out of here?"

I left dejected. I walked outside and stumbled around. Soon, I came across a couple heading toward the parking lot. Well-dressed, sober people.

"Oh, excuse me," I said. "Are you heading to Sudbury?"

"Yes, we are," the man replied tentatively.

"I'll pay you $20 to ride back with you."

"Are you going to be sick in my car?"

"No. I will not get sick." I was so insulted. I eventually did get sick but not in this car.

He drove a big Cadillac and I climbed in the back seat. I was on my way to a fine night of dancing, wining and dining. There was mud on my denim jacket and jeans. When we got to Sudbury, I went to a hotel, paid the cover charge, went upstairs to dance, stopped into the bathroom and that is where I got sick. I was so proud of myself that I didn't get sick in the man's car, just as I promised.

Picture this: a 34-year-old man who had been drinking for 16 hours by this time, mud all over his pants and on his jacket up to his shoulder, who has just barfed and he asks a woman to dance. Amazingly, she declined.

I was so dejected about being rejected, I couldn't believe it. So I drank more to get over my rejection.

There were many episodes like this. I was ashamed of myself in some ways. In other ways this kind of thing had been happening for so long that it felt quite normal to me. When I was drinking heavily and staggered or slurred my words, I would be so embarrassed that I would leave the bar and find another.

My whole world revolved around drinking, whether I drank with someone else or alone. It made me feel like I could survive, that I was okay. I wasn't happy, but I could survive by living a life of lies. That is how far down my addiction was taking me.

Breaking Through

CHAPTER 20

WELCOME TO HELL

A Dungeon horrible, on all sides round
As one great Furnace flam'd, yet from those flames
No light, but rather darkness visible
Serv'd only to discover sights of woe,
Regions of sorrow, doleful shades, where peace
And rest can never dwell
—JOHN MILTON, *PARADISE LOST*

THE CONDITIONS OF WORKING UNDERGROUND are difficult to explain. The degree of darkness is hard to fathom. The mine stinks, the noise is cacophonous, the place is dank and musty. There is a smell to it that I cannot describe, and a mine is a terrible place to die. Nobody wants to die underground.

What's more, mines are hot. Sometimes it was 95 or 100 degrees down there and I would have been drinking the night before until two o'clock, gone to bed, risen at 4:00 a.m., eaten breakfast and then driven a van of men to work because, in my mind, I had a responsibility to them.

In 1980, I became an entrepreneurial alcoholic. That year, I paid $18,000 for a new Dodge Maxi Van and began carpooling men to work. I drove 14 men to and from work, each of whom paid me $20 a week for the privilege. It was 30-some miles one way to the mine and I always had a case a beer in the back that I sold during the ride. It was a dollar a beer and two dollars for a shot of whiskey. There was a waiting list for men who wanted to ride in my van because they could smoke and drink. At one point, I was asked to put another vent in the van ceiling because of the cigarette smoke. Sometimes we drank on the way to work, and we always drank on the way home.

Even though I felt like hell most mornings, I felt a duty to the men to get them to work and I always did. Because we were on a strict time line at the mine—the cage went down at a specific time to each level—if someone overslept and made us late there was a fine that they would pay of 12 beers that the rest of us shared for free.

The mentality of the miners at the time was that a carpool of men would invariably stop for a beer on the way home. As drinkers know however, there is no such thing as one beer if there are six men drinking. What happened is that I took over three carpools and the wives and families of these men were very happy with the arrangement because I never stopped at a hotel bar. I always left the parking lot after work at the same time every day and on the drive home they could have one beer or ten, but I always had them home in time for dinner.

This worked well for three or four years and I gained the reputation of being a very entrepreneurial drinker. I was somewhat proud of that. I received recognition for being not only a big drinker but for being a responsible drinker and creating a business enterprise with my van.

The more recognition I received externally though, the deeper I was drilling and blasting into a dark, painful, lonely stope of my own making.

I would get up at four o'clock in the morning and take a shower, shave and make myself look presentable, even though I was dying on the inside. I thought I was okay. I really did think that I was holding my life together. I never wanted to look like the stereotypical alcoholic.

Part of the charade was to make myself a big breakfast, a bacon omelet that I ate about 4:30 in the morning. Depending on my condition, I would drink two or three beers while showering and shaving.

I would travel down the ramp at Levack West to my level swearing that I would never drink again. At 6:30 in the morning I would be so sick and hung over that I didn't want to be seen by my supervisors. I would feel just terrible. Hangovers are bad enough on the surface, but you can magnify that a thousandfold underground with the diesel fumes, the heat, the sweat, the urine and the oil smells. I used to smoke at least two packs a day and the taste in my throat, lungs and mouth was awful. I would grab my drill and begin work, sweating, puking, urinating and crapping.

The only water I would drink was from the hose hooked to my drill, and it was warm and tasted like rubber. By 10 o'clock in the morning though, I was feeling good again as the alcohol was metabolized out of my system through the heavy sweating, and this is how the addiction took over my life.

Other miners brought water, tea or lemonade down with them, mostly in white plastic jugs, and drank continually. One time, a miner needed hydraulic oil for his equipment and brought some down in a white plastic jug. His partner didn't realize it and took two or three big gulps of hydraulic oil. "Man," he said the next day, "that was the best laxative I ever took in my life. I was shittin' all night long."

What probably saved me is that at lunchtime, I would really eat. I always had a huge lunch: a 28-ounce can of Habitant pea soup plus a can of stew, three sandwiches, two hard-boiled eggs, topped off with an orange, banana or apple and some pickles. Besides the soup, the only liquid I drank was a thermos of tea at lunchtime. There would be two or three packs of cigarettes in my lunch pail just in case we got stuck underground, in a power failure or a cave in or some sort of incident were we couldn't get to surface. I would eat my lunch at 11:30 and, honest to God, I would not have another drink of water the rest of the day, even though I was sweating profusely. I knew there was cold beer in the van at 3:00. Surprisingly, I never once had heat exhaustion. What a contrast in thinking from – 7:00 a.m., and "I'll never drink again," to 11:30 a.m., "I can't wait to get a beer in my van!"

When I got out of the shower after work, I just about ran to the van to open up my first beer, which was always a big "Wow." I never even tasted that first beer when it went down. It just went down. I have been drinking with friends and been told that a bottle of beer turned upside down takes 7.4 seconds to drain with the force of gravity. I'm telling you that I have gulped a beer in 7.5 seconds. The first or second beer, I never even tasted. But, I could actually feel my body settle. That was my routine for years.

My week would unfold on Monday morning. Mondays were the worst. I'd been drinking since Friday after work and felt near death. My wife was pissed off about my weekend antics, I was dog tired and I often went to bed straight after work on Monday evenings. On Tuesdays, I didn't drink much, only a few, and I'd play with the kids and hit the sack around 9:30. On Wednesday mornings I would feel so good—no hangover, no remorse, and work would go great. Usually, there was a union meeting on Wednesday nights and I would be feeling a little antsy because I was feeling so good. If I was now feeling good, why not go out and celebrate with a drink or 10? Then came Thursday, which had become our new payday and the cycle would begin again. I drank to celebrate feeling good and I drank to numb the pain of the terrible days.

Friday night was power drinking night, and repeated on Saturday. I told my wife that Saturday afternoon was reserved for me alone. I would head out to a country and western bar and get half loaded, really buzzed, then go home and take a nap. I would get up at 8:00 on Saturday night go out and get buzzed again. Less often, I would do something with the wife and kids.

One time, we went to the drive-in. I took a bottle with me, fell asleep and passed out. I woke up at 4:30 the next morning. My wife and the kids were gone. A neighbor had been parked next to us and the family drove home with him. No one was around. The drive in was deserted except for me. I was apprehensive about driving home under the influence but eventually made it home and blamed my wife for leaving me in that situation. I always had a reason why it wasn't my fault.

On Sundays, I would drink beer at home. In the afternoon, I would go to town to do my laundry. The laundromats in Sudbury had machines expressly for miners. Our clothes would have ruined other washers, so we couldn't use the machines at home. Of course, the laundromat I patronized was right next to a bar. It would cost me $20 a week to do my laundry, $18 of which was spent on alcohol. Sometimes I would lose track of the time and come back to find the Laundromat closed. I would have to drag the owner back down to unlock the door so I could get my clothes for work the next morning. I would come home late for dinner, half in the bag and my wife would be so angry. The only day I felt good was Wednesday.

My days were spent digging deeper into the earth; my nights and weekends I spent diving deeper into a bottomless bottle of alcohol, trying to somehow fill the growing cavern in my soul or drown it in the attempt.

As I've said, the Levack West Mine, where I had been transferred in 1976, was a very mechanized operation. Instead of blasting six feet at once, the stopes were 40 feet wide, 16 feet high and as much as 400 feet long. Hydraulic drills put 2-inch wide holes throughout the roof, which we packed with dynamite. It might take three weeks to load the blast and the whole mine was evacuated before the fuses were lit. The blast would shake the surface and register on Richter scales.

After blasting, massive front loaders hauled the ore away, loaded it on trains that transported it underground to the crusher at Levack Mine, miles away. The buckets on these loaders held 8 cubic yards and in seven trips to the ore pass, the loaders paid for themselves. The driver could not see anything within 300 feet of him because of the massive bucket, so we had to be extra careful working around these monsters and shine our cap lights on the roof when walking in front.

After the blast, we would bring in a four-inch air line and come in with our handheld drills to install the head cover. This was metal screening with four-inch squares that was bolted to the ceiling for safety purposes. It came in rolls 50 feet long and 5 feet wide. Standing on uneven rock, we drilled upwards six feet into the roof. Then we bolted the screen to the rock using bolts like huge wall anchors and torqued them to 100 foot-pounds. Each bolt supported 22 tons, providing there wasn't a crack above the hole. We would sound the rock with a long metal bar and listen for the distinct hollow sound that told of a fissure.

We could install enough screen in a day to advance 20 feet. All we did was scale the loose ground and secure it. It was very demanding work, standing on unsteady muck, hung over and miserable. Many are the days I wished I had gotten a better education and worked at a drafting board up top as an engineer.

Despite everything I was going through personally, I managed to have some fun down there. It was a different life and a close-knit bond existed among the men. We stuck together, and as I said, we ran the mine. The supervisors knew that and didn't bother us. The ones who came in intending to make sweeping changes didn't last very long.

We'd be sitting in the eighth-of-a-mile-long lunchroom and a new supervisor would come down, usually an engineer or some young man who had never mined a day in his life but who knew the mining textbooks by heart. One of the supervisors would climb on a desk to introduce the new man.

The supervisor would holler or shake his light to get our attention.

"Okay, everybody, this is Bob Smith. He is our new supervisor. He'll be working with us for a little bit and take over this beat. He has his degree from the university and we look forward to working with him. We just wanted to bring him down to introduce him to you."

Then Bob Smith would start off, "You know, I'm glad to be here. We're going to make some changes. I've been in school for 6 years."

We'd be in the back laughing and carrying on. The foreman would get upset. He'd say, "Hey, McDougall, what the hell are you guys doing back there? Pay attention! Show some respect."

We would holler back, "We're just making a pool back here to see how long this guy's going to fucking last. Do you want to be part of it?"

Supervisors would ask a miner who had missed a day, "Why do you only work four days a week?"

The answer was invariably, "Because we can't afford to live on only three days' wages."

Had I been a new supervisor in the mine, I would have done things much differently. I would have met the men, worked with them, listened to them and talked with them, not at them. I'd say, "I got this new job. I have no idea what goes on down here. But I need your help." I would be on the beat with them for six months learning how to work the mine. I might know the textbook descriptions of mining, but a textbook is so much different from the practical realities of the situation.

A cardinal rule was that we had to move all the equipment safely out of the way before we lit the blast. One time, we were in a hurry and I had a scissor truck in the stope but lit the blast before moving it. We always watched the fuse to see if it would connect all the other fuses on the face before we left in case there was a misfire. We took extra time to look for that, which didn't leave us much time to get out. I jumped on the piece of equipment and discovered a dead battery. There I was, trying to start this scissor truck while the blast was about to go off 50 feet away.

What's more important at that moment—my life or the equipment? I ran out of there and the blast went off. We had a good laugh about it and went back in afterwards, never mind the 30 minute waiting period. The machine was covered in dust, rocks and nickel and had been severely peppered. There was a hole through the gearshift box and a hole through the transmission. We had to deal with this, so we called another miner who was working down the drift. He had a front-end loader and came over, looked at the mess, laughed about it, hooked on and pulled the scissor-lift truck around the corner.

After he left, we went to the lunchroom and told the supervisor, "We had an accident down here. We don't know what happened." Of course, we covered up all the tracks where the other guy had pushed the truck out of the way. With all the dust and rocks, that was easy to do.

The supervisor came down and looked at the thing and knew, guaranteed, that the truck had been in the blast. But he couldn't prove it because there wasn't any other piece of equipment around. The guy with the front-end loader had gone back to where he worked, maybe a half mile away. A mine is not like a factory where you turn a corner and there's 10 other men working. It might be half a mile or a mile down the tunnel where someone else was working. The Levack West Mine was like a city; the ramps even had a network of stop lights.

"Oh, my God, look at this!" the supervisor said, half drenched in sweat. "How did that happen?"

"I don't know. I can't believe it. Those rocks must have ricocheted off of that wall and around that corner and I thought the scissor truck was safe." There was probably $60,000 worth of damage to the machine.

Before you feel too sorry for INCO, realize that they paid for the damage in the first ton of ore they pulled out from the blast. We would have brand new equipment come down worth $250,000 and it paid for itself in the first half hour of taking ore to the ore pass. It was unbelievable. There were fourteen minerals in the mine and they always said that they mined enough gold in a year to pay all the expenses of that mine for the year. All the other minerals, the nickel, the platinum, the copper and the cobalt, were pure gravy.

It sounded like a huge amount of damage was done to the scissor truck, but it was nothing. The supervisor never even wrote us up. He walked away shaking his head. We stood there knowing, "We run the mine."

That episode never made it to the "collar." The collar is the ground level where miners go into the mine. Management never found out what happened. Of course we went to the van after work and had a great laugh about it on the way home.

Management had various tactics they employed to weaken

the unions. One was to take a union activist and promote him to a supervisory position for a year and then fire him. I was asked once if I wanted to become a supervisor, but suspicious of their motives, I declined. Managers had no wage protection. Union members had a protected wage. USW Local 6500 had a hall with a bar downstairs and I often went there to drink. Sometimes there wouldn't be enough members downstairs for a quorum at the monthly union meeting, so they would call me down to fill in and that is how I became active in the union.

In 1983, I was transferred to another mine called Stobie, where I worked for about a year. I hated it and put in a transfer back to the Levack West Mine, where I liked it a lot better. While I was away from Levack West, they brought in a new mine manager. I didn't know him, of course. One day back at Levack West, I was on a scissor truck putting support bolts into the roof where there was bad ground overhead. The ground was cracked and falling, snapping and very unstable.

The new manager came in with all these management types on a jeep. We could always tell when the safety foremen or supervisors or visitors were coming around because they never had their lights on their helmets; they held them in their hands to look around and see what was happening.

This new manager came up on the scissor truck and said, "What's your plan of attack today?"

I looked at him for a long time. I was hung over and sweating. There was loose ground coming down around my ears. It was bad ground, cracking and snapping.

"Just what fucking status do you have around this place?" I asked.

"I'm so and so, the mine manager," he said. "What's your name?"

I just looked at him with a look that said, "If you don't have anything better to offer about how to help us secure this bad ground that's coming down and scaring me to death because it's about to cave in, then you don't deserve to be here."

Even though he could smell booze on my breath (he probably knew my history of drinking), he just walked away. I never got written up, never got reprimanded, because a miner's job is to make money but it's also to save lives. Anybody who has any experience with miners will know that there's a time to talk to them and a time to leave them alone.

Above ground, the camaraderie and solidarity was near absolute, and it carried over into the bars at night. There might be four or five miners sitting at a table and someone else would come in and try to cause trouble. If they picked on one, they picked on them all.

I'm sure that's the same with other trades, but what keeps miners connected is the risks that we take and the dangers of the job. That and breathing the putrid air and the diesel fumes knowing that it is aging us. Some miners come out of the ground with lung diseases and cancers or they've got sinus problems and it is killing them.

There's a song called "Working Man," by Rita McNeil that tells the story of young kids going in to the mine at the age of 16 and coming out at the age of 64, if they lived that long. They're dead before their time. She sings about coal miners from Nova Scotia and even though I've been out of the mine for years, when I hear that song I get goose bumps and my eyes tear as I am transported back to the mine. I've heard other people say that when they hear "Amazing Grace," it has the same effect on them as "Working Man" does on me. That song describes everything.

My life went on like that for years, but around 1984, something began to change in my love affair with alcohol and that led me to a darker place than anything I ever met with underground. Mining mishaps trap miners underground; my life had essentially been one long mishap and I was trapped in it and about to be buried.

CHAPTER 21

THE BEGINNING OF THE END

The years teach us much, which the days never knew.
—Ralph Waldo Emerson

HERE IS ANOTHER ILLUSTRATION of the degree to which alcohol had a hold over me and how messed up things were:

After my father was hit by lightning, he began having blackouts, as I've mentioned. In 1977, he had a serious episode and I drove home in the middle of winter to help get him into a hospital. He and my mother were fighting a lot at the time and my sister called and asked me to come home and help her put Dad into the hospital. We put him in the psychiatric ward in a hospital in Goderich.

Right then, a record blizzard crippled the entire area around Lake Huron and Lake Erie. Everything came to a standstill. I was caught, too, and had to stay an extra week. The storm interfered with everything but my drinking. In fact, when I heard the storm was coming, I didn't want to be stuck in Auburn with my mother, so I moved in with a friend in Goderich on the pretense of visiting my father, which I did every day. However, it was also much closer to the alcohol. We have state-run distributors in Ontario and one can't buy beer or whiskey at the grocery store, and my supply would have been limited had I stayed at my mother's house. So, I lived in town for the week and, as you can probably guess, we had a wonderful party.

One night, the storm relented and the snowbanks were way up. I was out drinking and drove down a road toward the beach. I was in my 1974 blue and white Dodge Charger, which I took good care of. I had a bottle of whiskey in the seat with me, a case of beer in the trunk and headed down the road. This was in the days of the CB radio craze. Everybody had a CB radio; I had one in my car and a big antenna in the middle of the trunk. We were all playing Smokey and The Bandit.

I had been drinking all day and took what I thought was the road along the beach. At one point, I said to myself, "My God, this road is rough."

It turns out I was driving down the railroad tracks. All of a sudden, the car hit four ties that were widely separated. The frame clunked down onto the rails. I couldn't go either backwards or forwards, so there I was—stuck on the railroad tracks. I hadn't been able to see the tracks because of the snow.

I jumped on the CB radio and called my drinking buddy. It was about 3:00 a.m., and we called another friend from high school who drove a tow truck for a scrap metal business.

We got him out of bed and he came to my rescue. He backed onto the tracks and let out his cable. He said he had 150 feet of cable. I was down the railroad track 147 feet. We had 3 feet of cable left over to hook onto my frame to pull the car off the tracks.

As we were towing it, a locomotive with a snowplow on the front was coming around the bend, very slowly, clearing snow off the tracks. When the engineers saw what was unfolding, they were on their radio calling the police reporting some idiot who had driven onto the railroad tracks and was stuck.

I don't know if it's luck or what, but I jumped into my car and drove it away. I couldn't believe there wasn't any damage to it. The oil pan and everything else was good. The frame had sat on the rails and that provided enough clearance to prevent any damage.

Chapter 21 - The Beginning of the End

I paid the tow truck driver and as I was driving back to town, I saw the police coming down the next street over. That was another near miss. For me, drinking and driving and getting in messes was a normal occurrence.

That was my thinking. I wasn't thinking about the wrong I was doing, or the damage I could have done. It was that I got away with it. That was just another example of my thinking at the time. I have heard it said that God looks after drunks and fools. I was both, so I definitely had Him in my corner.

Every morning for the last four years of my drinking, when I woke up I knew I had a big problem. I didn't want to admit it and I didn't want other people to know that I knew it. There's a quotation: "The anticipation of change is worse than undergoing the actual event." That's what I was living for the last four years of my alcoholism.

I tried to maintain some sort of normalcy in my life. I knew I was drinking far too much. Alcohol was no longer having the effect that it once had and this was a terrifying realization. I had to drink more and more to achieve less and less of the desired effect.

Imagine you truly love someone and one day they tell you they have to leave. The prospect of an impending loss is what I began to feel. For half my life, I had been involved with an affair with alcohol deeper than any I had experienced with another human being, and I realized that it was ending.

Every day I woke up feeling remorseful and full of justifications such as, "last night I promised I wouldn't," or "something took over," or "what happened?" or "how come I do this? I only had so many beers." I was truly beginning to fall apart. I would go out drinking and wind up in places I didn't want to be with people I did not necessarily know or care for, doing things I normally would never do. Still, I kept drinking. Even with all the misery I was causing myself and my family, my desperation to somehow fill the emptiness in my soul outweighed the harm I was doing.

I was terribly, terribly unhappy and over those last few years grew more so.

Near the end, my bosses began to realize that I did have a serious drinking problem. There's an old joke I used to tell, "Nobody knew how much I drank until they saw me sober one day." That might seem funny, but there's no fun living it. I went to work under the influence and lived my life more under the influence than not.

Later on, when I finally went to rehab, they asked me what my drinking pattern was like. I figured out that I was alcohol-free a total of six days in 17 years and those six days I was in the hospital with a broken leg.

It was December 22, 1984, and my foreman had invited four of us out for drinks and dinner as a Christmas celebration. We began the festivities at 11:00 a.m. and the evening ended around 10:00 that night. You can imagine how much free alcohol I drank that day. While walking unsteadily home, my leather-soled cowboy boots slipped on the icy sidewalk, I fell hard and broke my leg in four places.

I looked down at my foot and saw that it was facing backwards. "This isn't good," I said to myself. I have to admit I sobered up real fast that night. A car came by and the couple driving noticed me and stopped to help. They hauled me up and pushed me into the passenger seat of their Honda Civic, which was quite a chore for them and very painful for me. They drove me to the hospital, made sure that I was being looked after and disappeared. I can't fault their hasty departure and felt indebted for their help.

In surgery the next morning, the doctors debated whether to amputate my foot, but fortunately decided to put it back together with a steel plate and six screws. After the operation, they said I would be allowed 12 shots of Demerol over the next six days. I could have them any way I wanted whenever the pain crossed the threshold into agony. A young man was in the same room as me with the same option. He wanted his shots intensively and received four shots a day for three days. On the fourth day, he was suffering severe pain and in great discomfort. I chose to have two shots a day for six days and told him that I wanted it to last. I would be playing cards down the hall, happy as a clam while he was a mess lying in bed. I was always thinking about how to fill that void with artificial happiness. Those were the only days in 17 years I was without alcohol.

At any rate, during those last years, my consumption increased to the point that when I arrived home at night I would have already had five or six beers or maybe ten. I would sit at the table and have dinner. If I wasn't eating I knew that I would be advertising my addiction, but I discovered that if I drank beer after work and had a meal I became sleepy. I did not want to waste the effect of the alcohol, so what I did was drink whiskey at dinner because I wouldn't become as tired.

Whiskey became a major problem. I drank whiskey like I drank beer earlier. Rye whiskey with a quarter ounce of Pepsi was my beverage of choice with dinner. I didn't want to lose the edge that I had gained on the way home from work.

After dinner, I would either go out and continue drinking or else sneak drinks while I was down in the basement. I would head downstairs to do something where I had stashed two or three bottles in the ceiling tile or behind the furnace. I'd sneak drinks all night long. Upstairs, I performed the charade of living a normal life with three lovely children and a wife who really didn't understand.

I guess I was somewhat successful with my drinking. If one considers the stereotypical life of an alcoholic, he or she reaches the pinnacle of success when they have nothing left. Somehow, I was able to avoid that. I could change my focus from drinking to working and remaining productive. I could apply the same energy and the same focus to one activity as to the other. I could reverse my focus from the destructive behavior that is alcoholism to being someone who brought some measure of value to his life and to the lives of those around him. I managed to pull this off for years.

But my addiction progressed, and finally took me on a downward spiral. I had increasingly more trouble the last four years that I drank. The alcohol wasn't having the effect that I wanted, that I *needed*. To reach a level where I could feel "comfortable with myself," where I would not feel that gaping hole in my soul, I had to drink more, and that began my whorl down.

As we know, alcohol is a depressant, so if one is sad or lonely or hurt and angry, by drowning these feelings with alcohol, one's life goes into a downward spiral.

Increasingly, I lived on the edge and one of the ways this manifested was driving under the influence. During my teenage years, it was always fun. I never meant to harm anybody, but during the last few years, I drove when I certainly shouldn't have. I am so grateful I never harmed anyone. I was blessed never to have involved another family's life through my drinking and driving. I drove the van to work and I was always under the influence, but I was always so proud that I thought I was a "functional alcoholic."

An epiphany of sorts occurred in 1984, but it took another three years to fully manifest itself. I was on vacation and celebrating. I was in Auburn visiting my parents. I had a case of beer in the trunk and a bottle of whiskey between my legs, and that night was clocked on the police radar doing 160 kilometers/100 miles per hour.

A cop saw me, turned around, put on his lights and siren and gave chase. I decided that I would give it one last fling and become that teenage rebel again. I was back home where my teenage years had shaped me and was determined to go out in a blaze of glory.

"They'll never catch me," I said. I was 34 years old, father of three, married, mortgage holder, some sort of parent but then I was back nearly 20 years earlier when I used to run from the cops as a teenager.

Except it wasn't fun anymore. I stepped on the gas and kept speeding away. Suddenly, I heard a voice somewhere deep, deep, deep in my head. Very clearly, it spoke to me, "Stop. You're going to kill someone."

That voice was as real to me as I am sitting here writing this book. For the first time in my life, I listened to somebody without arguing. I pulled over to the side of the road and waited for the flashing lights to pull up.

There were two officers in the car. The younger cop jumped out from behind the wheel of his cruiser and approached my car. There was an older cop, about my age, running my license plates. They had no idea what I was running from or why.

The young cop came over with a gun in his hand. I couldn't believe he had a gun so I tried some levity to break the tension. I leaned my head out the window and said, "What took you guys so long?"

His gun was in the middle of my forehead and I could feel it shaking. I wasn't shaking, yet I was the one drinking. I was the one under arrest but I was comparatively calm, cool and collected.

That gun in my forehead gave me a moment of clarity and I thought, "Man, I've got to change this situation in a hurry." They hauled me out of the car and had me spread-eagled on the hood. I had to blow into the mobile breathalyzer four times because they couldn't believe the readings. My blood alcohol content registered at .328, and an hour later at the police station it was still .311. The legal limit in Canada was 0.08. I was more than 4 times over the legal limit. Scientists have done tests on laboratory animals and determined that .40 was a lethal dose for half the test subjects. Mothers Against Drunk Driving states that a .16 BAC puts a person at serious risk. I was more than twice that.

I was guilty. I was caught. I wasn't about to argue. I just wanted the problem to go away. The older officer said, "You should be in a coma, Mr. McDougall."

"I was just getting started," I replied.

I tell that story only to impress upon you the commitment, the time, the money and the energy that I put in to be able to drink the way I drank. The police took me off to the station and leveled five charges against me. I pleaded guilty to them all. I didn't even have to appear in court. I lost my license for three months, paid a $400 fine and that was the end of it. I was very, very lucky that night. That voice in my ear made me stop and listen. You would think that would have caused me to look at my drinking but I kept on drinking creatively, and powerfully, always for effect, never for pleasure, for another three years.

Work didn't bother me much because I remained under the radar. I did my job. I didn't make trouble. My job was my means of having money so I could drink. I gave my wife my paycheck but my bonuses were the gravy I used to fuel my addiction. I never wanted to attract attention to myself on the job. I never missed a shift. I never got called on the carpet for disciplinary reasons.

The last year however, 1986, my supervisors began watching me more closely and attempted to broach the subject. One supervisor wanted to talk to me about my drinking and I told him, "I have it under control. I'm working on it now, and thanks for your concern." That was good enough for him.

People do not like to confront someone with an addiction, or else don't know how. In my case, they didn't call in the Employee Assistance Program (where I ended up working later). They only casually approached me about it and talked about it briefly.

I was perpetually fearful they would call me into the EAP office, but somehow I managed to elude the outstretched arm that would drag me to sobriety.

Most days during those last years, I continued to leave my house every morning, pick up the other men and drive to the mine. The last couple years though, I was really, really sick and on Monday mornings adopted a new routine.

The first passenger I picked up every morning was Crusher, my drinking buddy of many years. He lived nearby in a boarding house run by a retired nurse named Peggy. Peggy was a bootlegger on the side and miners knew they could go to Peggy's for a drink pretty much any time of day or night. I often took advantage of her consumer-friendly business hours. Often, I brought my daughter Angie with me and Peggy loved her like a granddaughter. I met Peggy soon after arriving in Sudbury and remained a loyal visitor for years. I even met my doctor there.

One day, a well dressed man came for a drink. He began asking if anybody there had seen a miner we called Popeye. INCO had a policy that if you were off work for more then 14 days without a doctor's excuse, you were automatically fired. The man was a doctor and looking for Popeye to give him a note. "Wow," I thought, "this is the doctor for me," so I bought him a drink and became his patient. When I got married, he gave me a note so I could take two weeks off for a honeymoon.

By 1986, things were not so carefree for me. The hangovers were getting progressively worse. My family life had deteriorated to nothing. I spent most of my time at home in the basement, going upstairs to eat and sleep, but never interacting with my family. I felt bad about that, but I always justified it in my own mind, "If you had my wife, if you had my childhood, if you had my job, if you had my bills, if you had my ..., my ..., my ..., my ..., my ..., then you would drink too." I surrounded myself with people who had the same problems and we could relate to each other.

So, there came many a Monday morning when I would pick up Crusher, get out of the van and let him pick up the others and drive them to work. Sometimes, I would have a few beers at Peggy's and smoke a few cigarettes to try to take the edge off my hangover. Many times, I would get out of the van and simply walk. I was too sick to work, but I needed to keep up the pretense of a daily routine, so I would start walking at 6:30 in the morning and walk and walk and walk. I had nowhere to go, there was nowhere I had to be and I was feeling so miserable that I wanted to be sick. There's an old line, "I had to die to start feeling better." I had to die to start living. That was a sad place to be, so I simply walked.

I was always afraid I would run into my wife or one of my kids in town when I was supposed to be at work. I walked in the park along the water. More than once, I considered committing suicide by jumping in the lake or buying a gun, but I was too afraid to do that. It was just a terrible, empty feeling. It's hard to describe the ache that I had in my heart from my life. I would walk until about 11 o'clock then go into another bar—it's legal to drink in Canada at 11 o'clock in the morning—so I would go in and drink.

I had to keep track of the time because Crusher would come back from work with my van at 3:30, pick me up at the bar and I would drive home as if I had been at work all day. I wouldn't be penalized for missing my shift because I would go to work on the following Saturday to make up for it. The mine wanted people to work overtime on Saturdays. That's how chaotic my life was. I would miss a good shift on a Monday with nothing happening and then on a beautiful Saturday afternoon I would go into work. My wife thought I was working overtime but I was just making up the shift that I had missed.

One reason I didn't drink very long at the same bar was so people would not know how much I drank. I never went into one bar and sat there drinking all night. I wanted to appear "normal." This was what I was doing by walking through the park all day long trying to live a normal life and then driving home at the end of the day pretending that I had a normal day at work. Meanwhile, I was out there in the city dying inside with my nerves shot, accompanied by my constant companions, the twins Remorse and Guilt. I was wasting money and emotionally estranged from my family. It was becoming overwhelming. The alcohol wasn't having any effect on that haunting, nagging pain in the pit of my stomach.

I drank alone because I never liked fighting or arguing. I'd had enough of that at home. It was all through my childhood and I knew that I could at least control myself when I was drinking because I wouldn't start any arguments. I was a peaceful drunk. I wanted the party to continue and have fun and watch other people and their actions. I also drank alone because I didn't want to drink with anybody else and then owe them money. I always paid for my own drinks; I didn't want to sit at the bar and then have it be my turn to buy a round. Oh, and one other reason: as I said, I didn't want them to know how much I drank.

In April 1987, just a couple months before I hit bottom, I went to a five-day conference in Kitchener for the United Steelworkers. I had applied to attend the Labour College of Canada and the people who would say yea or nay were there to meet the applicants. My parents came to visit and I was somewhat embarrassed by my condition.

Many things happened to me that week, but attending even a single seminar was not one of them. I spent the week trying to drink myself into oblivion. I removed the bottles from the mini bar in my hotel room and in their place I put bottles of rye so I wouldn't need to pay the exorbitant hotel prices. That mini bar needed to be used for its proper purpose, a refrigerator. The seminars took away time from my drinking, so I skipped every one.

For the most part, I just holed up in my room and drank. I was terribly unhappy. I knew I didn't belong anywhere, that I didn't fit in. I knew I was in really bad shape. The last four years I drank, I knew I was in trouble and needed to change, but every time that terrifying realization began to bubble to the surface, I'd go out and drink and forget that I was in trouble. It was just a bottomless void where there was no hope and that was a terrible place to be.

Kitchener became a new low. Needless to say, my application for Labour College was turned down. Still, I considered that their rejection was politically motivated—denial can be amazing!

I ran completely out of money. I had brought only so much to the conference and spent it all. On the second to last day I was flat broke. There were no ATM machines, there weren't any credit cards in my name and I was hurting. I was shaking inside. It was the first time I had ever laid in bed and just vibrated from the inside out and thought that I was having a heart attack. Maybe I was, but it was probably more of a panic attack or the DTs, which I had never experienced up to that point and never will if I continue to live one day at a time.

I phoned my cousin Dorothy's husband, Stan, who lived in Kitchener. Stan had come to visit us in Sudbury occasionally, and he and I connected on many levels and still do today. That day, I simply started walking over to meet him. My nerves were shot. He picked me up in his car. I was in terrible shape. Dorothy and Stan still talk 24 years later about how deathly ill I looked that day when I walked into their place.

"Stan," I began, "I need some money. I'm out of money and need some to get back home."

I had a ride home but still needed the money to taper off on the drinking. He lent me $100.00. Here I was, age 37, made very good money in the mine, had a home just about paid for, had an apartment rental and had to borrow $100.00. Stan later told me that at the time, he felt I would never remember the loan because of my condition.

The day before I called Stan, I was sitting in a bar. I had heard about a shooter called a B-52. For those unfamiliar with the terminology, a shooter is a mixed drink and a B-52 is a three layered drink in a shot glass with coffee liqueur, topped with Irish cream and, on top of that, Grand Marnier. That was the first (and last) shooters experience I ever had. There I was in a bar on a Wednesday afternoon, by myself, drinking shooters.

At one point the waitress came over to me and said, "I'm kind of worried about you, young man. You have had 21 B-52s in an hour and a half."

Chapter 21 - The Beginning of the End

"Well, I'm going back to Pepsi and rye," I replied, "because this is too much for me."

That shows where the addiction had taken me. I was near the end. But not quite.

BREAKING THROUGH

CHAPTER 22

Lying in a Ditch Looking Down on the World

Lost in a Roman wilderness of pain
And all the children are insane.
–Jim Morrison, "The End"

I WENT BACK HOME after the conference and continued drinking.

One night, I came home drunk and staggered down to the basement. There on a shelf were two clear glass jugs, neither one labeled. One contained paint thinner and the other contained homemade moonshine. I had forgotten to label the jugs and there they sat. I couldn't trust my sense of smell, so I sat there for half an hour wondering if it was worth the risk. Finally, I just went to bed. There was a 50/50 chance I could have poisoned myself.

Not long after my return from Kitchener, my wife and I got into an argument one afternoon and I just walked out. I didn't know it would happen that particular day, it simply did. It was my daughter Marcie's sixth birthday and I walked out on my family. I had set them up financially. We had income property. I didn't want them to lose the house. I had sense enough about me as a father and husband that I didn't want my wife and children to have to move because I didn't want to live.

It wasn't that we never had good times as a family. We had wonderful Christmases and birthdays. I would play with my kids in our yard. I remember setting up one of those Slip 'n Slides on the back lawn and turning the yard into mud with them. We had barbecues, we had good times on vacations, but that day was not one of those good times. It was traumatic for the whole family, moreso for me, since I was the perpetrator.

As I've said, I have never done well in confrontations, but I was sick of them and the wife had grown weary as well. I had built a bedroom down in the basement and I spent most of my time there drinking and trying to find people to talk to on my CB radio. I had run through the scenario of leaving a hundred times in my mind and finally, this argument was when it came to pass.

So, I walked out and promptly decided to drink myself to death. I became an alcoholic on a mission.

Those days and weeks are still vague for me. I lived in a little one-room apartment in a friend's house for a couple of days, and then moved into a $20 a week room in a skid row flophouse. My credit cards didn't mean anything by this time. At the end of it, I was dipping into the bank account where I had placed money for my children.

I was taking $50 out of their account at a time, fully intending to replace it. My intentions were honorable, but the addiction just took over. It was overpowering. I lived in this one room and the sad thing is today, when I go back to Sudbury I drive by that flophouse and it is still standing and there are still people living in it.

My room didn't even have a toilet; the bathroom was upstairs, a shared bathroom facility. My hovel was so dirty that I called up my oldest daughter to meet me in a restaurant and she brought me a blanket because, even though I was drunk, disheveled and at my wits end, I knew that I couldn't sleep in a filthy bed. The sheets were so stained that I refused to lie down on them.

The walls in the room were paper-thin. Plywood flooring showed through the holes in the worn-out carpet. A two-element hot plate, with one of the elements burned out, was my stove. A tiny beat up refrigerator and a small table with two chairs completed the furnishings.

The closet was made of wall paneling with a worn-out dingy gray curtain on a wire rod for a closet door. Not that I had an abundance of clothes. When I moved in, my wardrobe consisted of one shirt, one pair of jeans, a pair of boots, two sets of underwear and a black leather jacket.

I didn't want to disrupt my family's home life any more than I already had, so I stayed away. I was never there for them emotionally. I paid the bills the best I could. Even that got to a point near the end that was debatable.

After twenty years of abusing alcohol, my world was falling apart. I had no credit. I had nothing. I remember waking up one day and looked in my pocket and I had 25 cents. That's a terrible feeling when you have no place to go and 25 cents to your name. You're 37 years old and you have no idea who you are, what you're doing or where the next meal is coming from. It's a very, very sad state.

At times, I couldn't afford the $20 for next week's rent so I slept outdoors, in my car or, literally, in a ditch. I lied there looking down on the world. It was the world that had problems, not me. The world was messed up, but I was okay. How little I knew. That's where I was. That was my denial, my way of coping and rationalizing to remain on my self-destructive course.

Over the last four years, my drinking progressed to the blackout stage. I'd be drinking and go into a blackout. My memory would go. I prided myself on being able to handle my booze, but the booze was finally taking over for real and beginning to mismanage my thinking. I would black out and wake up in places not knowing where I was or how I got there. Just as my jackleg drill was running me for the first six months I used it, booze was running me during the last six months of our affair.

I took to borrowing money. Sometimes, I'd be drinking at a bar, run out of money and have to borrow $50 or $100 from someone. The next day, I would have completely forgotten. Someone would come by and tell me, "Hey, you owe me $100," and I wouldn't remember. My pride and my ego were eating me alive.

During these last months, coming out of a blackout, I wouldn't know if owed anybody. I'd be sitting in a bar and wonder, "Do I owe any money here?" I was scared to ask my circle of drinking friends because they would automatically say, "Yes!" whether it was true or not. That's the circle I surrounded myself with.

I ran into my wife's cousin one day and said, "Man, it is great to see you. I haven't seen you in months."

"What are you talking about, Al? We drank together just the other night," he replied.

I was devastated.

I didn't get in trouble every time I drank, but every time I got in trouble I'd been drinking. To lose control like that really tore up my mind. Even though I had experienced sleeping in a ditch, I maintained that I had class because I slept in ditches in front of five star hotels. No one ever caught me sleeping in front of a dump. I say that with humor, but there was a side to me that would not admit to my situation. Pride goes before the fall, as the saying goes, and when I fell, I fell so hard I never even bounced. I landed on top of my pride. It wasn't much of a cushion, but it was a cushion.

It's hard to believe that where I was sleeping, where I was staying, where I was in my head, that I still had a job. Somehow, I managed to keep my job.

Whenever the supervisor would come up to me and say he needed to talk to me about my drinking, I would come back with, "Hey, man, I'm so glad you brought this up. I've been looking at Alcoholics Anonymous and I've been to counseling."

They would be glad to hear that and say, "Hey, great. Hurray. We don't want to interrupt you. We don't want to bother you. We just wanted to talk. If you have a problem, come and see us."

I think they were sincere. I know that one supervisor was very sincere. However, I think they were also glad not to delve into it too deeply because it's a topic that was, is and probably always will be difficult to broach when you're digging into someone's personal life but not trained to do it.

I really needed help. I couldn't live like this any longer. One of the best things I ever did was move into that flophouse, which was clearly physical evidence that I wasn't just pretending. My decisions had brought me to that level where I lived and it became a great awakening for me.

I drove an old beat up car, a 1973 Buick, on which part of the car body had rusted away from the frame. Every time I needed to change a tire, I had to use an axle jack because, if I used a bumper jack, only the body would lift. I bought the car for $250 and that's what I drove back and forth to work.

My van had since disappeared out of my life. At one point, I was making $400 to $500 a week extra driving guys to work in that van. One afternoon, the bailiff came by. He was a bartender I knew, called Hooker because of his pool-playing ability.

"Hey, Hooker, what brings you by this way?" I asked cheerily.

"McDougall, I came by to repossess your van for not making your payments."

"Oh, shit! Hooker, I can take care of it. Give me a break, will you?"

"Okay, Al. I just missed you. But take care of it."

There was a little restaurant on the hotel strip—a dive, really—that I knew and that is where I ate soup or a hamburger, whenever I got too hungry, usually on credit. The flophouse was not too far away from the hotel strip. So, everything was quite convenient.

At long last, a close friend talked to me and said, "Allan, you really, really need to go and seek out help."

My wife and my family had told me that to varying degrees, but hearing someone else say it to me in my own circumstances and knowing I couldn't live like this anymore, the timing was right for me to seek help.

That is where my life had brought me. Somewhere in my mind, however I still thought that I was okay. Somehow it was everybody else causing my misery.

Then, on Sunday, May 31, 1987, at long last, I met up with myself. I was sitting in a bar, alone, in a run down establishment and there was whiskey and Pepsi on the table. I took a sip and swallowed it.

My mind told me I had to have the effect, but for the first time, my body no longer listened.

It rejected the sip. I went to the bathroom and vomited. For some reason, my body couldn't handle it.

I went back to my table, sat down, steadied myself and took another sip.

Again, my body rejected it, and back in the bathroom, I again vomited. "What the hell is going on?" I wondered.

I sat back down and stared at the glass. Whiskey and Pepsi, as always. My mind commanded me to drink, as always. I reached for the glass and raised it to my lips, hesitating for a bit. The characteristic smell filled my nostrils. The warm burn as it slid over my tongue and down my throat was a sensation more familiar to me than the taste of water.

Again, my system rebelled. Within seconds, a wave of nausea rose from my gut and once more I hurried to the restroom. Crouching over the dirty toilet, I heaved for the third time in 15 minutes. Mixed with stomach acid, I could taste the alcohol as it flew from my mouth into the bowl, and the sensation made me retch again.

The spasms subsided and, somewhat dizzy, I stood up and leaned against the door of the stall. What was happening? I wiped my mouth with the sleeve of my jacket and made my way back to the table where the whiskey and Pepsi were waiting, two old friends now transforming into adversaries.

It went on like this for hours. Take a sip. Throw up. Take a sip. Throw up.

There may have been others in that bar, but I didn't notice. I was locked in what had turned into a life and death struggle.

Again and again, my body cried out, "I can no longer handle the booze!"

"Drink more for the effect!" my mind screamed back.

So it went, my mind and my body battling like two desperate beasts.

Finally, after five hours of this pathetic dance, I broke down and cried. It hit me—I had just lost the best love affair of my life. After 20 years, it was over. Alcohol did not work for me anymore. It could no longer cover up that hole in my soul. The bandages had been ripped off for the last time and there was my emptiness for all the world to see, raw, red and hurting like you couldn't believe.

It was over.

BREAKING THROUGH

CHAPTER 23

DESPERATION

The best place to find a helping hand is at the end of your own arm.
—SWEDISH PROVERB

WHEN I LEFT THE BAR, it was dark outside but darker still inside me. I have been thousands of feet underground when my cap lamp went out and I had to sit there in the darkest blackness you can imagine with only the dank smells of the mine and the unstable rock underfoot to keep me company. One couldn't move in those situations because a blackness that deep is disorienting and the ore pass might be just a stumble away. So, one would just sit there until help arrived.

That night back in my flophouse room, I had three choices. I could continue drinking and end up in an institution. I could commit suicide. Or, I could stop the drinking and try to find some way to claw my way out of the cave-in that had nearly buried me alive. I had narrowly avoided a cave-in underground in the mine but couldn't avoid where I now found myself. I had absolutely no faith that I could dig myself out.

What a terrible place to be.

I could no longer deny that I needed help. I have always been a strong union man. I believe in unions. I believe in the collectiveness of people and their strength when united. On Monday, I called the union hall from work and said that I needed help. They couldn't see me until

Wednesday morning, so I set up an appointment and waited.

Believe me, I was scared. There were six beers left in my refrigerator. I was working the afternoon shift at the time and that night when I got home, I drank four of the six.

Tuesday night, I got home at 12:30. There were two beers left and I drank them. The bars wouldn't close until 2:00 and I considered heading out for one last drunk. I sat there at my beat up table and thought about if for maybe 10 minutes. Finally, I said, "That's enough. I quit."

June 3, 1987, at 12:30 a.m., the moment my life turned.

I used to joke, "Enough's enough, and too much is just right." That night I simply said, "Enough's enough."

I went into the Steelworkers Union Hall at 10:30 the next morning. I had often been to the union hall because it had a bar. I went to union meetings because they gave me an excuse to get out of the house. I was actively involved in the workplace as a union steward and I knew the terms of the current collective bargaining agreement. I had always supported decisions that they made at meetings for the betterment of the union members and society.

Rather than come in the front door, I snuck up the back stairs so no one would know that I was seeking help, even though everybody knew that I needed it. I walked up to the door of the Employee Assistance Program office and knocked.

It opened into a small office. I stood in the doorway, still on the hallway side of the threshold. Two men were standing a few feet inside the door to greet me, Dave and Bob. They looked clean. Their eyes were their natural color, not the bloodshot redness that I'd grown accustomed to every morning in the mirror.

"Come on in," they invited.

"No, I'm fine. I'm fine right here," I asserted, suddenly feeling the need to hang on. I didn't want to be prompted. I didn't want to be pushed. The alcohol had pushed me too much and beat me up. I didn't want to be beat up any more. Dave and Bob recognized this, and they had compassion and, I suppose, took pity on me. They knew the things that a man is feeling when he hits bottom in his life.

"That's fine," they said and went back to their small desks. I lit a cigarette and stood in the doorway. The office was simple and tidy, about what you would expect in a union hall. I mentioned some of my issues to them. Even though the booze was absolutely killing me, I downplayed it, saying only, "I've been told I may have a drinking concern."

"That's okay," they said. "That's what we're here for. If you want to come in, please come in and sit down and we'll talk."

I stood there and finished my cigarette. I stood outside the door on Wednesday morning, June the 3rd, 1987, and then I took that step over the threshold from dying to living.

Now, I would love to put pen to paper right here and say that all my issues and all my problems magically dissolved when I walked through that doorway. I'd love to say that I got my house back. That I got my psychological health back, my mental health, filled my emotional void, became spiritually whole, returned to my family, became financially solvent again and that everything came back to me. You will notice though, that you are only halfway through my story. None of those things happened right away. I'll be honest, I had my worst days at the beginning. I've had terrible days sober, but the worst days sober have been much better than my best days drinking.

There was a chair along the left-hand wall and as I sank down onto it, I felt utterly defeated. These two gentleman, Bob and Dave, were kind to me and just listened. I didn't want to share too much, of course. My pride was still in the way.

They handed me a sheet with 20 questions on it. It was written by a doctor working at Johns Hopkins University at the time and was an assessment of a person's drinking patterns. To those 20 questions, I answered "Yes" to 17 without hesitation. I've always joked since that was the best grade I ever got on a test, but the sad thing was that only three Yes answers on that sheet was a strong indication of a drinking problem. I had 14 more than the three. The assessment and my answers are in the Appendix.

Keep in mind, I wasn't in trouble at work. I wasn't yet in their progressive disciplinary system. No court had mandated me to go for help. I had hit my own bottom. Unbeknownst to me, my wife had gone into the hall a month or two earlier and met with these people and told them that I had to stop drinking, that I was going to kill myself. I didn't know for a couple more years she had done that.

So, besides the friend who told me to seek help, I had these two men in my corner. We talked a little bit more and it was now about 11:30 a.m.

Bob said, "Well listen, Al. This will be a great day for you to go to an AA meeting."

"Oh m--m--m--my g--g--g--god, I c--c--c--c--can't do that!" My stutter returned with a vengeance. My mind was scrambling for an excuse. I always looked for excuses when faced with the inevitable. I was scared, and when I was scared I stuttered.

"Oh, I'm s--s--so so--so--sorry," I said, though I wasn't. "I have to g--g--go to work on the afternoon sh--sh--shift."

"Well, what time does your cage go underground?"

"Th-th-three-thirty." I was hoping that the meetings were at nighttime.

Suddenly, I felt back on top of my emotional game. I felt back in control. "I just can't do this. I just have to go to work and I'll be okay. I'll quit drinking on my own."

Dave had mentioned earlier that one of the things he did to change his life along with attending AA meetings was to work out in the gym.

"That's what I'll do. I'll join a gym," I said to myself, "a workout place that I'll go to every day and I'll get physically fit. I'll feel better. I'll look better and I'll get my life back in order by working out at the gym every day. Anything was better than attending Alcoholics Anonymous meetings."

I was so anti-Alcoholics Anonymous that I had a T-shirt silkscreened about two years earlier reading, "Alcoholics Unanimous." I often wonder whom I offended with that shirt. When I went to one meeting during my first months of sobriety, I met a friend who said, "Hey, Al. We've been waiting for you." I guess my drinking was not that invisible.

That day, June 3rd, was a pivotal day in my life. I didn't know it at the time. It was a beautiful sunny day, but all I was aware of were clouds of despair. I certainly can't claim that I experienced any moments of particular clarity, but I remember it like it was yesterday. For someone of my generation, it was like the day John F. Kennedy was assassinated or, for younger people, September 11, 2001. You remember it. June 3, 1987, was that kind of day, the day when 'ol Allan decided to go to an Alcoholics Anonymous meeting. It was, at once, both profound and nerve-shattering.

The elation furnished by my excuse that I had to go to work was short-lived. In response, they said, "Hey, we've got good news. There's a meeting in town here at noon."

What were the odds that on Wednesday, June 3rd, that the only AA meeting on the entire week's calendar in Sudbury, population 100,000 plus, was on Wednesday at noon? The other thing that later struck me as odd was that the meeting was held in a hotel. The hotel donated their restaurant space to AA. People would show up and talk about their issues every Wednesday at noon and have a buffet lunch. It was called the Lunch Bunch.

The only reason I agreed to go was because, if I didn't like it, I could get a drink from the bartender at the hotel bar who I knew on a first name basis. Since it was at noon, I had the option of going there before work. Now, what were the odds of that?

I told Bob and Dave, "I'll meet you there," and left the office. I debated all the way down the stairs whether I would actually go or not. Finally, I decided, "I'll try it." I gave my commitment, and a promise made is a promise kept. Not that I wasn't a master at breaking promises.

I trucked down to the hotel and arrived at 10 minutes to 12:00. I walked in embarrassed, very downtrodden and extremely beat up. I didn't want anyone to know who I was. Bob and Dave had arrived already and met me at the door. They took me under their wings and we sat down and ordered lunch. Then the AA meeting started.

I looked around at all these people and I thought, "Wow. I don't know if I can relate to this." Everybody was a stranger. They were well-dressed. They seemed respectable and responsible. I felt totally out of place. I heard some of the stories, but it was really all just a vague blur. Part of me wanted what they had and part of me was scared that I couldn't attain it, but a few days earlier, I had become painfully aware of what my alternatives were.

In the 37 years of my life up to that day, I had never opened up my mind to any message of help. Then, one gentleman spoke up and said, "My name is Mike and I'm an alcoholic. Next week, I will have had four years of sobriety."

I looked at Mike as he sat there and said those words. He did not know me from Adam. He was just making an announcement, but I took those words and brought them into my heart and said to myself, "Wow. This program does work. Maybe, just maybe it will work for me."

People talk about the power of words to have an impact on us for the rest of our lives, and Mike unknowingly did that to me when he said, "I will have had four years of sobriety." One of the reasons I continue to go to Alcoholic Anonymous meetings with more than 8000 days of sobriety behind me is that I believe we need to bring longevity to the equation to show people that it does work. As well, we need to hear the newcomer's story because the people who are just entering the program are the ones who are most lost and hurting, just like I was that June day.

For certain, I didn't have a story that day. I was so overwhelmed; I didn't have anything at all to say. I was just there in body, or what was left of it, not necessarily in spirit, in mind or in emotion. I merely landed there and was eating a dinner. Though everything was a fog, I do remember Mike's message with clarity, a moment of clarity in my life just like the voice I heard the day I was driving my car in a high speed chase that said, "Stop. You're going to kill someone."

Mike's message of four years sobriety really helped me. I often wonder whether had he said, "two years," or "six months," or "90 days," that his message would have sunk in as much as it did. Whatever, it resonated deeply within me and became the touchstone I took with me from that meeting.

Years later, I read a quote by the American mystic Charles Fillmore that made perfect sense considering what Mike said that day: "Words are the most powerful agents of mind. Every time we speak, we cause the atoms of the body to tremble and change their place. Not only do we cause the atoms of our own body to change their positions, but we raise or lower the rate of vibrations and otherwise affect bodies of others with whom we come in contact."

As much as I scorned the AA program, scoffed at it, detested it—in fact, everything in life that I looked upon with distaste, didn't believe in or voiced opinions against when I was drinking—99 percent of it I have learned to adopt into my life and to love and cherish. I thought sobriety was a total waste of time. I thought it was boring. Little did I realize it was the beginning of a new life, a brand new life, one day at a time.

BREAKING THROUGH

CHAPTER 24

FIRST STEPS

When the pain of change is less than the pain of staying the same,
then people will change.

−ANONYMOUS

I LEFT THE MEETING WITH A TINY BIT OF HOPE but I was still really scared. I picked up my three passengers on the way to work in that old beat up car of mine. None of these men drank anything other than occasionally; they weren't problem drinkers. They were just miners who worked underground with me, and I loved and respected them very much. I wanted to tell them about my eventful day but was afraid of the teasing I was certain would come my way. I am sure they were aware that I seemed distracted during the drive.

Finally, about ten miles from the mine, I gathered my courage and said to them, "You won't believe what I did today . . ." They were expecting a story about drinking. They didn't know where I was living. I had never told them I was separated from my family. I said, "I went to my first Alcoholics Anonymous meeting this afternoon before I came here."

I half expected some humorous dig. They were miners after all. Instead of laughing at me they said, "Hey, great! Wonderful. Why don't you try it for a while? We will help you any way we can."

They were incredibly supportive and their words impressed me enough to remember them more than 24 years later. I have kept in contact with some of those men over the years, meeting them on happenstance, or perhaps to give them a call to thank them for their support many years ago.

On the anniversary of my sobriety on June 3, 2010, my 23 year anniversary, I called Mike. I had the opportunity to become acquainted with him a little over the years and subsequently learned his last name. Even though I moved to Pittsburgh and live 12 hours away, when I celebrated 23 years of sobriety, I said to myself, "I want Mike to know what an impact he had on my life." I had never told him before, so I called him at his home and as the world would have it, or as a God of my understanding would have it, he answered the phone.

"Hi, Mike, how's your day going?"

"Great." He had no idea who I was.

"My name is Allan McDougall. I don't know if you remember me from years ago, but we belonged to the same fraternity. You probably won't recall, but I just wanted you to know that on June the 3rd of 1987, you announced that you had four years sobriety in another week or two, and that statement was such a remarkable moment in my life. I wanted to call you up 23 years later and thank you for what your words did for me, and what you unknowingly and so graciously gave me, a message with realistic hope."

I believe in a message of hope, I believe in hope, I live by hope, I live in hopes and dreams and aspirations and trying to get to the next level and having fun while doing it. There's a big barrier between hope and realistic hope, and Mike gave me realistic hope.

"My God, Al, I don't remember that," he said, "but I remember the meetings at the hotel that we went to in the afternoons, and soon after that meeting they moved the location."

I often wonder if I would have gone to a meeting on a Wednesday afternoon that wasn't held in a bar. I didn't have to make that decision and I'm glad I didn't, but I have to be honest, I went to AA because the location was in a bar.

It's important to tell people our success stories because the world will certainly tell us what we're doing wrong. We are a very negative society. If you have ten things you need to do on a list and you only get nine done, what's the one you remember? Which is the one other people will remind you of? Which is the one that remains foremost in your mind?

I think baseball has a wonderful metric for success. In baseball, you go to bat three times but you only have to get one hit to make tremendous money. You're a star if you are successful one-third of the time. True, baseball is hard. They say that hitting a round moving object with another round object is the single hardest thing to do in sports, but life is hard too. There is a saying, "If we do what is hard, life will be easy. If we do what is easy, life will be hard."

Alcoholics Anonymous had been around since the 1930s, but I knew nothing about it beyond my own narrow-minded prejudice that a sober life was not worth living. Through involvement though, I learned that AA is a fellowship with the simple purpose "to stay sober and help other alcoholics achieve sobriety."

I told the guys on the way to work that I was going to try AA for a couple of weeks to see if I could start to feel better. I worked my normal shift, and just continued on with my life. I started attending meetings every day and INCO was supportive.

Through reading the book, *Alcoholics Anonymous: The Story of How Many Thousands of Men and Women Have Recovered from Alcoholism*, I discovered that I was living in its definition of addiction. It fit me to a T: "an obsession of the mind coupled with the allergic reaction to the body."

My mind was telling me, "I need more, I need more, I need more, I need more." My body was telling me, "Allan, I can't take this anymore." That last day it was getting rid of the alcohol as fast as I put it inside me.

Though the bottom had fallen out of my life, I still didn't want to admit that I had a problem. When I looked at the first step of

Alcoholics Anonymous' famous Twelve Steps, it read, "Step 1. We admitted we were completely powerless over alcohol—that our lives had become unmanageable." I did not want to admit that I could not manage my alcohol, but I could certainly admit that my life was unmanageable.

Whether I came into AA under the second half of the first step or the first half of the first step, who cares? I arrived. I was ready. No one wakes up in the morning at 5 or 10 years old and says, "You know what I want to do with my life? I'm going to become a member of Alcoholics Anonymous." Everyone who does become a member though, ends up there beaten, bruised, empty, null and void, with no self-respect. AA is a door that is opened to you if you want it opened.

I continued to live in that rooming house, that flophouse. Upstairs lived a schizophrenic nymphomaniac who, whenever she was off her medication, became a terror. I witnessed a stabbing in the flophouse parking lot, a non-life threatening stabbing, but a stabbing nonetheless.

It was a moonless night but there was a street light outside and I heard arguing. I went to the window and looked out. My window was so filthy with dirt and fly shit that I could hardly see out of it, but I saw this woman stab a man in the leg. I had come from a small village, I had been in a mining camp, I had lived in the city, I had a house and an income property and here I was living in this filth. I was witnessing something I didn't want to see, but I didn't drink, I did not drink. Instead, I thought, "Wow, what have I done? What have I gotten myself into?"

I became very afraid and was scared to go out to my car. When the man staggered away and she ran back into the flophouse with the knife, I drove to a 24 hour restaurant and drank coffee until it was time to go to work the next morning.

I really did want sobriety, I didn't even know what sobriety meant, I just knew it was a different feeling than when I woke up with all that guilt and remorse. I still had lots of guilt and remorse but I had a new pathway to walk, I had new ideas, new guidelines, and a couple of friends who truly cared for me.

The week after my first meeting I was back on the day shift. I told my boss that I was attending AA meetings and the company offered to put me on steady days to accommodate my attendance. I declined, saying that wasn't necessary because AA's meeting schedules were made around shift workers like myself.

There is an old saying, "When you start to help yourself, people come out of the woodwork from the strangest places to offer you help." They say the world favors a risk taker. Maybe I'm perceived as a risk taker, but I tell you, my choices were made at that very tenuous place between life and death. There was nothing glorious about any of it; it was simply a matter of sustaining my life. I had to die to start feeling better. That's a deep, dark place to be.

Bob and Dave picked me up sometimes to go to meetings and they would introduce me to people. They really went out of their way; that United Steelworker Employee Assistance Program went the extra mile. Often, I would walk to meetings, farther than I ever would have walked to a bar, so I must have really wanted to succeed at sobriety. Each day that I made it through without drinking, I was proud of the accomplishment.

Those first couple weeks of sobriety I was attending meetings and counting each as a victory, but life was still a blur. One day, I went to one of my old haunts, the bar at the Steelworkers Hall and told Fats the bartender, who used to serve me vast quantities of whiskey, and who had tried to quit himself, "Fats, I have been sober 15 days today."

He stopped wiping down the counter and looked at me. "Allan, stop your counting. Just live one day at a time. I had a brother in Alcoholics Anonymous who used to count the days and he got up to 60 days and then he went out and celebrated. I'm proud of you but stop the counting, for fuck's sake."

The people in my life that drank and the people who didn't drink, both types gave me great words of wisdom at different times, especially when I needed it.

My mind was still in a fog but I knew that my vacation time was coming up in July. I had four weeks paid vacation, and I knew the odds were that I would go back on the bottle. I didn't want to lose my meetings or continuity they had begun to bring to my life.

I had started to develop some friendships with people around the tables at AA. One great thing about an AA meeting is that everybody greets you, gives you a smile and honestly asks, "How are you?" Then, they really listen to your answer and care about you. That was something new to me.

The friends who drank with me, and I with them, only cared about how much money we had and how much booze we consumed together and how we could get the most out of our time for our own self-serving purposes. By contrast, Alcoholics Anonymous seemed to me, at the beginning, and has turned out to be in the long run, a very other-centered organization.

One day, a few weeks into my sobriety, I was having a really hard time of it. My financial obligations were getting the best of me. I was having a terrible time of dealing with the thought that I could never again have another drink. I was in a shopping mall in Sudbury and in that mall was a bar, Dangerous Dan's. I was sorely tempted to go there and have a drink to settle myself down. Sorely tempted. In fact, I was heading up the escalator to the bar.

As fate would have it, just about to step onto the other escalator coming down was an old pack sack miner I knew. Keith was an itinerant miner, the kind who drifted from mine to mine, never joining the union, never stably working. They came in, made a pile of money and drifted on. Keith was on and off the wagon and back on. A revolving door drunk, we called them. Sadly, he died drunk. That day, he caught me in one of his sober periods.

"Hey, McDougall," he called out. "Where you headed?"

"I'm on my way to get a drink," I replied in all honesty. "Things aren't going well for me. I'm thinking about having a drink."

"Come and have a coffee first, Al."

We went for a coffee and talked about different things. I told him all the stuff that had been rattling around in my head during my pity party. I told him about my job, the bills, the child support, an upcoming court date. Keith sat there and listened. The act of unloading all that to somebody helped me come out of my funk.

Then he said, "Al, live one day at a time. If you drink today, tomorrow you will still have all your problems but you'll also have a hangover. Just live today."

I began to hear what he was saying. Finally, he added, " But Al, if you really want that drink, I'll come to the bar with you and I will buy you your first drink."

"Absolutely not," I said, my spine straightening. "Absolutely not."

Who knows what would have happened had Keith not run into me that day.

Fifteen years later, I ran into Keith in a bar as I was about to celebrate my 15 year anniversary of sobriety. I had heard he was drinking again and went looking for him. I knew all the old haunts and sure enough, there he was.

"Hey, Al, you old shit. I know why you're here. You're trying to make me stop."

"No, Keith. I'm just here to spend time with a guy I respect. Whether you drink or not is immaterial."

"You're just trying to get me sober."

"Keith, no. I don't know if I would be here today without what you did for me many years ago. My 15 year anniversary is coming up and I would be honored if you would attend to witness it."

Keith never received much positive affirmation during his life and he agreed to show up and did so, albeit somewhat under the influence.

My family was there, my mother, my sister and my kids along with other friends. I reserved a seat for Keith in the front row.

When I received my medallion, it was emotional for me. It always is.

"I want to thank everybody who has helped and supported me. But there is one person who deserves this medallion more than me and I want to give it to him."

I got Keith up there in front of everyone and gave him a big hug and we both shed a few tears. A year later, he was dead, but that moment was a big deal for Keith, even under the influence. It certainly was a big moment for me. But for Keith, I may have gone back drinking that day. Keith saw me through and my life began to even out.

I knew that with vacation time coming up, I'd have a few extra dollars. I was paying support to my family. I had not been to court yet, but I was still paying a considerable amount regularly to my family.

I had been visiting them off and on and it was very painful, but I think they were somewhat excited, as I was, because I had new hope, I had new breath, I was doing something that I had never done before and it was exhilarating to a degree because I was having success.

Each day was another day of continuing sobriety and new friends, new concepts, new ideas, a new life. I kept in close contact with the employee assistance office at the Union Hall. I would call them or go in and have a cup of coffee.

Bob and Dave were very gracious with their time and allowed me to help them as a volunteer. They said I was helping them, but I was really only sitting there and listening and talking, discussing life, talking about our drinking and how it wasn't working for us anymore. They gave me passages to read from the Big Book of AA. I would tell them something about my life and they would say, "Read page so-and-so."

I had many opportunities to have sober people around me. I made as many friends in that first month of sobriety as I did in the old days when I was drinking.

A couple of these new friends were both single and essentially, so was I. We went to meetings together, went out for coffee and talked and became a little support group for one another.

July, and my vacation, was fast approaching. I was apprehensive about losing my routine of the past month. To avoid what I feared would happen when I would be on my own with extra money in my pocket, I decided to enter a rehab program. My life was about to change, but not how I imagined.

Breaking Through

CHAPTER 25

BREAKING THROUGH

In times of change the learners inherit the world,
while the learned wake up to a world that no longer exists.
–ERIC HOFFER

DURING THOSE FIRST COUPLE OF WEEKS while attending AA meetings, I made some new friends and saw other men that I had known in the mine, men that I drank with 10 years previously but had lost track of, and now, here they were in the AA program. They had probably been going to AA for that amount of time but we didn't associate with the same circle of friends anymore. I found it interesting to reconnect with them again.

I went to the EAP office to talk about my fear about having a month off work without any structure. I talked to some friends there and said I wanted to go into a rehab program. One person said yes, go. One said no, it was too soon, too early.

I picked up the telephone myself—quite amazing to me—and referred myself into a 28 day rehab program located in the town of Elliot Lake, about 100 miles west of Sudbury.

July arrived and I left work. My good friend drove me out there. She was very encouraging to me throughout this whole period; she became the backbone that truly helped me with my sobriety. We spent a couple of days in town before I went in. We talked a lot about the present, we talked a lot about the future and she drove me up to the door that morning. It was the 5th of July 1987.

Elliot Lake was another mining town—uranium, which gave it a good tax base, and it also had excellent medical facilities to deal with the particular hazards of uranium mining. The Camillus Center occupied one wing of a hospital in town and used the AA Twelve Step model. Responding to the concerns of the area's mining operations about the high rates of alcoholism and drug abuse, the local order of nuns opened the center. They named it in honor of Sister St. Camillus whose pioneering efforts had led to the establishment of the hospital in the 1950s.

It was a two-story 30-bed facility, cafeteria on the first floor, therapy rooms on the second, two beds to a room on both floors and a basement with a library and reading room. Out behind the hospital was a fenced off wooded area where we could see Elliott Lake and take walks during breaks. There was no way out except through the front door.

I had been sober a month, a longer time than any since my early teens, and I was terrified. I was scared to death, but my friend was there for me, and I give her eternal credit for that. She was motivating, she inspired me, she gave me hope, she gave me encouragement, and above all else, she was someone that cared enough to listen.

We hugged and I turned and walked toward the entrance. I never turned back to wave good-bye because I was worried that I would falter. I forced myself to head toward the entrance.

I walked slowly up to the door, wanting to appear confident that I would follow through. With each step though, my heart pounded harder, sweat appeared on my forehead, I was scared. I was not sure what was behind that door. What was I getting into? I was fearful that I couldn't go through with it, that I would fail to complete the program. It brought me back to the anxieties of my school days. Somehow, my sweaty hand reached out to the door buzzer and pressed. There was a wait of maybe 30 seconds that might as well have been 3 weeks.

A man opened it and ushered me in. The place was well set up. Those who were near the end of the program had the duty of greeting new arrivals each Sunday. He gave me a genuine smile as he shook my hand.

"Hi, how are you? My name is Kevin. I'm an alcoholic. Welcome to the Camillus Center. Here's where you check in." Then, "Here is where you put your clothes. Here's where you register." It was a very nice introduction.

I was never alone. I've walked into some hospitals where I had to find my own way—"Please follow the green line. Please follow the yellow line for the next 552 yards, and then take an elevator up, get off at the third floor, follow the burgundy line over another 1002 feet, and you'll be at the nurses station." None of that at all, it was very hands on, very personal. They made me feel that I belonged. The only other place where I felt that to the same degree was in the Steelworkers Union.

A typical day began at 5:00 a.m. We rose, made our beds and headed to breakfast. After that, there was time for reflection, meditation and reading from the Big Book of AA. From 10:30 to 11:15 was group therapy, more quiet time and then lunch. The same routine was repeated in the afternoon and after dinner, we went to an AA meeting in town. They wanted us to see what long-term sobriety looked like.

There were definitely rules and regulations. Any medications, even mouthwash, had to be dispensed by a nurse and taken while they watched. We had responsibilities, too, such as making our beds in the morning or cleaning up after meals.

One recovering alcoholic was a volunteer assistant to the attending counselor, and his name was Sergeant Bob. He'd been sober for 20-some years and used to tell me that he was so dry he was a fire hazard. Sergeant Bob inspected the beds and then went to the breakfast room, where we were sitting eating breakfast cafeteria-style.

With a military demeanor, Sergeant Bob would announce, "Al, Bill, John, you don't know how to make your beds. You have to do extra kitchen duties today because your beds weren't made right and..." It was embarrassing, but I think it was a test to see how we could take directions.

We had 45 minutes of therapy twice a day every day, group therapy, sitting around discussing our lives with counselors and peers. I just hated that because I never wanted to disclose what my life was like. Mostly, I sat there and listened. I dreaded the open therapy groups and discussing what my life was like or how much I was accountable for my actions. These therapy sessions were right up there with Oral Composition Day in grade school.

During my first two weeks, we had a daily break of an hour after lunch and we used the time to walk out of the hospital to a 7-Eleven convenience store in a nearby strip mall. We wore bracelets on our wrists and we had to go in pairs, so that if one person wanted to go drinking, his buddy was supposed to stop him.

At the 7-Eleven, I would pick up lottery tickets, scratch tickets, cigarettes and real coffee. There was no caffeine allowed in the center, and I had major headaches my first two or three days, not from the disclosure of things I had been carrying for 37 years, but from the lack of caffeine. We all looked forward to our daily journey out into the regular world for real coffee or chocolate bars. We could bring things back as long as we gave them to the counselors to check to make sure we weren't bringing in any mood-altering chemicals.

I would buy a lottery ticket or the equivalent of a power ball ticket, and pray, "Hey, God, I've been sober now a month. Why won't you let me win a million dollars so I can help my family, I can be a responsible citizen and I'll never drink again."

Imagine if I'd won a million dollars on a scratch ticket with six or seven other recovering alcoholics. We would have been off to Mexico, and all of us would have either died there or died trying to get back. That was my sincerity level at the time: "God, just let me win a million dollars so I can help some other people get out of their addiction." I truly believe a person needs a strong foundation and great support group to handle any unexpected gain of wealth. Simply throwing money at someone is a recipe for failure.

Though I like to tell people about the lessons I learned in rehab, I don't generally promote that people should go into rehab right away. There seems to be a myth about rehab as the magic cure and truthfully, I can only speak from my own experiences. I'm so glad that I had those first 30 days behind me before I entered the program.

I had a roommate who turned out to be Kevin, the man who first greeted me at the door. One day he said, "Al, I am really going to achieve sobriety because I have faith. I have just discovered faith."

His words had a profound effect on me but in a disconcerting way. I woke up about 2 o'clock the next morning in the next bed and said to myself, "I won't make this, I'm not going to reach sobriety, I'll fail. I'll go back out there and drink and die, because I don't have faith. I don't feel what Kevin said he felt."

I was devastated. Looking at it now, I was scared. Sometimes it was the same fear I felt in school, in that one-room school, where the bullies, in my mind, were ten feet tall and 500 pounds of muscle, but who when I look at the class pictures weren't much bigger than I. I couldn't sleep, so I got up about 2:30 a.m., and went downstairs where Sergeant Bob was the attendant on duty.

"What's on your mind, Al?" I told him the story about Kevin finding faith, that he had everything down pat because he had seen the light.

Bob said, "Well, let's talk about that." So I pulled up a chair and sat down.

Bob then said, "Stand up." I stood up.

"Sit down," he said, so I sat down.

"Stand up," I stood up.

"Sit down." I sat down.

"Stand up."

"Honest to God," I said to myself, "this man is crazy. He's better off drinking. If this is sobriety, it's not for me." Still, I followed his directions.

After five or six times he said, "Now, just stay seated. Allan, you have all the faith that you need to achieve sobriety. Not once did you ever look back to see if that chair was there."

His last statement stunned me. Then I remembered Sunday School as a young boy when the minister spoke about the Parable of the Mustard Seed, the lesson being that even if one's faith was only as large as a mustard seed, which is a very, very tiny seed, that it could grow and eventually become great enough to move mountains.

That sleepless night became one of the important lessons I learned in rehab, so much so that today I use it in my motivational talks. I see people writing it down, so it must be of value. When I talk about simplicity being profound, this is one of the examples I use.

One of the many lessons I learned is the value of living one day at a time. I've had to relearn this lesson two or three times in my life, and in that first year, I had to have that lesson hit me more than once just to get it into my thick skull.

Another night, I woke up in despair. "Oh, my god," I thought. "I won't make this and it's just overwhelming. I won't make it because I won't be able to drink at my daughter's wedding." That thought took over my whole mind. It became an obsession: I won't be able to drink at my daughter's wedding.

I grabbed my pack of cigarettes, pulled on my jeans and headed downstairs to see, guess who—Sergeant Bob.

"How's you're night going right now?" he asked.

"Not that great, Bob."

"What's wrong?"

"I'll never make this, Bob."

"What's the issue?"

"Well," I began (and I was so earnest and so sincere), "I won't be able to drink at my daughter's wedding."

"How old is your daughter?"

"Twelve," I answered.

Bob started to laugh. "Does she have to get married?" he asked.

"Of course not," I snorted indignantly.

"Al, live one day at a time. Live today," he said. "You're missing a great day. Al, live today. If your daughter's 12, don't worry about drinking at the wedding. Be here tonight. Be here in the present with me."

The irony is that my daughter is now 35 and not married, not because she couldn't be, but because she chooses not to be. She's studying for a wonderful career and is living a rewarding life.

We had speakers come in, volunteers from an Alcoholics Anonymous group in Elliot Lake who were giving back to the community. We had to go to AA meetings every night. Some were "in house" and sometimes we went out to other meetings and were always welcomed warmly. In one meeting, a man got up and spoke about how he had always committed himself to quit drinking tomorrow but of course, tomorrow never came.

That brought me back to one of my experiences when I was drinking. I frequented one bar and would sit on an old bar stool looking at the whisky bottles lined up and wonder whether I could take one drink out of every bottle on display. Behind those bottles was a big sign on the mirror behind the bar that read, "Free beer tomorrow." I kept coming back to that bar, and as we all know tomorrow never came. It's always today, which leads to the old saying, "Yesterday is history, tomorrow is a mystery. But today is a gift. That's why it's called the present."

There was another speaker who came in, and his talk literally made me stop breathing. I'd never met the man before, yet he told my story. The speaker at an Alcoholics Anonymous meeting ordinarily has half an hour to 45 minutes for his talk and there are three things that he focuses on: 1) identification of oneself as an alcoholic and a sharing of one's experiences as one, 2) what brought one to AA, 3) one's recovery in AA and the knowledge gained from the program.

Within that framework this man, who was about five years older than me, proceeded to tell my life story. I couldn't breathe, and in my little paranoid mind I was sure that someone had told him to tell my story so that I would realize that someone knew all of my secrets.

Like me, he grew up on a farm. He was abused as a child. He was passionate about cars. He even owned a 1969 Camaro, the same make of car as I once owned. I couldn't believe it; I couldn't believe that he knew my story. It irritated me that the counselor would pay someone to come in and tell my story just to make a point with me. I went up to him afterwards. "Who told you my story?!" I demanded. He just laughed.

After some dialogue however, he convinced me that it truly was his story. Although I was basically mistrustful, there was a glimmer of hope that, "If this guy can go through what I did and quit, and has five years of sobriety. . ."

It wasn't all life-changing lessons, though. The therapy sessions were extremely uncomfortable for me. Sometimes people were challenging or crying or wildly laughing. We had a counselor named Art. I love him to death today but didn't love him in those days. At one time, I detested the ground he walked on and today I kiss the ground he walks on. There was no change in Art, the change was in me.

Then however, he was overbearing. He challenged me and stripped me of all my defense mechanisms.

"McDougall, you're awfully quiet today. What's going on with your life?" he would start in.

"Oh, I'm fine," I would say noncommittally.

"Well, what are you doing here if you're so fine? None of us here are fine. What the fuck are you doing here if you're so fine?"

This went on and Art reported that I wasn't making progress. In our two 45 minute sessions a day we sat around in a circle and everybody talked about their feelings. Some people cried but I just couldn't cry. As much as I wanted change, and I knew I had to change, I just could not get in touch with my emotions. I had bottled them up. I had buried them. I had drowned them. I had packed them so tightly inside that I couldn't open up. I really wanted to, I really needed to, because they were getting ready to throw me out of the program. There were other people waiting to get into the rehab program and if a person was not committed 100% to changing their lives or actively seeking help, then it was time for that person to leave and I didn't want to leave. But I didn't want to touch those feelings, I knew they would be too overwhelming.

They switched me from Art to another counselor, Collin. I just could not connect with him, either.

Sister Jean was the executive administrative assistant, and one day she called me into her office. "You know, Allan, you're going to have to leave because you're just not putting forth the effort. You're not making it."

I was so disappointed. A familiar feeling began to well up inside, the same humiliation I would feel each Oral Composition Day when I would drag myself home and tell my mother that, once again, I had failed to deliver my speech in class. I literally ached in the pit of my stomach to finish this program because this was my chance for renewal, my chance to leave that scared little boy behind forever. "But I don't want to leave. I want this sobriety, and I'm really working at it."

"But they said, you haven't shown any emotion," Sister Jean came back.

"I said some things about my childhood with my parents and my mother's anger," I pleaded.

"Okay," she said. "We'll give you one more chance." I felt so relieved.

"Write down your life story with your mother," she directed me.

She gave me a three ring binder and some paper. I left her office and sat down in the cafeteria with a cup of coffee and I started writing. I wrote and wrote and wrote and wrote and wrote, for at least 12 hours straight. The people in the center knew I was on a mission and didn't make me do my cleaning duties that day.

The exercise of writing about my relationship with my mother was more intense digging than anything I had ever done underground. I kept digging and digging but still had not struck the emotional ore I was now searching for so desperately.

That Thursday, I got a letter from my son, Shane. He was seven at the time. In his letter, he included a picture. He and I had gone fishing on the Spanish River with a neighbor about a year before I walked out on my family, and he had written me a letter, printing each word the way a kid will do. I was in the basement of the rehab center by myself when I opened the envelope.

"Dear Dad," it began. "This is Shane. I want you to know I love you and I don't want you to forget me."

There was a picture of him standing on the bank of the river fishing. He was standing there with a smile on his face holding his fishing pole, but he was all by himself. His father was nowhere around. He looked so alone.

The picture of Shane, alongside the Spanish River, that enabled me to break through to the pain that had ruined my life.

An overwhelming sadness rose up and swamped me. His letter touched a place I didn't know existed. Right then, the dam broke.

Pent up waters flowed and flowed and flowed. With the writing I had been doing and having been away from the booze for five or six weeks, all I needed was the catalyst of that photo and my son's pleading words. I cried and cried and cried.

When I looked up, one of the counselors, Collin, was watching. He came over and put his arm around me, and I just cried some more. I sobbed uncontrollably. My shoulders were shaking. Through my tears, I kept writing about life with my parents and my mother's influence on me.

The next thing I knew, they called me in and said, "We'd like you to stay one more week and we're assigning you to a new counselor." The counselors met every day and talked about their clients in the group, and after my lack of connection with Art and Collin, they decided to switch me to a counselor named Elaine. I moved to a group of six people, included in a family program, which included spouses or partners of alcoholics.

I walked in and saw this was more group therapy. I thought, "Oh, my God, here we go again." Elaine never said a word to me the first day, never confronted me at all. I sat there sharing only a few inconsequential things but actively listened to the others. My secrets were my secrets. There's a slogan in AA: "You're only as sick as your secrets." If this is true, I was still very sick.

The next day, I was sitting in the group waiting for it to begin, thinking, "Oh, my goodness, this is the day. I've only got four days left, and I have to do some work on myself."

Elaine walked in and walked right over to me, took my hand and said, "Allan, you're not a bad man. Actually, you're a very nice man."

Again, I just lost it.

I broke down and cried right in front of everybody. I couldn't remember a member of the opposite sex ever giving me a compliment. I'm sure they had, but a lot had been churning inside of me. I had just experienced being physically ill due to my drinking, which was very uncomfortable and centered in the pit of my stomach.

My son had recently sent me his letter. I had been journaling and getting in touch with my feelings about my mother, my childhood and my past. I'd been alcohol-free for less than two months and Elaine's statement triggered all these pent up emotions.

The people in that counseling group just loved me to death, and so I cried and cried. I couldn't stop, and every time I tried to speak I began to cry again. There was so much inside of me.

Underground in the mine when a waterline broke and was under pressure, the water gushing out of the split was hard to stop. We could put a little patch on it, but then the pressure would build up again, burst and spray all over. Finally, we'd have to shut the valve, drain the line and fix it properly with clamps and gaskets. I didn't have any clamps and I didn't have any gaskets. I had only myself, my feelings and the sadness of 37 years.

Elaine sent me back to my room and said to lie down and relax. She told me I was doing great. I couldn't believe the relief I felt at that moment. It was like 50 tons of rock had been lifted from me and I was floating. I felt good but terribly tired. Exhausted, I laid down on my bunk and slept. I cried some more. Slept again and cried again. Journaled more and that was the beginning of getting in touch with my feelings, the feelings that I had buried long, long ago.

I had finally broken through. Those eighteen inches from my head to my heart were the hardest distance I have ever travelled. More unyielding rock than I ever encountered underground. After more than twenty years, I am still mining that vein, still extracting its wealth and I am convinced that it is a bottomless source of personal riches.

CHAPTER 26

Beginning Life on the Up Ramp

Birds sing after a storm. Why shouldn't we?
–Rose Kennedy

The mining process at Levack West had become much more mechanized; I no longer went down in the cage but rode a low-profile bus down a spiral ramp. At the end of a shift, I rode the same bus back up to surface, and my life after rehab began to parallel that movement upwards. The ramp in the mine was a steep 20-degree slant, however my life did not take off at such an angle. Some days it was one degree.

My first year of sobriety, I had such a haze and fog around me that all I could do at meetings was sit there and listen. It was like living in the smoke that filled the stope after a blast. I asked Jim, who later became my sponsor, when I could begin speaking at meetings. "What the fuck do you know, living in a flophouse? Just sit back and listen. You have nothing to contribute because your best thinking got you lying in ditches looking down on the world."

So, I took Jim's advice and simply listened during meetings. My recommendation to anyone in a similar situation is: when you go to a meeting, take what you want, take what you need or take whatever applies to you and leave the rest, but keep it on the shelf. Someday, you may need it.

I have seen many people go to Alcoholics Anonymous meetings

and say, it's not for me because the person speaking is wrong, has a bad outlook, wasn't right, it's too spiritual, there's too much religion, or whatever. I say to them as someone who was a firm defender of drunkenness, that all those objections boil down to grasping for an excuse of any kind not to attend further meetings and thus, avoiding sobriety.

The treatment center I went to followed the Twelve Step model of AA, the first step of which is, "We admitted we are powerless over alcohol, that our lives had become unmanageable."

I still didn't want to admit that, even though I was in a fog, every day the sun shone a little bit brighter. I was born in August, and the sun means a lot to me because that is my birth sign, Leo. Slowly, I began coming out of the haze. Sometimes it was beautiful and sometimes it wasn't, but I was moving and struggling and continually reaching.

If you're in jail, or stuck in a bad marriage, a dead end job, or in an addiction, you feel as though you can't move. You're trapped, and I had been totally trapped by alcohol. So, coming out of this was a step, no matter the direction. Sometimes my life moved sideways, sometimes it moved backwards, but I was moving. I didn't want to admit that I was powerless over alcohol in the beginning, but I could certainly admit that my life had become unmanageable.

I had finally gathered enough gumption to peek out of the hole I was in to see what others were doing to "peak" there lives, that is, to make improvements. I still do that today; I peek to "peak."

Then there were steps Two, Three and Four as described in AA's Big Book. For those fortunate enough not to be familiar with the Big Book, it originally contained the stories written by 100 alcoholics and was co-authored by two people, Bill W. and Dr. Bob, the cofounders of AA. Every person who follows the Twelve Steps has their own experiences with them and these interpretations are mine.

Step Two is "Came to believe that a Power greater than ourselves could restore us to sanity." Some people dispute the existence of a power greater than ourselves. The simplicity of this step is profound. I didn't really believe there was a God. I didn't know what I believed in. I had believed in the "magic" of alcohol and that finally let me down. I was believing in myself for a long time but that had let me down, too. I always say that I left my ego in rehab, and another acronym for ego is "easing God out."

Again, I'm not religious, however I am spiritual and another definition of spirituality is, "People helping people to better their lives." Someone once described the difference in this way: religious people are afraid of going to Hell and spiritual people have come back.

My eventual sponsor, Jim once told me, "If you don't believe that there's a power greater than yourself, go down to Main Street of any city, take off your clothes and stand there. A power greater than you will come along and take you away."

That was the simplicity of a power greater than me. It was simply a faith in something or someone greater that one can turn to in a storm.

Step Three was that we "Made a decision to turn our will and our lives over to the care of God *as we understood Him.*" Those last four words I have italicized were very important in my case. AA is very tolerant how a person understands God. It has encompassed nature, consciousness, existential freedom, God (in the conventional Christian sense), science, gravity, Buddha and others. "As we understood Him" allows for a great deal of latitude and I needed that.

Step Four was to "make a searching and fearless moral inventory of ourselves." Unknowingly, I was doing this through journaling my relationship with my mother. In rehab, they didn't tell me to sit down and do a moral inventory of myself, they just asked me to write my life experiences with my mom, my dad, my family, my friends, my circle of influence and my life.

When I began keeping a journal back then, the focus tended to be on what I didn't have or what I had lost. I was focused on the glass being half-empty instead of being half-full.

Today, when I do journaling or recordings, I notice that it's extremely difficult for me to focus on the negative, or what I don't have, because it's just not in my life anymore. Not only have I reinvented myself, I've also reinvented the world around me. I can't take credit for that. It's because I've listened to people who are much smarter, wiser and more experienced than I.

That first searching and fearless moral inventory was tough to do, but I did it and it has become a positive habit. For me, it is a process worth repeating and I try to do it on a six-month or an annual basis at a retreat. I also try to do a mini-inventory each night. In the last five minutes before I go to sleep, I look over my last 24 hours because I firmly believe that's all we are guaranteed— one day at a time.

I look back on my last 24 hours and since I have probably slept 8 of them, there are really only 16 hours to consider. Did I hurt anyone? Did I offend anyone, and if I did, do I need to say I'm sorry? Do I need to apologize or make amends? If so, I make a conscious decision to do so at the earliest opportunity. Then, I also ask, "Have I helped someone today? In the last day, have I reached out my hand or listened to someone or given someone a smile? Maybe given someone some insights, reached out to a family, reached out to my own family or even reached out to myself?" That would be my interpretation of a mini-inventory.

Step Five was a tough one. In the Big Book it reads, "Admitted to God, to ourselves, and to another human being the exact nature of our wrongs."

That step was ordinarily done one or two days before graduation from the 28 day program. I'd been there 30-some days, while most people completed in 28. I tell people they kept me there because they liked me, not because I was remedial.

They set aside half a day for this step but would allow me as much time as I needed. As it says in the Big Book, you have to admit your wrongs to another human being and to God. I was hoping to restrict my confession to God only so no one else would have to hear. I was so ashamed of some things that weighed heavily on my mind.

For my confession they selected a nun. Her name was Sister Margaret, and she was about 4'6" tall. I'm 6'2" and I was smoking at the time.

She came into the room where I had been waiting anxiously and I thought, "Oh, my God. I've had issues with women, and now I have to tell a woman all my stories." What's more, she's a Catholic nun, the iconic representation of religion. She was a very kind woman, though very direct.

She sat down across from me and said, "Hi, I'm Margaret,"

"Hi, I'm Allan."

"Do you smoke?" she asked.

"Yeah."

"Over by the window," she said with a dismissive wave of her hand.

I sat by the window and talked for the next three and a half hours. I spilled my guts to the best of my ability. I related what I had done, what my life was like, all my sins and all my thoughts. Some people in rehab told me that when they completed that fifth step, they felt exhilarated. Afterwards, they went to church or a spot in nature and sat there and shed tears of joy, they felt so uplifted.

I don't know if I set my expectations too high. Sometimes, we do that in life and therefore, our disappointments equal our expectations. That makes for an up and down emotional day or an up and down emotional life. When I was finished with my arduous task, yes, I was extremely happy. I felt good, but I went to sit under a tree in a place of solitude, and didn't feel any special exhilaration or any particular "Wow." The thought went through my head, "Oh, my goodness.

Maybe I'm not doing it right. Maybe I'm going to go back out and drink again, and maybe this is all for naught."

How many of us have ever said that? "Maybe this is all for naught." I went back and saw my counselor. Elaine asked me, "How did you feel after your Fifth Step?"

"I felt okay," I said, "but there wasn't any white light or any sparks or shooting stars or anything."

"Come with me," she said and showed me in the Big Book something called "Spiritual Experience." I read that most victories over alcoholism are not of the "burning bush" variety, but instead develop slowly over time.

After that fifth step, I was in counseling one more day, then we had graduation on a Friday morning. We weren't allowed visitors or phone calls the first couple of weeks and I had left my family in disarray. I certainly didn't feel I deserved any contact with them and they never visited. However, my son got that card to me through his mother and I'm eternally grateful to them for that because it really helped me.

The friend who had helped me came to my graduation. She had come to visit on the second weekend and spent the afternoon, and I told her my experiences at the center. Once again, she gave me hope, motivation and inspiration.

There were five of us graduating out of a group of about 40. During my fourth or fifth week I greeted people coming into the program and helped them register and settle in. It gave me a glimpse of being outside of myself and reaching out to help somebody else. So, I was there at the door when they came in and it was a quite an experience to see the fear, uncertainty and hopelessness in their eyes, just as I had in mine when I came in such a short time before.

I have a photograph from my past, when I was working in the mine. Around 1984, I lost my security badge and I had to get another picture taken. I have that picture today in my office and, talk about dead eyes, my eyes were as dead as a shark's. There was no life in them compared to today. In truth, I looked younger at 44 with several years of sobriety behind me than I did at 34.

After I finally quite drinking at age 37, I became interested in my health. I had a complete physical and the doctor told me what saved my life was my age and my large appetite. I ate big lunches underground and always had breakfast and dinner because I worked hard and, probably just as important, I knew that it was a sign of normalcy to eat three meals a day.

Those factors, plus the fact that the mine was so hot. The sweating I did every morning helped flush the alcohol out of my system and limited the damage to my liver. My liver was diagnosed with some problems, borderline damage that was just beginning to cause me difficulty. My doctor was young, supportive and energetic. She wanted to try new treatments and prescribed a medicine that I took for five years to nurse my liver back to health. I seem to have lived on the edge and obviously I have that mentality but I always seemed to go just far enough and then I would stop and rehabilitate my body, so I have been really blessed that way.

During my physical, the doctor told me that I wouldn't have lived past 41 if I had continued my lifestyle. Today, I'm 60, so, I've had 19 years of bonus living. I would have missed those 19 years. I would've missed my older daughter growing up, my other daughter growing up and the birth of her son, my first grandchild. I would have missed watching my son develop, the little boy who gave me that picture of himself with a fishing pole, and how he developed into a wonderful young man. I would have missed all that, not to mention the other beautiful people who have come into my life.

My graduation from rehab just so happened to occur on my birthday, August 3rd. The significance was not lost on me.

One of the important lessons I learned in rehab was that a person stops growing emotionally when they begin drinking for effect. A 50 year old on the outside may be only 10 on the inside emotionally.

Sister Jean was there for the ceremony and afterwards, I told her that it was a great day because not only was I graduating but it was also my birthday.

"Congratulations on finishing the program, Allan," she said, "and by the way, how old do you think you are today?"

Trying to impress her, I gave her a grin and said, "Thirteen."

"You think very highly of yourself, don't you?" she replied, which stopped me in my tracks.

Afterwards, I said good-bye to the staff and signed out of the center. My friend and I spent the weekend in Elliot Lake relaxing and having fun. I slept a lot. I was totally drained after the experience, but I felt better and more at peace than I could ever remember.

For the first time in my life, at the age of 37, I connected with myself. Those 18 inches from head to my heart took a long time to travel, but the ride has been upwards ever since.

CHAPTER 27

BACK INTO THE WORLD

When I hear somebody sigh "Life is hard,"
I am always tempted to ask, compared to what?
—SYDNEY J. HARRIS

THE FOLLOWING MONDAY, we drove back to Sudbury. I didn't have a place to live. I sure wasn't going back to that flophouse with the filthy bed and the one element hot plate. I would never have any part of that again if I could help it. Even though I was only 35 days in rehab, the promises of the Twelve Step program were working to a degree and somehow I knew that everything would be okay.

I stayed in a hotel that first night, and the next day, Dave from the Employee Assistance Program drove me to the bank where I withdrew some of my vacation pay and we found an apartment. It was a quantum leap above my earlier hovel despite its yellow living room, purple kitchen and orange bathroom. It was a triplex, which I shared with two other families. Fortunately, it was furnished because I owned no furniture. I had no credit cards at the time and was paying child support and alimony, even though my wife and I had not yet been to court. That wild-colored apartment became my home for the next year of my journey forward.

Alcoholics Anonymous regards milestones as significant and these vary depending on regional ideas. In Sudbury, they awarded a medallion at the end of three months of continued sobriety. The recipient stands in front of the meeting and says a few words and can choose who else will participate.

Between my first day of sobriety in June and my five weeks in treatment, I didn't have very long to reach 90 days, so it was a goal I could set. I went to meetings every day. It was quite a milestone, considering that not a week had gone by during the past 20 years that I hadn't had a drink.

Physically, I was feeling better than I had in a long time. Often, a person entering detox or rehab will experience allergic reactions like the shakes or DTs. I never did. The doctors attributed that to my hard work in the mine and a relatively healthful diet. I was able to work now without the hangovers and the sickness but I was tired and drained. My years of drinking began to catch up to me. I would go to a meeting at night and nod off at times. Mentally and physically, I felt drained. My energy level was out the bottom. I saw an iridologist who prescribed a regimen of vitamins, and that helped.

That first year, I ate cruller donuts every day; I was substituting sugar for alcohol and ate as many as I could get. Today, I can't even look at them. I was still smoking at the time, and at the Camillus Center they recommended that people not try to quit smoking right away. They advised me not to make any major decisions for the first year. So, I kept smoking but felt an urgency to begin taking care of my body.

When I left rehab, they gave me a sheet of paper with four recommendations on it: 1) attend 3 AA meetings each week, 2) attend aftercare, which was a follow up program of group therapy at a local detox center, 3) obtain a sponsor (a sponsor is someone you admire for their words, ideas and personhood and who agrees to stick with you for a while and help you get on your feet) and 4) return to the Camillus Center for a week-long relapse prevention program after three months' sobriety.

I do not like to give advice, but the best suggestion I can give if you are choosing a sponsor or mentor in your life is to gravitate to people who are successful in their own right. This doesn't only pertain to someone in Alcoholics Anonymous or who is dealing with any sort of addiction. It applies to any area in life.

As my own life evolves, I continue to choose different mentors or sponsors. An important one for me is Les Brown, the motivational speaker. I belong to his Platinum Speakers group today and one of his promises is that your life will unfold like you never expected and you will live your wildest dreams by following other successful people.

I have traveled with Les and worked together with him for PBS and BBC. We have nothing in common except public speaking. He's not in the addiction circle that I am, but as he always states, "If you're the smartest person in the group, get a new group."

When I consider the different mentors I have had, I remember one in particular. It was a Sunday morning at an AA meeting at the Steelworkers hall. There were maybe 50 or 60 people there, and among them was a young man who had the happiest eyes I had ever seen. I've mentioned my dead eyes. When I saw this young man, I thought, "Wow, he's got happy eyes." I shook his hand and made certain to remember his name. I listened when he spoke at meetings and found out which meetings he attended. In Sudbury, we had about 75 meetings each week to choose from, depending on what shift you were on or other factors. I have since lost track of him, but I wrote down the titles of books he mentioned when he spoke about some of his principles and traditions. I read the books, took many of his ideas as my own and today, I have extremely happy eyes. He didn't realize he was mentoring me, but perhaps he will if he reads my story.

I had some mixed reactions from my friends when I quit drinking. One drinking buddy has not spoken to me since that June day in 1987. Another friend was named Paul, who used to ride in the van with us to work. Paul had his own drinking issue, but throughout our entire association, he had never once bought me a drink. Two or three months after I quit drinking, I was in a hotel bar to visit an old friend and Paul was there.

"Come on, Al," he said, "I'll buy you a drink."

"No, Paulie," I said, "I've quit."

He went to the bar anyway and bought me a double whiskey and Pepsi, which he knew was my favorite. He walked over and plunked it on my table.

"Al, be a man."

The guy had never bought me a drink when I wasn't trying to quit, so why would he buy one now?

I looked at him and I looked at the drink and sat there for 10 seconds. "You're right, Paul, I'll be a man."

I got up and walked out. When that door to the bar closed behind me, a door also closed on another world that I left forever. There was a shift at that moment and I realized that I had just passed another test on my way to lasting sobriety.

It became clear to me that in recovery, I was associating with a different group of people. My point is that all the sponsors in AA had something to give. I took it all in, all the ideas, concepts and strategies, slowly but surely. I begged, I borrowed and I stole. Many of the quotes I use are ones I've learned from others and incorporated into my life to share with others.

Who cares where they came from? Anyone can own any idea, make it their own and use it in their lives. That's one of the beautiful things about an idea. Anyone can own it. All my sponsors had something I wanted and I took it. When I seemed to have incorporated it into my life and had it down to the best of my ability, then it was time to move on. As Tommy Douglas, the father of the Canadian healthcare system, said in the famous fable, Mouseland, "You can lock up a man, but you can't lock up an idea!"

Life can be likened to riding on a train. You're in a seat and someone comes and sits beside you. They'll stay for a while and you may get off at the next station or they may get off. You may be sad to see them go or you may be relieved to see them get off. I believe we're beside each other for a reason—to share our experiences, our strengths and our hopes, not necessarily only in the field of addiction, but in the wider field of life.

Sometimes you say, "My god, I hope that person will get off at the next stop," and they won't. Maybe they have one more lesson for you to incorporate into your life or you may have something for them, unbeknownst to you. It's not all about taking. It's all about giving.

So, there I was, attending AA meetings and living in my multicolored apartment, which were my first clean, quiet living quarters since leaving my family. I was going to meetings at night and working during the day.

The next step for my success was to go to aftercare, and one day, a couple weeks after I graduated rehab, I went down to the local detox center. When I was drinking, that is one place I avoided at all costs, because if I had ever ended up in detox, I would have been forced to realize that I did have a problem. I avoided that detox center while drunk, but I went to it sober. Sometimes, I think my life is a paradox.

Not long into my sobriety, I bought a book called, *The University of Success,* by Og Mandino. Standing at the cashier's, I explained how happy I was to buy it when I noticed that the cover was glued on upside down and backwards. The cashier said, "Oh, I'm sorry, sir. I'll exchange that book."

"Not on your life," I replied. "That's quite symbolic for me. I've lived my whole life upside down and backwards!"

I still have that book and will never lend it to anybody because it's so special to me.

At any rate, I went down an alleyway to the back door of the detox center in Sudbury. The center was not far from the EAP office downtown. It was early evening towards dusk when I pressed the buzzer to be admitted inside. A voice came over the speaker mounted on the outside of the door.

"Who's there?" It sounded chilling to me, but only because I was already apprehensive.

"McDougall," I replied.

"Come back when you're sober!"

"What?!" I hadn't been this dry since I was 18.

I said to myself, "Wow. What is this?" I looked around to see if anybody was standing behind me. Maybe they had a camera and were looking at another person thinking it was me. No one else was there, so I shuffled around feeling puzzled and thought, "Well, they told me to be here and I have a commitment, so I'll try to fulfill this commitment." I pressed the buzzer again. Again the voice said, "Who's there? Who is it?"

Tentatively this time, I said, "McDougall."

"I'll be right down," he said.

A man disabled the alarm system on the steel door and opened it. The door was locked and alarmed because of the center's policy that if someone left of his own volition before they were allowed, they could not return for three more days. It made sense. You could stay as long as you wished but could only leave with their permission. Otherwise, there would have been a revolving door parade of drunks who go out and get plastered, come back in, sleep that night, go out, get drunk, come back, sleep, get some food, etc. Hence, their 72 hour policy.

The man who let me in was Don D. who has since become one of my closest friends. He took a good look at me. "Oh," he said, slightly puzzled. "Come on in."

I entered and looked around the facility. It was one large room with about 25 beds, no partitions and seemed somewhat the worse for wear.

"I apologize," Don said. "I have a story to tell you. The reason I asked you to leave and come back when you were sober is that we just had a gentleman in here with the same last name and he was trying to get sober. Just a few minutes ago, he started tearing the place apart and was fighting and yelling and screaming and causing damage."

Don and someone else had personally evicted the man just before I came around the corner. When I buzzed, he was cleaning up from the fracas and still had blood on him and his hair was messed up. We still laugh about that today. I never got to see detox while I was drunk, but I went when I was sober and they wouldn't let me in.

Whenever a person came in under the influence and things turned ugly when he began to sober up, Don was the type of person who never called the police. Invariably, that would wind the man up in jail. Instead, Don would turn him out onto the street and if he carried on fighting there, he wouldn't have to call the police.

Don was an industrial mechanic who maintained and repaired equipment at the mine. He had quit drinking by age 24 through the same EAP office as I. At one point earlier, he had been off work for 23 days, drinking heavily the entire time. After 14 days absent from work, INCO fired you. Don was sitting in a bar one day when one of his foreman came in.

"Christ, Don, where have you been? I thought you died!"

"No, I've just been off. I'm probably fired by now," he replied.

"Hey, man, get your ass down to the EAP office. Go talk to them tomorrow. See what they can do. You don't want to quit the mine, do you?"

"Well, I dunno —"

"Listen to me, Don! You go down to the office tomorrow and that's the end of it!"

The next day he went down to the Union Hall and talked to a guy at the EAP office named Alex, himself a recovering alcoholic. Alex smoked a big cigar, and his idea of compassion was hitting you with a baseball bat instead of an iron pipe.

Every time Don opened his mouth, it was, "Shut your fucking

mouth, asshole! You've been drunk 23 days. What the hell can you tell me? You listen good, prick: you drag your sorry ass back down to the mine tomorrow and get back to work!"

"But ... but ...," Don started in protest.

"Shut the fuck up and get out of here! Don't embarrass me."

Don was trying to tell him that tomorrow was his regular day off but Alex wasn't having any of it. The next morning, he showed up for work and nobody there knew him, but he eventually got himself straightened out and was back on the payroll. He became one of my first new friends in sobriety and remains so to this day.

Another miner he worked with was named Mike, who also had serious issues with alcohol, so much so that he was admitted to a sanatorium and placed on heavy medication. One day, Mike got a day pass to leave the hospital and Don came to pick him up. This was before Don got sober, and the first thing they did once out of the hospital was to buy a case of beer and drive over to see Mike's girlfriend.

Mike had been on a heavy regimen of medication, including Librium, and the beer had the effect of slowing his central nervous system way down. His speech slowed way down and he became a classic stiff. Real stiff. His body became increasingly rigid and he could hardly move.

Don became worried and drove him back to the hospital, but knew he would be in big trouble for bringing Mike back in such terrible condition. So, he drove around to the back of the hospital where the loading dock was. Don knew about the loading dock because he had been hospitalized there himself once when drinking. He backed his car up to the dock and managed to pull Mike out of the seat and lean him against the wall next to the delivery door. He rang the bell and drove away to the far side of the parking lot, keeping a watchful eye on his friend in the rear view mirror. Slowly, Mike began to sink down the wall and when someone answered the buzzer he was still sliding ever so slowly down towards the cement.

Don landed a job at the detox center years later when INCO laid off a group of workers and he was caught in the net.

After that first experience at detox, I attended aftercare meetings twice a month. It was an in-depth therapy group for people who had been through the treatment center at Elliot Lake. The same diocese that ran the Camillus Center funded the program in Sudbury at the detox center. Those of us in aftercare met in a conference room and didn't sleep there overnight, though one more binge would have put us there. The facility provided a clear reminder what could happen to us if we returned to drinking.

That went on for 10 or 12 weeks. I felt that I was really getting my act together. I was working, had my apartment, was dating and attending aftercare meetings. I was spending much of my time at the Steelworkers hall where I originally sought help. I talked with them a lot and they had me come in and volunteer my time.

One day, I was in the office when a miner named Robert came in. He was white as a sheet. His wife was with him and it looked like Robert had received the rolling pin treatment from her.

"Sir," Robert said to Bob, "I think I killed a cow last night." He was distraught.

He had been out drinking and blacked out on his way home, ran through a farmer's fence and hit a cow. The farmer had threatened a lawsuit. On top of that, Robert and his wife were getting a divorce. Apparently, it was not amicable because when it came to dividing their property, Robert had taken a chainsaw and was literally cutting the house in half. He cut some electrical wires, nearly electrocuting himself. For eight years, Robert thought that he was driving the night the cow was killed. Finally, someone confessed that he had only been a passenger. Watching this unfold, I had a hard time keeping a straight face. Ah, the disadvantages of blackouts!

He happened to be a good mechanic and at the time, I was still driving that rattletrap '73 Buick. I told him that the steering was loose and he agreed to look at it. He took the car for a couple days and then came into the EAP office very excited, exclaiming, "I found God! I found God! McDougall said his steering was loose. There are supposed to be four bolts on the steering wheel. There was only one on his. There has to be a God otherwise McDougall would be dead."

Robert fixed my steering, and in October, I went back to Elliot Lake for my one week program. I learned more about how to live life on life's terms. I was now moving forward, moving on an up ramp.

I knew I still had to go to court. I knew I had to accept the consequences for deserting my family. That wouldn't be easy, but I was starting to believe that it was possible.

CHAPTER 28

LIVING WITH ACCOUNTABILITY

*Fair play is primarily not blaming others for anything
that is wrong with us.*
–ERIC HOFFER

STEP NUMBER 8 OF THE TWELVE STEPS was to make a list of all people we had harmed and become willing to make amends to them all. The most important word in that sentence is "willing," simply to become willing.

One amends was to a man to whom I owed $50. When I was drinking, I once borrowed $50 from him. I felt embarrassed one day during my last year of drinking when I ran into him in a bar I frequented. I didn't have the money to pay him back. Soon after, he moved to Ottawa, which is a 6-hour drive from Sudbury, and we lost contact.

After several months, I had saved up some money and it was in the back of my mind to pay him. I had lost track of the guy, however I knew where his mother lived, so I called her and asked for his contact information in Ottawa. I cut a check and included a note saying that I had changed some habits in my life and had made the decision not to spend my life drinking anymore. I also wrote how sorry I was that I had owed him the money. I mentioned the shame I felt and included the check for $50, adding that I'd gladly pay him the interest that was owing along with my phone number and to give me a call back if he so desired. If not, I wrote, I completely understood.

I sent the letter off not really thinking anything more about it. It was humiliating to have been making good money before, yet now owe a man $50 for more than a year or two and then pay it back through the mail.

About a week and a half later, my phone rang and a voice asked, "Is this Al McDougall?"

"Yes."

"This is Wayne from Ottawa," said the voice.

"Oh, my God, Wayne, how are you? I haven't spoken to you for a couple of years. Did you get my letter?"

We talked and talked. He was so exhilarated that I had made a change in my life. Here was this man who I owed money to and he probably thought he'd never see it again. We drank together from time to time, though not often. At one point in the conversation I said, "Wayne, this $50 that I paid you is being eaten up by this phone call."

"I don't care. I just don't care," he replied, "I just wanted to call and tell you how proud I am of you and the changes that you're making and I wish you well."

It was a complete and utter surprise and I'll never forget it.

I hope when he reads this he'll remember. I confess there may be others I borrowed money from during a blackout and have completely forgotten about.

I tried to reach out and became willing to make amends to them all. There are some people out there to whom I still need to make amends. Some I will never be able to because they have passed on. I hope that through changing my life though, and where I am today, that maybe by helping other people or taking time with other people will clear those accounts. I'm not sure how it all works, but it gives me some hope that they're at peace with themselves as much as I am at peace with myself.

Besides making amends to others, I also learned to make amends to myself for all the mistakes that I made and for hurting other people. That eighteen inches from my head to my heart is so important to me. Conducting my regular inventories and asking, "Who am I? Where am I headed? What's my purpose, if there is a purpose?" Truthfully, all those questions, I don't know much more about them today than I did when I began asking them, but asking them sure has helped me along my path of recovery.

When I speak about myself as a man who drank years ago, it is like looking at another person; it's like looking at a third party. So, I definitely know that I have made changes. I think differently. I act differently. I am different.

In those early months, as the fog in my life began to lift, I began to see more clearly how my actions over the years had harmed the people I was closest to. While I was drinking, my viewpoint and attitude was mostly focused on what others had done to me. Now, I became able to look at things from the other way around.

Highest on the list of persons I had harmed through my drinking were my children and my wife. My daughter Marcie turned six the day I left, and I spoiled what should have been a moment of joy in her young life. As it turned out, she handled it a lot better than I did. On subsequent birthdays, I occasionally asked if she thought about that day.

"No, Dad," she told me one year. "It's over. I only think about it when you mention it."

I believe her statement came as the result of hours of conversations, tears, taking her to my milestone ceremonies and counseling. I haven't brought it up since.

I took my children to my three-month anniversary of sobriety and gave them some information and pamphlets on Alcoholics Anonymous. I talked with them at length to try to rebuild relationships with them.

To be sure, my leaving was traumatic for them but I think they probably handled it better than either my wife or I did. About two weeks after I quit drinking, there was a big summer festival on Lake Ramsey in Sudbury with folk singers, booths, games, food and all kinds of fun. Dave suggested I take the kids, so I did, and we had a great time.

I never learned whether they sided with me or their mother. Even from the early days of my sobriety, though they wanted me to come home. They knew my wife and I were finished but still they wanted me to rent the apartment upstairs.

About a year later, while visiting Shane at his mother's house, he said, "Dad, I really miss seeing you."

"Shane, I miss seeing you too. If it is any consolation though, see that antenna tower over there? I can see that from my apartment, so we are connected."

That made him feel closer to me, and he still mentions that conversation today.

I went to the kids' PTA meetings. Angie even tried to set me up with one of the school teachers.

"She's single, Dad," Angie said. Her statement indicated to me that there was a level of acceptance of my divorce.

Early on in my sobriety, I remember talking with them in the backyard when I went to visit. I asked them if they believed that I would stay sober, and they said, "Yes." My wife was there that day and she said, "I've heard this so many times that I don't believe it."

That hurt, because I still wanted a relationship as a mother and father raising our children.

But why would she have had any reason to trust me? She had heard this all the time and now that I had left, her life was in an upheaval.

I went back to Don D. at the detox center and said, "You know, my wife doesn't believe that I quit drinking or that I will stay sober."

"Why should she?" he replied. "How long have you been drinking?"

"Fifteen, sixteen years," I answered.

"Well," he said, "if you stay sober for 8 years, 50% of that time, she might just start to believe you."

That made me face my impatience to have everybody trust me at the age of 38 where I had never before kept a commitment. Although I had wanted to, I couldn't seem to keep a commitment to stay sober for any length of time, even so much as a single day, so why should anyone trust me this time?

My marriage was finished, by mutual agreement as much as anything. My wife had had enough. Given the opportunity to visit me in rehab, she declined and I don't blame her at all. As a result of our divorce, I thought she was much better off materially than me. She kept the house and most of the furniture and our joint possessions, and I never begrudged her that. Perhaps it is a relationship that was never meant to be, and my affair with alcohol guaranteed as much. I sincerely hope that her life after our marriage has become as fulfilling as mine has.

Later that year, I was back in Auburn for another family get together, my dad's birthday. Stan and Dorothy had driven over from their home in Cambridge, Ontario. I went to the trailer park, walked over to Stan's RV and knocked on the door.

"Stan, I need to talk to you," I began. I was apprehensive about how he might react. I had worried about this conversation the entire drive down. "I have been sober now for a while. I quit in June, went to rehab in July and this is the end of October. Stan, I haven't drank now since June 3rd. I am doing much better, but I owe you $100 and I don't have enough to pay you today. I have only $50."

That was another blow to my ego: that I didn't have $100 to pay him.

"Man, I am even surprised that you remembered," Stan said. He thought I was in a blackout at the time and never expected the money back and yet he lent it to me.

"Here, Stan, here is $50. The next time I see you, when I save up $50, I will pay you the rest."

"Hey, if you have $10 in your pocket or you want to write a check and mail it to me or whatever," he said, "that is great."

The next year, I drove back to the village in my old rattletrap. It was another family gathering and we were in a restaurant. Stan and Dorothy were there. He and I were talking outside the restaurant and he said, "Wow, Al, you need a new car." Stan was a used car dealer.

"Yes, I do, but I can't afford it."

In the 12 months since I had seen him last, I paid off the other $50, so now we were even. I gave him $10 interest but he refused it, saying, "I'm not charging interest to a friend who is trying to get back on his feet again."

Walking out on the sidewalk that Sunday morning, he repeated, "Man, you really need a new car."

"Yeah, but guess what, Stan, I can't afford a new car. I've gone to the bank. They won't look at me."

It was quite something to be the breadwinner in the family and have to go to different places to borrow $2,500 for a used car because the one I was driving was so unsafe. I went to another bank and even a finance company. I didn't want to use a finance company and have to pay their exorbitant interest rates. I went back to the bank that I had been dealing with since 1970 when I got hired on at the mine and talked to this well-dressed man, the type of person that I term a polyester floor manager.

He said, "I would like to help you so much, Mr. McDougall on behalf of the bank. However, you need to go back to the banking institution you usually deal with, and they will help you, I am sure."

I said, "I'm standing here."

His face turned red and he started to stammer and stutter. I ended up having to pay off some bills through a finance company. I am eternally grateful to them because they lent me money when I didn't have much collateral. When I signed my divorce papers, I didn't have a home, I had hurt my back so I didn't have a job per se as a production miner, I was still gainfully employed but was no longer married, renting an apartment, no house, no savings and my bank wouldn't lend me $2,500. I am very grateful to Diane who worked at the finance company. I would go in every month and make my paltry payments and she and her financial institution helped me get back on my feet again by giving me an early return on my income tax so I could stay afloat.

At any rate, I said to Stan, "Guess what, I don't even have $1,000."

"I tell you what," he said, "I will look in my lot and pick out a car for you. I'll drive it halfway to Sudbury and you meet me down there and pay me what you can, no interest."

I was dumbfounded. "Wow," I thought, "here is a man who would do that for me, not even a blood relative." It made me think back to a parable I learned in Sunday school, the parable about reaping more than you sow. I wasn't looking for that, but Stan, in paying him the $100 over time gave me back tenfold what I owed him. Stan drove up in a '76 Chrysler and it was a beautiful car. It was a 6 cylinder, sturdy as a rock, 12 years old, one owner with miles left on it. I drove it for eight years until I saved up enough for another car. I have been told I am a humble and grateful man and, if that is true, I have these life experiences to thank. My life's decisions had beaten my ego out of me, but the Law of the Harvest was beginning to play out in my life.

I learned another lesson from those early days: when you sincerely begin the effort to bring change to your life and when you are truly trying to change the condition you are in, people will notice that and they will help you.

Another example was the woman who ran the Boomer's Restaurant I frequented in my drinking days. It was your classic high cholesterol, greasy spoon eatery. In the early weeks and months of my sobriety I was making high payments, dealing with bills and money was real tight. When I would drop by to treat myself to a cup of coffee, she would make me lunch but not charge me for it.

"Just stay sober, Allan. No need to pay me back," she would say.

Cynics may doubt the decency of the human heart. Not me, brother, not me.

CHAPTER 29

Out of the Mine and Into the Classroom

Change in all things is sweet.

–Aristotle

Working underground hoisting a 110 pound pneumatic drill while standing on unstable ground took its toll on my back, as it does with many miners. Over the years, there were five or six times when I had to have it treated. I would have to take time off to see a chiropractor or acupuncturist, do light duty work for a while and only return to work underground when my back was better.

Emotionally, things were much better on the job since I had quit drinking. I had better relations with my foreman. They would come up and ask, "How ya doin', Al. Still behaving?" That was how they phrased it. In other words, was I still sober?

Every day that I went underground following my sobriety it was feast or famine as far as my back was concerned. Some days, I'd climb out of the bus that brought us to our level and almost have to drag myself to the stope. One immutable law of the mine was: the more you produced underground, the more money you made. On a good month, I was able to double my wages over my base salary in bonuses. When my wife and I decided on a fair support payment for my children and her, it was based on the amount I could make with incentive bonuses added to my wages. In my financial situation, I needed all the extra money I could get to pay my family's expenses, both legally and morally, and to eke out some kind of living for myself. That situation continued to plague me. Whenever I was off work for a couple days on light duty or sent home for rehabilitation I would go to the union hall to work in the office.

Finally, on August 8, 1988, I was at work drilling and my back went out. I had a severe muscle spasm like I'd never experienced before. I threw the drill down and stumbled sideways to the lunchroom. "Take me to surface," I told the guys there. That was my last day underground until I retired from the mine in August, 2006.

The doctors examined me and discovered that I had two herniated disks. I would never go underground again on full duty. I would be able to go back to some kind of work because of a law called "duty to accommodate," which mandates that an employee who is hurt on the job must be given a meaningful job and retain his or her salary.

I hadn't saved anything, as you can well imagine, and then I lost that extra thousand dollars a month in bonuses, which really hurt. I had debts to pay off. The ironic part was that I didn't have enough money to go back to see my lawyer to get my obligations reduced in line with my reduced income. I had to learn to cut corners and it turned out to be a great lesson for me. It taught me humility, it taught me the value of a dollar and it taught me the value of being other-centered, not to be so self-centered.

I had become involved with the union in a more active role in 1977 when a union official approached me and asked if I would be on the health and safety committee. There were numerous injuries and fatalities in a mine with 20,000 workers. The United Steel Workers Union fought hard and bargained for workers to have joint health and safety committees. The composition was 50 percent management and 50 percent labor, in our case the Steelworkers, and we met once a month to resolve safety issues brought to our attention by the miners. Such things as poor ventilation, bad ground, poor lighting and better sanitation systems were issues for discussion and resolution.

In answer to the man's request, I said, "Sure." I was already involved with the local union primarily because there was that bar downstairs and I always wanted an excuse to get out of the house. I saw on the bulletin board that there was health and safety training, so I volunteered. If someone wanted to be on the committee, two health and safety instructors at the union hall offered training and you could sit in a classroom for 30 hours to learn about health and safety laws and regulations. I wanted a reason to be away from home, so I attended the classes. However, I also truly wanted to make a difference in the conditions in the mine. I finished and received a certificate, Level 1 Health and Safety, which was recognized by the Ontario Federation of Labor. So, I had that under my belt and I was on the committee.

We held an election very shortly after I joined the committee. I attended six or seven meetings and the chair retired. Another person wanted to be the next chair but others encouraged me to run as well. So, I ran. I never thought I'd win; mind you, I was still drinking heavily then. I ran in the election and won. The vote was determined by the occupation health and safety committee members, maybe ten in all, and I won. The man who lost appealed, saying that the union bylaws required that I had to have educational training in the health and safety field.

My drinking wasn't an issue, but he said, "The reason I'm appealing is that you don't have the education."

I went back to my locker and pulled out my certificate. "There's my credentials," I said.

That taught me a valuable lesson. It has been said that, "Luck is when preparedness meets opportunity." Looking back on those days, as much as I simply wanted to go down to the basement and drink, I also wanted to be a good member of the health and safety committee. That was maybe forty percent of my motivation. Sixty percent was for the convenience of my addiction. It taught me a lesson that I had to be prepared when an opportunity presented itself. The reason I won the election and became chair of the health and safety committee was because I had that bit of education.

After a year of AA meetings an average of five times a week, I didn't want to continue on that near daily schedule. To be perfectly up front about it, without being judgmental, I met people in AA who traded one addiction, alcohol, for another, Alcoholics Anonymous. Perhaps I've been guilty of that over the years, too. I didn't want my addiction to switch from seven nights of drinking to seven nights of AA meetings. I'm not speaking on behalf of AA or those with addictions. I'm just speaking on behalf of myself.

With that in mind, I thought, "Well, it's time I go back to school."

I had a wonderful opportunity in the spring of 1988. I reapplied to attend the Labour College of Canada, which offers education to trade unionists. Located in Ottawa, it provided classes when regular students were on vacation and they offered a two-month residential program in different subjects: Industrial Sociology, Labour History, Labour Law, Political Science and Economics. I had applied the previous year as part of my efforts to be prepared for opportunity. I really did enjoy being an advocate for the underdog, for working people and for people who are too shy to speak up for themselves.

Of course, that 1987 opportunity was squandered because of my drinking. The union however, stuck by me through all my problems and I kept my interest in going to school. I went to the health and safety director of the union one day and told him that I couldn't cope with everything happening in my life and that I wanted to quit all my union activities.

"Allan," he said, "don't quit everything. Take yourself off as co-chair of the health and safety committee and just be a regular member, but don't lose all your interest in everything."

I was so glad that I took his advice, which proved very wise. I thought I had to focus on getting sober, which was true, but I also had to have something besides Alcoholics Anonymous. So, I kept up my union involvement and made a difference in the workplace, to a small degree. Because I remained active and involved, and because the union didn't judge me, I still wanted to attend the program at the labor college. I applied once more and was accepted.

I began my studies at Canadian Labour Congress Labour College in May 1988, and it proved to be quite a test. It was my first time away from Sudbury, my first time being away from AA meetings and my sponsors. I was away from the relationship I was in at the time. It was a good test of my commitment to refrain from alcohol.

There were about 75 students from unions all across Canada and we made a very diverse group. We each had our own dorm room and I diligently applied myself to my course work and did quite well. I challenged myself by writing papers, something I hadn't done since Grade 12. I visited the parliament buildings and made new friends who had a singular focus: helping people in the labor movement.

I celebrated my first anniversary of sobriety on June 3rd 1988, at Labour College. Amongst the group, there was socializing that took place, which included drinking, as you can well imagine. I was never shy about telling people that I didn't drink. I would tell people upfront, "I can't drink at this time, I have a problem with alcohol," and they totally respected that. On my one-year anniversary, somebody brought a cake and balloons and they had a little party for me in the classroom. It was a sign that even though I was accepted at Alcoholics Anonymous meetings, I was also accepted in the labor movement, as a person who had a problem, not a problem person. That's very important—we are not problem persons, we are persons with problems. In that distinction lies a world of difference.

I was very excited to graduate. I attended the graduation with some good friends who were staunch supporters. The organization was with me. The Steelworkers Union was there to celebrate with me. My parents drove a considerable distance with close friends of theirs to attend, which meant a lot to me.

One of the factors that motivated me to continue my education occurred during my rehab one evening when a man came to relate his story to us. He did his presentation as a lecture, not simply as a retelling of his life story. His lecture had highlights, takeaways and quotations; it really made an impact on me.

Afterwards, a thought came into my head, "Why can't you be a speaker like that and inspire and motivate people?" Then came another thought, "Why not write a book?"

I haven't seen that man since, but he left me with the impression of the power of words. He doesn't know the effect he has had on me even today. I had the sense to know that if I wanted to be a living success story, quitting drinking was not success enough. Individuals successfully quit drinking every day. It's a great milestone and I don't diminish it. I'm very proud of the fact that I quit and it changed my life. However, I wanted to base my success on what I've accomplished since I quit drinking.

Today, I can speak to people and if I talked only about getting sober, many might say, "Well, that wasn't such a big deal. It was a moral issue. He was weak willed…" or whatever their interpretation might be. Sobriety, in my mind, wasn't enough to consider myself a successful motivational speaker. So, I set out to accomplish some things that society would classify as success.

At the time, I had a friend who worked with the union and who was having trouble with his addiction. He'd been more involved with the union than I had. We befriended each other in the world of AA.

His wife was a community college teacher and taught a class for women who had come out of abusive relationships and homes for battered women. She was looking for someone to speak at her class, so she called up the union office one day while I was there. Bob often spoke to her class and he took the call. They chatted for a minute and then I heard him say, "I can't make it, but I have a young guy here who has been sober about a year. He has a good story and he'll go and speak to your class."

He hung up the phone. "Guess what, Al? I just volunteered you to speak to this class of 25 or 30 young women who have come out of abusive relationships. Most of them had some addiction issues, either with themselves or their spouses."

I was stunned. "Oh, my goodness! What do I say?"

"Just get up and tell your story," Bob advised.

Off I went. I did a lot of praying driving the five miles from the union hall to the community college. I walked in and met the class professor. I talked to her class about leaving my family on my youngest daughter's birthday. At that point, I lost my composure and broke down in front of the class. It still brings a wave of sadness to think of that time, but today my daughter and I are very close. We call each other often and we love each other. She is the mother of my first grandson and it's an amazing comeback story, my own growth, as well as my daughter's.

The college professor befriended me and I spoke to her class often after that. We always went for coffee afterwards and one day, she asked me, "What are you going to do with your life?"

"I'd like to work at the union hall in the EAP office where I sought help, either part time or when they're on vacation until a full time position is available."

"I know of a very good, brand new course, a four year course coming up put on by the Addiction Research Foundation in Ontario in conjunction with the Cambrian College. I think you'd be good at it. I'll get you an application form."

She mailed a form, I filled it out and off it went.

Here I was, 38, someone who hated school, now facing the prospect of going back. When I graduated high school in 1969, it was the happiest day of my life. I had my Grade 12 certificate and never had to do any more homework for the rest of my natural life, or so I thought.

It is funny how life presents opportunities when you least expect them. All you have to do is keep an open mind and live in the moment.

The next step was an interview with the course registrar. I walked into my interview and the woman asked me what my background was. "Are you in social work?" I chuckled because I gather she assumed that anybody enrolling in a four-year addiction studies course was involved in social work.

"No," I answered, "I have seventeen years of very personal research in the world of addiction and I'm coming here to try to understand the things I did that I can't remember doing."

She had a great laugh at my answer and welcomed me with open arms to the course. There were thirty-three of us who started class in September, 1988. I worked steady days and went to Cambrian three nights a week from September to May studying addiction intervention. Four years later when I graduated, there were six of us left. That old cliche, "Showing up is 50 percent of success," holds true. What I mainly did was show up.

It was quite an accomplishment for me because, besides the four-year night school and work, I also became very involved in the community. At Alcoholics Anonymous meetings, there was often talk about giving back. Giving back through my volunteer work led me to different opportunities that have improved my life.

I tell people that I was born on a Tuesday after a long weekend. In other words, there were parts missing. What provided me with the missing parts was a new circle of friends, which involved looking closely at the principles and traditions of Alcoholics Anonymous. I'm not an advocate for AA, but I want to declare that it gave me good guidelines, some valuable principles and ideas about giving back to others with no expectation of receiving anything in return.

During those four years of night school, I made many connections throughout the community. Our final course module focused on working with alcoholics and others with addictions. The instructor asked me if I would participate in the module. I did a two-hour session, and it was quite interesting to facilitate a trainer's role in a course in which I was about to attain a certificate.

A lot happened to me during this time, but I remained focused on my Cambrian College program in Sudbury. To bring it full circle, I met Marcel's wife during this time. She had told me about her husband and his problems, and she and I became friends. She would tell her husband things like, "Marcel, it's too bad you couldn't meet Allan. He's turned his life around. He's made big changes in his life...."

I knew what that was like from my wife. She really tried her best to help me with my drinking and often said to me, "You know, you ought to meet this guy Rick...," or "You ought to meet this guy Bob...," or "You ought to meet this person Bill. He's really turned his life around."

The last thing I wanted to hear was how someone else had done something that, inside, I really knew I needed to do. I couldn't work with that, I couldn't handle it. My mind would just touch on it and bounce off.

So, Marcel built up a resentment for me, even though we did not know each other. If I met him on the street, I wouldn't have known who he was. That's the thing about being a functional alcoholic—you can function, so from the outside, you look like you're doing well but on the inside you're actually dying.

My experiences since sobriety have led me to the realization that education is a lifelong process. What is more, it does not all have to occur in a classroom. In the mid-90s I began a relationship with a very successful woman who opened my eyes to many things culturally and emotionally and who pointed me in the direction to further my classroom education, too.

We became friends after meeting at a union/management seminar in Sudbury. She was from Toronto and over the course of a few years, introduced me to many different things such as fashion and style and the difference between them. Fashion changes but styles stay the same. She also opened my mind to the importance of good food, healthy eating habits, travel and hiking and I started to get myself back into physical shape. My stamina improved. I began to feel the benefits of quitting smoking and cutting down on salt. My back was feeling better and I obtained some long-overdue dental work. After years of neglecting and abusing my system, I was taking care of it for the first time in my life really. Everything in my life was headed in the right direction, and in large measure, I have her to thank.

On her suggestion, I enrolled in a two year study of general psychology at Laurentian University in Sudbury, beginning in September, 1995. I had some superb professors and the experience introduced me to a new world of workshops with local leaders in the community.

One night, she and I were talking and we uncovered a deeply buried emotional wound. Whatever it was hit me full force and without knowing what happened, I suddenly found myself sobbing uncontrollably. There was so much heat pouring off my body that I was sweating profusely. Finally, she had to put me in a tepid bath to cool me down. It was all quite unexpected but afterwards, it seemed as though many layers of the onion at my core had been torn away. That was really something, another breakthrough. Not a lesson you could ever learn in a classroom, but educational nevertheless, because it represented a quantum leap in my understanding of myself and who I was. That night, I slept the sleep of the dead. I was out for 14 hours and awoke feeling light and renewed, as though a ton of muck had been lifted away.

Part of education, I could say, is being willing to experience anything and remaining open to whatever lessons that life or a teacher may present.

At Laurentian University, I was the oldest in my class. I sat in the same seat every night up in the left-hand corner of the auditorium, a theater-style classroom.

One of the reasons I wanted to return to school at university level was I thought it might help me become a success and progress closer to my dream.

There I sat at the age of 44 or 45 in a class with much younger students. I was amazed at how many didn't show up for class; I didn't know if it was because they could learn quicker or if they were in a similar place to me 30 years before. On the first day, there were a hundred students, and age-wise, I could have been the father of most of them. That first day and the last day, however, were the only times I saw the classroom full.

My professors spent much time with me and encouraged me to keep coming back. Many were much younger than I; however, I guess they saw something in me, and I just kept showing up. I never thought I would pass some of the tests, but I did, so I seemed to have developed the desire and the diligence.

I learned never to give up on doing the homework assignments. I never fell behind. I set aside so much time every day to do my assignments, to do my reading and to write my papers. I had people check the grammar in everything I wrote. I had them check the way it was laid out. I never sent a paper in without it being reviewed by at least two people, not so much that I wanted them to change the content, but to make sure that I had not driven myself off track from the intention of the assignment.

I heard many good arguments and debates in class. However, at the end of the day (and I said this to other people), the professor had what I wanted, so why would I debate him? Why wouldn't I simply listen? In that sense it was like rehab—the people who were sober had what I wanted, so why wouldn't I listen to them? Why would I debate? I would bring up points for discussion, which I think is healthy, but never to the point of creating resentment or shutting down communication.

Being motivated after this latest course of study, I enrolled in the next step of my education, which was to get my undergraduate degree through the National Labor College in Silver Spring, Maryland. After my second year at Laurentian, I began facilitating educational programs, not only in Canada, but in the United States as well. As a result of now spending half my time in the U.S., I ended my studies in Sudbury and transferred my credits to National Labor College. It is the only accredited higher education institution in North America devoted exclusively to educating union members. I was with other union people and labor associates of mine from different unions across the United States and Canada, mostly from the U.S.

I was scared to death at first. I was in a new country with its own history, with new laws, its own labor history and with unfamiliar studies. I didn't know US laws, policies and procedures, but it amazed me how people seemed to come out of the blue to help me.

I walked into the university and the first thing I saw on the wall was a United Steelworker poster with its logo. That gave me such a feeling of confidence and comfort because it was a symbol I was familiar with. It was similar to walking into an AA meeting and seeing the Alcoholics Anonymous slogans and the Serenity Prayer on the wall.

That is one of the important aspects of symbolism. I never had a particular familiarity with symbolism before I discovered who I was. I'm still discovering who I am, still making that 18-inch trip from my head to my heart. Every time I make the trip, every time I think about it, or do an inventory, or a mini-inventory of myself, I am pleasantly surprised at some of the discoveries I make.

Something that became symbolic for me were the sights and sounds of airports, train stations and highways. My speaking opportunities began to take me farther and farther afield. I'd be working in the amphitheater at the Creighton Mine. The USW would ask me to drive to Toronto to conduct a seminar. I'd drive past the airport and see a six lane highway and the Amtrak, or the "Go Train," as they call it in Toronto. I'd see and hear airplanes landing. (I always stayed in a hotel near the airport.) Two or three times a year, during the first half dozen years of my sobriety, something would happen. Seeing all these signs of life around me, my body would begin to vibrate. My eyes would tear up and I would get goose bumps.

"Look! Look!" I would say to people who were with me. "See that plane? See those cars? Look at that train! These people are alive!"

My friends looked at me as though I was a wee bit like Forrest Gump. I was so grateful just to be alive. The excitement of the planes, the takeoffs, the landings, the trains, the cars, the trucks. Everything was alive. I can still see that. I was so close to dying that when I came back, seeing these signs of life was overwhelming. Many people are deeply affected by babies, but for me, these were the symbols of life and movement, new beginnings and new changes.

There's an old saying, "Follow your bliss." I had been following my bliss for a while now. In May 2001, I became the first Canadian Steelworker to graduate from the National Labor College, when I achieved a degree in Labor Administration, which I considered quite an honor.

As I walked across the stage during the graduation ceremony, I deliberately took my time. I wanted to savor the moment. For a split second, I could smell the dustbane and see the chalk dust from the erasers in the afternoon sunlight back in USS #5. What I didn't hear was the derisive laughter of the bullies. The little boy inside had finally gained confidence.

The local newspaper in Sudbury wrote an article on me and asked what was the key to my success. That was tough to answer. One of the keys, I said, is that I now know what I don't know and I surround myself with people who know what I don't know. The universe has brought people to me that can help me do what I don't know. I can admit that I need help.

Following the principle of "success breeds success," I enrolled at the University of Massachusetts Amherst in their graduate program in Labor Administration, from which I graduated in May, 2005.

Again, I applied the same principles that I use every day in my life, which is to dedicate time daily to my goals. I never got behind in my work. Each morning and without fail, I asked myself, what's my intention today? I set a goal to obtain my degree, the equivalent of an MBA, before my 56th birthday and did so with three months to spare.

Good friends from Pittsburgh attended my graduation, as did my sister and her family who made the long drive from Auburn and other friends from Sudbury. Again, I was thrown back to my little one-room country schoolhouse and reflected on how much my life had changed.

Those years at the university gave me self-confidence because people valued my opinions and I was heard. It was a whole new world compared to where I had been only a few years earlier. It needs to be made clear though, that I had much help along the way.

CHAPTER 30

My Sponsor, Jim W.

Whatever you may be sure of, be sure of this,
you are dreadfully like other people.
—James Russell Lowell

Even though I held my one-year anniversary of sobriety in Ottawa, I still had a little celebration in my AA "home" group. We have seventy-some meetings in Sudbury and I joined the Thursday night group. It's a very supportive group of people and still continues to meet every week in Sudbury. I still maintain good friends and connections there.

A home group is a little bit different from other AA meetings because those who join one have accountability and responsibilities to the group. One arrives early, makes the coffee, sets up the tables, helps tear down after and clean up the room in the church or the hall or wherever the meeting is held. One would also attend a business meeting every month to assign who would chair the meeting next month, who would be the greeter at the door, etc. I'm still a member there, even though I live in another country. I go back every so often to visit. They are gracious enough to allow me to receive my medallions there every five years.

Throughout my first year of sobriety, Bob and Dave temporarily acted as sponsors for me. However, with increasing numbers of employees coming into the EAP office for help, it became time for me to seek a more permanent solution. An important aspect of Alcoholics

Anonymous is for a newcomer to find someone who will become his or her sponsor. A sponsor is a fellow alcoholic who has been in AA for a while and helps the newcomer understand the AA program, answers any questions pertaining to the program, gives them rides to meetings or other such assistance. It is my belief that a sponsor should be of the same gender as the newcomer, though this is not mandated.

My very first week in AA, I met someone who would have a great impact on my road upward. Jim W. was at that first meeting along with Mike, the man whose words had cut through the fog and reached me. I happened to meet Jim later that week, and he and I connected.

Jim was a character and had been sober approximately 13 years. I liked what he had to say at the meetings. I listened to his stories, his words of advice and his humor. Jim had a very, very interesting story. There's an old saying: "If you fall down make sure you land on your back because if you can look up you can get up." That's a perfect introduction to Jim's story.

He was a financial planner in his professional life. He could have played professional hockey as a goaltender; however as a teenager alcohol became more important than hockey practice, and he squandered the opportunity.

He married and had a family. From the outside, Jim appeared successful, much as I did. On the inside though, everything was falling apart, so much so, that in 1974, Jim went into a bar and paid a complete stranger $50 to end his pain, to kill him. The stranger readily took the money.

Jim's plan was to lie down in the street and have the stranger run over him. It was raining that night and he lied down in the dirty, wet street. Jim had a poetic sense about him and he laid there with an empty wine bottle on his chest—a metaphor for the emptiness of his life. How full or how empty do you see your wine bottle as you read this paragraph?

Jim laid there waiting for his pain to end. He heard a car approaching closer. . . closer . . . closer . . . .. He closed his eyes. He took his last breath. He braced himself for the end. All of a sudden, he heard the car stop. He heard the door open and a heavy footstep coming across the pavement. A deep, deep ominous voice said, "What are you doing?"

Jim opened an eye tentatively on that rain soaked street and said, "I'm committing suicide." He saw a black shiny boot and looked up to see a police officer standing over him.

"Do you have a place to stay tonight?" the officer asked.

"I didn't intend on being here," he answered in a voice so low the officer could barely hear.

The officer looked down. "Come with me and I will get you a hotel room. I get off at midnight and I'll be over with the drinks."

That was Jim's hook to live one more day. What's your hook to live one more day? What keeps you going? What's your motivation? For Jim that night in 1974, it was the promise of another drink.

Jim picked himself up off the street, set his wine bottle on the sidewalk and walked with the officer to his cruiser, ego bruised, overcoat sopping wet, down to his last thought of hope. He thought he would be dead by this time, but the idea of having one more drink kept him alive. What a power an addiction is.

He checked into the hotel room, took a shower, cleaned up and waited impatiently until midnight when he heard a knock on the door. He was elated because he wasn't sure if the guy would show up or not; maybe it was just another empty promise. We hear numerous empty promises in the world of addiction.

Jim opened the door and, lo and behold, there was the officer, off duty, with two steaming cups of coffee. That police officer turned out to be a recovering alcoholic of six years. He wasn't the guy that Jim paid the money to. The man that Jim paid certainly didn't call the police. It was a lucky coincidence that this police officer, who happened to be driving down that street, on that particular night, at that particular moment, when Jim had decided to end his life saw Jim and stopped.

As a result of that caffeine-laced conversation, Jim never took another drink, though he never found the guy to whom he gave the $50.

These are the stories we hear around the tables at Alcoholics Anonymous. The stories are of complete giving up, utter exhaustion with life, complete devastation, complete "kill me now," or "take me out of this mess," that turn into stories of a life of vibrancy and new hope.

"Possibility thinking"—how powerful those two words are. Possibility thinking. What's possible? What's attainable? What can I do today? What can I do today to help someone else in their life? What can I do today to help myself? What can I do today to help my family? What are some goals that I can set? What a way to build self-esteem, by reaching goals, attainable goals, by giving the power of example. With just a little space and a little refocus, the word "impossible" becomes "I'm possible." Same letters, totally different meaning.

Jim used to say, "Shoot for the moon because if you miss, you still hit the stars."

I don't believe that we are aiming too high and missing; we are aiming too low and hitting. I used to aim too low. I was aiming just to have a drink to end the pain, end the misery that was drowning my miserable life.

When I heard that story about Jim I said, "Man, I can relate to him. I'd like to have him for a sponsor." A week before my one-year anniversary celebration in Sudbury, I asked him if he would become my sponsor.

"I'll think about it and get back to you," he said, and he made me wait.

I anxiously anticipated his answer and even though I didn't particularly want much to do with people in recovery, I was anxious for him to become my sponsor. Down deep, I really did want recovery.

A couple days later, Jim came back and said, "I gave it some thought and, yes, I will be your sponsor."

My sponsor, mentor and great friend Jim. W. This wonderful man had a profound impact on my life.

That told me a couple of things: Jim took the job of sponsorship seriously. It wasn't just something to give a perfunctory yes or no to right away. That made me feel good. He took responsibility for it, and was serious about the idea of sponsorship. Jim had 13 more years of sobriety than I did and therefore had some experiences in his life that he could help guide me through in my own life, and his sponsorship grew into a wonderful friendship. Jim was willing to share his experiences, his strengths and hopes with me on a one-on-one basis.

It's wonderful to go to a group meeting and engage in a collective session sitting around the table and listening to different people. It's also great to have one-to-one relationship where you can give a person a call and say "Jim, I'm having a bad day…can you help me with this?" Or "Have you had any experiences with . . .?" Or pick up the phone and have someone to listen to you. That was so rare in my life experience because I never opened up, I kept all my feelings inside.

I think back to that day in my living room with my wife when I was trying to open up, was ridiculed and shut down my feelings. With Jim as my sponsor, attending AA meetings, still feeling beat up and carrying all this guilt and remorse, I found that I was becoming more emotional. All this began to surface. Alcohol was no longer burying my thoughts, my feelings or my pain. I could feel myself beginning to dig out from under my self-created cave-in and I was starting to feel things again. Often though, it hurt. It hurt a lot.

CHAPTER 31

A Lifetime of Living in One Year

Fame is what you have taken. Character is what you give.
When to this truth you waken, then you begin to live.
—Bayard Taylor

LIFE IN 1988 BEGAN TO LOOK VERY DIFFERENT from life one year earlier. I had a new sponsor. I had a certificate of graduation from the Labour College of Canada's labor studies program. I had one year of sobriety under my belt. I had a year invested in my community college program. I was still seeing the woman who had helped me in the beginning of my sobriety and I decided to quit smoking.

She told me about the hazards of smoking and said that it would be good for me to quit. You'd be healthier, she told me. I tried to quit three or four times during that first year, and I would get so discouraged. Here I had quit drinking, but I couldn't seem to quit the cigarette habit. I still smoked at least a pack and a half per day, sometimes two. Earlier, every time I had a drink, I sometimes had two or three cigarettes burning at the same time: one in my mouth, one in the ashtray and, depending on how loaded I was, one in my fingers.

On July 17, 1988, after my graduation from the Labor College, my friend and I went out to stay at another friend's cottage. We climbed into a paddle boat and made our way out on a lake. I said that I had a surprise for her. I wasn't about to tell her, I would show her. I paddled a little ways out; we didn't go too far because I am not a swimmer. I don't particularly like water and I don't even like paddle boats. We talked a bit and were just having some fun in the sun. I smoked three cigarettes, then picked up what was left of the pack and threw it into the lake. At first, she thought that I had dropped them until I threw my lighter over the other side.

"That's it," I said. "I just quit smoking." She was so surprised.

I had smoked so much since my first cigarette in that old driving shed when I was in Grade 7. My nicotine addiction became so strong that once, when I was stuck underground for about five hours because of a power failure, I missed the cigarettes more than I did the food. That is the craving I had for nicotine. My fingers were a yellow-brown from the tobacco. I used to coat them with toothpaste and iodine, which was supposed to clean the stains. It didn't work, but they smelled clean.

We paddled back to shore. "That's it," I repeated. "I will not smoke anymore."

It was a little more than a year after I quit drinking. I will be honest, the main reason I wanted to quit was that if an overwhelming problem arose, I would use smoking as a security blanket instead of going back to the bottle. That would be my source of comfort, the lesser of two evils. It was like an insurance policy. If something happened that I thought I couldn't handle, I could pick up a cigarette instead of picking up a drink.

I have always been a deal maker. When I quit smoking, I said a prayer, not from just my head but from my heart. I said, "God, if you'll take 80 percent of the pain and misery, I'll handle 20." That was the deal that I made with the God of my understanding, or Higher Power.

They say that tobacco is one of the hardest addictions to kick, but believe it or not, for me it wasn't that bad, although, about two or three weeks after I quit I said, "My God, why didn't I make this deal with you: You take 90 percent and I'll take 10?"

My cigarette of choice had been Player's Light. They came in packs of 25 and the day I quit, unbeknownst to my friend, I stashed a pack, unopened, under the seat of my car just in case I had a real panic attack. However, with my commitment and her encouragement, I kicked the habit. A year later, I discovered the unopened pack—I had totally forgotten. To think that at one time I missed cigarettes more than food!

To recap my first fourteen months of sobriety: I was going through a divorce, I had quit smoking, I was living in my apartment, trying to build a bank account and trying to rebuild my life as the father of my children. I had parted ways with that '73 Buick with the unattached frame. I was more concerned about the Ministry of Transportation stopping me than I was the police because they would have pulled it off the road on the spot. I now drove a 1976 Chrysler New Yorker, only 12 years old at the time.

For sure, I had made significant improvement, but I felt I should have made 100 times more. In this regard, I was caught up in the instant gratification attitude that seems to permeate our society. Sobriety plus mining taught me the value of one day at a time.

I spent a great deal of time in physical therapy that year and, over time, my back improved. The doctors assessed my condition and said I would never work on full duty underground again. I had always been proud to work underground and been productive enough to make good bonuses. Then, there was the macho status of being a hard rock miner. My new job was hosing floors and cleaning up an old pump house in a sand plant.

A sand plant is the facility above ground where sand and cement are mixed with water and pumped into the voids where ore has been extracted. The object was to prevent the ground from caving into open stopes. A slurry of sand, cement and water was pumped from the plant for miles on surface through 36-inch pipes and then underground in 6-inch pipes to a mined-out stope that had been prepared with timbers and burlap.

Once a stope was open, that is, all the ore had been removed, timbers were laid against the walls the entire length of the stope. Then, logs that were the width of the stope were laid on top of these timbers every few feet. On top of the logs, burlap was laid down and cemented part of the way up the side of the stope, creating a seal. Next, like a massive cement pour, the stope was filled with slurry, excess water drained off and the resulting mass shored up the ground, which made it possible to extract ore from neighboring stopes and to enable undercutting to reach the ore below. In the latter case, the floor of the now-filled stope became the roof of the new stope being excavated below it.

Every mined-out stope was treated this way and, over the course of decades, the original ore body would become replaced by a mass of hardened slurry.

The function of the sand plant was oddly similar to what I was now doing in my life—filling the voids that I had drowned in alcohol for nearly 20 years. Instead of a slurry of sand and cement, I was using honesty with myself and others. I was using the process of making amends to those I had harmed. I was opening my mind to education and to change. I was making a journey repeatedly, traveling the 18 inches from my head to my heart.

In time, what I thought was the worst day of my life, being transferred to this "mundane" job, turned out to be one of the best days of my life. Mind you, I was eternally grateful for the opportunity to go back to work at all, even in a mine that I had never worked in before.

There were eight or nine mine sites around Sudbury along with one or two refineries, a couple of mills and a smelter. The policy was that wherever a miner got hurt in that complex that was the plant he went back to. I was way out in the Levack West Mine, about a 30 mile drive from the city.

During my year off on disability compensation, I volunteered a lot for the Employee Assistance Program filling in for people on vacation. When I went back to work, one of the HR people who was directly associated with the EAP had been watching me. Unbeknownst to me, Mr. Poland had a close affiliation with Creighton Mine. In late summer 1989, when he heard that I was going back to work, he knew I wanted to stay involved with EAP as much as I could. He went out to the complex in Creighton and lobbied for me to get a job there. It gave me some leverage to have an ally in Human Resources and to be much closer to the union hall. I could be there in 10 minutes instead of the 40 minute drive from Levack. The job he lined up for me was working in the sand plant as a pump man, which, in time, allowed me some latitude to work between there and the union hall.

This plant was a huge brick building, three or four stories high like an old steel mill, musty smelling with not a working light in the entire place. It hadn't been operated as a mill for nine or ten years and was in severe neglect. Two small sections of it were being used, one as a sand plant and the other for fabrication. It was filthy, absolutely filthy.

Huge pumps that needed tending were beneath the main floor and because there was no natural light down there, I had to wear a cap lamp to be able to see. I didn't want to fall into a hole or get caught in a piece of equipment. "My goodness," I thought, "if I am spending the rest of my years up here in the sand plant," which was my destiny as far as I knew then, "I don't want to wear a cap lamp."

When my pump man duties were officially done at the end of each shift or in the middle of each shift, I began cleaning up the place. I have always had a good work ethic, being raised on a farm and working in the mine, no matter how drunk or sick I was. However, I think I did the extra work just to keep my sanity, bearing in mind that in a year I had quit drinking, quit smoking, had a relationship change, a job change and was struggling to get back on my feet. I didn't do much with my life for 37 years and then within 14 months I tried to do everything. My stress level was high and I have learned that whenever I get anxious or become nervous or feel over-stressed, I work, which gives me a sense of accomplishment and peace of mind. Work gives me something to focus on. So, I began cleaning up the sand plant and again, I was amazed to find that when I started to take these positive actions, people came into my life to help who I didn't even know.

I also learned something about human dynamics. I went in there as a relatively young man of 38, while the other men who worked there were quite a bit older than me and closer to retirement. They performed their jobs but never went the extra mile. They thought that an honest day's work for an honest day's pay was fantastic.

On the other hand, I just kept working. Even if I was on break or during lunch, I would get up, probably because of my bad nerves, and start cleaning. I received some static for that and the others were calling me names. I was a stranger in that complex and they didn't know my history. They knew I had a problem with alcohol because I was very open about it. However, my extra activity drew comments such as, "What are you doing that for? You're making us look bad." I had that to contend with and my bad back as well.

There was unmixed cement that had been sitting in ditches for 8 or 9 years and it had oxidized and hardened. While remaining careful of my back, I broke it up with a scaling bar, which is a six-foot bar with a point on one end and a pry bar on the other. I drove holes into the mass, placed electrical blasting caps in the holes that friends would pilfer from the explosives magazine underground and set them off on night shift when nobody was around. That loosened the sand and cement, which I then shoveled into a dumpster. My work was spent cleaning the floors and breaking up the cement, and then for good measure, looking under old walkways for garbage to throw out.

One day, the electrical foreman came over and said, "I will make a deal with you, Allan. The more you clean up this area, I will send my crew over to put lights in."

That was wonderful as far as I was concerned and it became an incentive for me to continue working. Every so often, he would send an electrician down to string more wire and install floodlights. I no longer had to wear a cap lamp. I realized that I was now on the surface! I kept track of the number of dumpsters I filled, along with the help of others who came to pitch in. We filled 43 industrial dumpsters with old parts, cement, dirt, rusted out pipes and junk from that mill.

Inadvertently, I began building a reputation. Even though I did the extra work simply to maintain whatever sanity I had left, I began receiving some positive recognition. I was on the health and safety committee at the Levack West Mine, but I did not go onto the health and safety committee when I transferred over to Creighton. I wanted to be involved only in one department in the union and that was the Employee Assistant Program; however, Health and Safety played a key role in my life when they did their inspections.

Every six months or so, the Health and Safety Committee would come down to inspect the sand plant, and over time, I developed a friendship with the coordinator. The inspectors hadn't been down there for about 9 months and they were used to seeing nothing but blackness, cement, sand, useless pipes and rusty chains. There were 12-inch pipes that at one time carried tons and tons and tons of water. During their next inspection, they noticed more lighting. They noticed the pipe removal, the ditches clean, garbage picked up and they entered all that in their report. They were supposed to report not only what was wrong but any positive changes as well. That is not why I was doing it, but it turned out that I received positive recognition for the extra work. I was still doing my pump man's responsibility but also cleaning up the sand plant itself.

A couple more bonus miners had been hurt at Creighton and they joined me up top. Their physical limitations were such that between the three of us we constituted one able-bodied person and we worked well together. We worked on different shifts and would surprise each other by doing something extra on our individual shifts that the others would notice when they came to work.

There was a huge container, a 100,000 gallon steel drum sitting on two cement abutments that was 15 feet long and made of heavy gauge steel but no longer used. We often teased each other about how we would dismantle the tank and bust up the cement to improve the plant. And honest to God, we did it.

I came in one night and one of the guys had started working on it, and before long we rolled it onto the floor, cut it up with torches and had it removed. It was lots of fun and hard work, but resulted in positive recognition for all of us, which turned into a very good thing.

Next door to the sand plant was the fabrication department called Divisional Shops that had front-end loaders and forklift trucks. The foreman there had an issue of his own with alcoholism and had been sober 10 years longer than I.

He came over one day and said, "You know, Al, you and the other men are really doing great work over here. If we can help in any way, if you need to take pipe or big stuff down, leave it overnight and we will come and take it out to our scrap yard at the next available opportunity."

Here we go again. One man comes over who I never met in my life and says he will put in lights. Another man I never knew comes over and says, "Hey, you keep cleaning up the heavy stuff and we will come over and remove it for you."

We had help coming in and it proved to me that when you do something positive, people will support you. It was another example of something I read in the Big Book of AA: you have to be the example and go the extra mile.

One day, I ordered yellow and blue paint from the electrical foreman and spent the weekend painting the pumps, the pump guards, screen guards, the wire mesh and the pump stands. These were massive pumps that stood four feet high and were mounted on cement pads, very high profile pumps. They pumped water for miles and miles up from the mines. When the pumps were shut down and I had some extra time, I scraped off the dirt and painted them.

By the time I left there in November of '90, the place looked good. I was still attending my four-year course at night and did homework assignments while working on Saturday mornings waiting for the tanks to fill. I would do my homework assignments and be on the phone with fellow students getting help from them. Looking back, it was a great time. I met many fine people there, some who still work there.

Every fall in October and November, the union conducted a United Way Campaign at the mine where the employees donated part of their weekly paycheck to the United Way Foundation and INCO matched it. We had an amphitheater that held 88 men; the number of seats equaled all the miners who could cram into the double decker cage at the Creighton Mine. The mine was so deep that it was more efficient to take twice the number of men down per trip. So the amphitheater was built to hold a double cage load of miners. They would come in their mining clothes before going underground and attend safety training or have other kinds of meetings.

People knew that I was becoming involved in the community and the gentleman doing the fundraising asked me to work in there for two or three months to help them with the campaign. Me, deathly afraid of public speaking from my grade school days, was being asked to stand in front of all these miners to explain the benefits of the programs that United Way helps to fund. I fully expected to go back into the sand plant, however some said I would never return. I thought it was pie-in-the-sky on their parts.

I left the sand plant went over to the amphitheater, where they gave me a small office. There were two of us in there. After the United Way campaign finished, management asked me if I wanted to do some health and safety instruction at the safety meetings the union put on and I said, "Absolutely." So, there I was, the stuttering, ringworm-infested, undersized, wimpy kid, 30 years later standing up and speaking in front of miners, not doing it very well, but standing up and taking that risk.

I think I went to the edge of the cliff, jumped off and grew wings on the way down. I never returned to the sand plant. I never put on my hard hat or my work boots again. I stayed over at Nine Shaft, as we called the amphitheater area, involved with training, the United Way and developing my skills as a facilitator and instructor. I also became involved in the education department of the Steelworkers Union.

Our Employee Assistance Program was set up in 1976 and I looked at the people who worked there over the years. Some did not have a high success rate in their own lives either while there or after they left. Some drank, others had nervous breakdowns and one attempted suicide. I am not blaming the EAP for that, I am just saying I looked at the history of that program. "Man, I have not come this far," I thought to myself, "only a couple years sober and going to school that I wanted to jeopardize my mental health over a job at the Employee Assistance Program, no matter how great of an office I think it is."

One example of the cases we had to deal with was a miner named Rollie who was having a hell of a time. His wife had left him and he was despondent to the point of suicide. He took blasting caps, drove his car out in the country, wrapped the caps around himself and prepared to detonate them and end his life. Fortunately, he left his car door open, a trick mobsters do when starting their cars, so I'm told, and when the blast went off, it blew Rollie out the door. He lived but when I visited him in the hospital the next day there were bits of gravel embedded in his chest along with dirt and lord knows what else.

I had no idea what to say to him so I said, "Rollie, I used to work with your dad at Levack. He could never learn to blast right, either."

That made him laugh, which he said hurt him worse than the blast. Eventually, he got his life back together. It is small wonder that the people running the EAP often had their own issues. It was apparent to me that to work in that office, you had to have a special personality to deal with the daily tales of misery.

I knew I had to have something positive in my life and that was

Me, sober. For the first time in my life, my eyes looked happy.

an instance where I found it beneficial to talk to mentors or sponsors or people who had been there before. Some people I talked to asked, "What do you enjoy doing?"

"Teaching," I answered, without thinking.

"Well," they said, "if you became involved with the union's education program there might be some balance in your life. On one hand the EAP can be a trying, draining job because people are coming to you at the last minute wanting you to save their jobs or save their marriages. On the other hand, you will also be in a classroom where you can talk to people and see a light come on in someone's eyes. That is very rewarding."

I have always said that no matter how far down the scale I went, if I could keep someone from traveling down the path that I did, then my life has been of value. It is not my intention to see through people, but to see people through.

I didn't know all that then, even though I was beginning to live it.

I continued with my education and with the health and safety training at the mine site, while still attending AA meetings.

Just as I had a sponsor in Alcoholics Anonymous, Jim, I thought I should have the same kind of mentorship in my education training for the union. One day, I went downstairs to the classroom at our union hall. I walked in and timidly asked the education coordinator, whose name was John, "Do you have five minutes?" and he answered, "Sure."

I sat across the table and humbly asked, "John, would you be my sponsor, my so called 'sponsor,' to help me with my training and educational seminars?"

"I will get back to you on it," he said, just like Jim had. He gave it some thought, which I took as a good sign because it was not just an automatic "Yes." He came back the next day and said, "Absolutely, I will help you in any way I can."

I took direction from him about attending union meetings and going to different conventions. He reached out and arranged for me to attend a program on how to train workers to become trainers. This program did not use the lecturing model as seen in most educational settings but instead used the facilitating model, and I have never looked back. John is still a friend of mine, and even though he is retired and I am not living in Canada anymore, we still keep in contact.

My first experience was anything but smooth, however. John asked me to do a 15 minute talk about the EAP during a day long seminar for union members. I agreed even though I was nervous about doing it. The morning of the seminar, John croaked to me, "Allan, I can't talk. Laryngitis. You'll have to do it."

Suddenly, that 15 minutes looked like a dream. I struggled through the entire seminar and what I feared would be my worst day after hearing John that morning, turned out to be one of my best days. At the end of the seminar I was exhilarated. The response was great. Nobody had a clue that it hadn't been planned for me to do the entire seminar. The boy who detested everything about school had caught the teaching bug.

The union noticed my enthusiasm and desire to continue along this path and offered to send me to other cities across Canada to deliver seminars. I was very tempted but in the back of my mind I knew that I needed a more solid foundation of sobriety in my life. It was a wonderful opportunity the union was presenting, I enjoyed traveling and I loved teaching, but I declined their offer. I felt I needed the stability that five years of sobriety would give me. The union rep said, "You know, Allan, that this opportunity might not be available in five years."

"I completely understand," I replied, "but I am unwilling to jeopardize my sobriety. Without that, I have nothing."

They understood my position and today, I feel that is one of the better decisions I have made.

My life continued to turn around: sober, nonsmoking, head clearing slowly, had a mentor, paying off my bills and getting some respect from the community. The bank started trusting in me as they saw I was changing my life.

Believe you me, I had gained a reputation around the mining community in Levack and Sudbury for prodigious drinking. People made bets that I wouldn't stay sober for more than two or three weeks. Regrettably, some of the people who made those bets are not living anymore, nothing to do with their bets against me so much as they didn't change their own lifestyles.

I walked into a bar one night when I had attained 7 or 8 years of sobriety. Some of the friends I had spent time with in the past were there sitting around drinking with the same problems from, what seemed to me, a lifetime ago. I sat down and bought two or three drinks for them and a soda for myself.

That evening, one of them looked up at me and he said, "Hey, Al, how long has it been since you quit now?"

I said, "I don't know."

"It must be two years," he said. In reality, it was more like seven.

"Absolutely," I replied, not wanting to embarrass him. "Yeah, it has been a couple of years now."

He looked up at me and a tear ran out of his eye. "You know what, Al," he said, "someday I'll do what you did."

Today that man is no longer living and I often think about the decision he never made. My sponsor Jim was fond of saying, "Don't worry, we all get sober. Some of us do it while we are still living."

So, while all this was occurring, I had these new changes and opportunities coming into my life. I never forgot that I still had a vision in my mind's eye. It was gray and clouded, there were curtains over it, but there was enough of a view. It was a vision of becoming a speaker and an author. That man who came that one night when I was in rehab back in 1987 to tell us the story of his life and battle with alcohol wasn't a motivational speaker per se. He was simply a man speaking about his experiences, strengths and hopes. It was enough to convince me that I could do the same. The prayer I used to say in the morning was: "God, please use my eyes to look at people through, please use my face to glow through and please use my mouth to speak through."

That was in addition to another prayer I said from time to time: "If You can use me as an instrument of change, please help me. I will be honest, open and willing and try all the opportunities that You bring my way no matter where it takes me." That has worked out quite well.

When I graduated from my four year addiction assessment and intervention program in 1993, another opportunity came along and that was another course called life skills coach. It was a one semester seminar on how to teach adults and make education fun. I took that training at the Cambrian College in Sudbury, twice a week, and met some great people from all kinds of backgrounds. Some are still friends today. As much as I detested school back when I should have liked it, I certainly got the bug when I was in my late 30s. My mother, being a big believer in education, was very proud.

BREAKING THROUGH

CLOSURE WITH MY PARENTS

He that cannot forgive others breaks the bridge over which he must
pass himself; for every man has need to be forgiven.
—THOMAS FULLER

ONE DAY WHEN I RETURNED TO MY APARTMENT, there was voice mail from my mother on my phone. The voice sounded negative, low-toned and depressed.

"Allan, do I have a son called Allan who I never hear from? I'd really like to hear if I have a son called Allan." Then she hung up.

It had only been 10 days since we last spoke and I knew she was trying to lay a guilt trip on me.

Before I called her back, I thought about it for quite a while. One of the slogans in AA is, "Think, think, think." I didn't want to call her back in anger because, as the saying goes, "Anger is only one letter away from danger." I didn't want to make a series of mistakes out of anger. So, I thought about it for a day. I had been sober for five or six years and had grown to love my mother dearly, but I wasn't about to fall into her negativity or her guilt-making ways. I said a short prayer and placed the call.

When she answered, I said, "Mom, we're going to have a telephone call and these are the rules: I'm going to talk, I won't be angry and you will listen. Then you can respond and I will not interrupt. The other choice you have is you can hang up the phone when we're done and take a day or two to think over what you want to tell me and then you can call back collect."

There was a slight hesitation on her part and she tried to interrupt, but I said, "No, this is my call. So, please have the respect for me that I deserve."

I told her about the many changes I had gone through, and that I refused not to be respected by her, but also that I loved her very much. She listened, though she tried to interrupt me several times; however, I was prepared. After I had said my piece, there was hesitation on the other end of the line.

"Do you want to talk with me now, or do you want me to call you later or would you rather call me back collect?" I asked.

"Oh, no," she said, "that's fine." She cried a little bit, and we talked and I cried a little bit, too.

My mother had a tendency to manipulate, but by now I had forgiven everything that happened between us. That took some time, believe me. It began in rehab when they had me journal about our relationship. I sought counseling from the EAP office, I heard others at AA meetings relating their parental stories and finally someone said, "You can't afford to let your mother keep paying rent in your head."

Our exchange over the phone that day sparked a new beginning for us, the renewal of a connection between a mother and her son. I had a wonderful relationship with her for the remainder of our days. I've been very grateful for her support as I was dealing with my struggles. She went to Al-Anon meetings and drove 12 miles at night as a 70-year-old woman trying to understand the difficulties of her 37-year-old son. There she befriended women who had sons and daughters or husbands in AA and became part of a support network. That helped her come to terms with what I had gone through and helped draw us closer. I love her for that.

People have asked me over the years, "Why were you an alcoholic?"

I always answer with great humility and a sincere look right in their eye, "I was an alcoholic because I drank too much."

The answer is no more complex than that: I drank too much. My mother used to say it's because I worked in the mine. I think she was trying to understand me and understand the addiction. However, I also think she felt some guilt about my childhood.

Answering my mother, I would say, "Mom, I drank because I drank, it's as simple as that."

Ultimately, that is probably the most honest answer of all. I never disclosed to her that the reason I drank was because of my childhood, growing up in Auburn or my school years or my poor grades or my shyness with girls or my shyness with everybody. If someone turned around and said, "Boo," I cried. I cried at the drop of a hat.

For many years, I solved those problems and many others with alcohol. I suppose I could have solved my problems in other ways, such as by throwing myself into a career, or by joining a monastic order or running off to the French Foreign Legion or any number of other solutions. To say simply, "I drank because I drank," has a truth to it that admits of no justification.

Often, simplicity is profound.

"I drank because I drank," is the answer that enabled me to take responsibility for the choices I made. It freed me from that dark period of my life rather than bury it with denial.

Some time later, I was visiting my family and my mother said, "Now that you've been sober five years and you're working at the union hall in the EAP office, are you now happy?"

Our relationship had improved. I had just finished my four-year course of studies and was interested in enrolling in Laurentian University in Sudbury. My dream of becoming a motivational speaker was still part of my vision. As I often say, "Good, better, best—never take a rest until the good is better and the better is best."

I think she was concerned that I would let myself in for

disappointment if I could not realize my dream of becoming a speaker. She feared that I might go back to my old habit of self-destructive thoughts and behaviors. She kept asking, "Why do you want to go to school and why do you want to do this and why do you want to do that? You have a great job; you're working in the office you wanted."

Even though she was elated with my educational success, she seemed to have a difficult time with my dream. Perhaps my reaching for my dream became a reminder of the education she abandoned so long ago.

I considered her question for a moment and then answered, "That was what I wanted five years ago. I'm changing."

I think the fountain of youth is in our imaginations, in our minds, to inspire, to create new plateaus that we want to reach.

"You have the job you wanted and a relationship. You're sober five years. That's a great milestone for anyone," she parried.

"Mom," I said, "I want to be a motivational speaker and an author. To be a success, I have to do something that society sees as successful so I can have the credibility to get up and speak, and not only to carry the message, but to be the message."

"Allan, that's not the real world," she said.

This conversation replayed itself every time I came down for a visit. I would drive down to Auburn and we would talk about it again. Routinely, she would finish the conversation with, "Allan, that's not the real world."

After several visits and hearing her same argument I finally said to her with real conviction, "You know, Mom, you're absolutely right. It's not the real world, but it's my world."

Even though I was frustrated with my mother at the time for debating my dreams, I was grateful for what she said. She was saying those things out of love. The woman who I feared as a little boy, the woman whose actions and behaviors had scarred me, I finally stood

Mom, about to cut the cake at her 80th birthday party.

up to. Not in anger, but with confidence. I stood up to her and said, "You're right, Mom, it's not the real world, but it's mine."

She accepted that and never brought it up again and was very supportive of me until the end of her days.

Mom worked at the post office in Auburn. She was always active in the church, playing the organ at services and working with the ladies' auxiliary. Sadly though, she always carried with her the feeling that life had passed her by. She had to quit her education at 18 when her brother Stewart was born because her mother had St. Vitus Dance and could not care for her infant son. I think that she was envious of Stewart's successful life, but she, too, was accomplished in her own right. She was gifted as a speaker, was well organized and used her talents in the community.

Late in her life, she developed congestive heart condition and passed away on April 28, 2001, at age 83. I was in Texas at the time but Bernice was with her in the hospital. Even then, Mom was still a fighter. The night before she died, Bernice went to visit and asked her how she was doing. "Terrible," she complained bitterly, pointing to the other woman sharing the room with her. "See that woman over there? She kept me up all night coughing. She's going to die!"

"No, Mom, don't say that. Calm down, calm down," Bernice said.

The next night Bernice went to visit again. My mother hated air conditioning and made the nurses stand on the bed and stuff pillow cases into the air vents. She and Bernice visited for a bit and my sister said she had to go. Her husband Gordon had suffered a heart attack and was in another hospital.

She left and fifteen minutes later, while Jeopardy was playing on the TV, my mother passed away.

The little old lady sharing the room later said, "I was talking to your mom and she turned her head and died."

I learned a lesson from that: Be careful when you point a finger because there will be three pointed back at you.

Mom's last wishes were to be cremated and that a memorial service be held in June when the weather turned nicer. We did so and it was a wonderful remembrance of her life. Mom was great in her own right. She had her own social circle and, despite her anger, made her own positive mark in the little village where she lived her whole life.

After the ceremony, we spent some time sorting through her belongings and packing up her house. A close friend who had gotten to know my mom came to the memorial service and went with us to Mom's house. In one of the bedrooms, she found all the letters I had written to her, AA medallions, articles about me from the papers when I graduated from my college programs and notices about my work for the union.

CHAPTER 32 - CLOSURE WITH MY PARENTS

After my 10th anniversary, she wrote me the following note:

> June 4/97
> 10 year sobriety
>
> Dear Allan: —
>   What a wonderful, glorious experience we enjoyed last night at your 10th anniversary. Thanks for the wonderful meal, all the fine friends of yours that I met. And lastly the kindest gesture of all in giving me your medallion. Some day you will have it back to keep for yourself. I am truly proud of all your accomplishments & the many great friends you have made. Love, Mom.

Amongst everything we also found the cards and letters my children had written to their grandma over the years.

"Allan, your mother created this room as a shrine to you," my friend said.

It was a poignant moment for all of us, especially for me. It helped me feel a closure with the mother who, despite all her troubles, had

Shane, Marcie, Mom, Angie and me in front of Mom's house.
My kids loved their grandma.

brought me into the world and, all things considered, did what she thought was right and did the best she could.

That evening opened a dialog of reminiscences about Grandma, something that is revisited even today when the family gathers at Thanksgiving, Christmas or other occasions. Hearing my children laugh as they share the happy times they spent with their grandma helped me see that the chain of sorrow and sadness had been broken. That is worth every tear that I ever shed.

Even so, she carried her anger and resentments to the end. Some situations in her life she found impossible to let go. AA has a saying: "Let go and let God."

There is a story about a lake somewhere in the universe called the lake of "Forgiveness and Forget." It is a deep and tranquil lake where people bring the issue that is "paying rent in their head," in other words, bothering them. They cast the issue into the lake and, while it may cause a ripple, it invariably sinks to the bottom.

People turn and walk away, but if they look back, they will see signs posted everywhere that read, "No Fishing." Hopefully, the signs prevent them from tossing in a hook and reeling their problem back in.

Sadly, my mother was great at fishing. Before she died, she made funeral arrangements and went to the headstone engraver. She paid him to engrave her maiden name, Toll, on her headstone in letters so large that there was no room to mention her husband, Ken McDougall, and barely enough to mention her daughter and son. Her anger must have run deeper than any mine shaft I ever descended. Sadly, she took this fight to the grave.

She never heeded the advice put forth by Samuel Johnson, the great man of English letters: "Let us not throw away any of our days upon useless resentment, or contend who shall hold out longest in stubborn malice."

The arc of my dad's life was decidedly different from Mom's. As I mentioned earlier, they stayed together for years after I left home for fear of the social stigma that divorce carried in our provincial little village.

After the farm was sold in 1965 and my parents relocated to Auburn, Dad became a tax assessor until he retired in 1975. Upon his retirement, the arguing increased substantially between him and Mom. One day in 1977, I got a call from Bernice. "Dad's in a bad way," she said. "Your help is needed at home."

I drove from Sudbury, upset about what I expected to find. Naturally, I stopped at a bar and put away 20 ounces of whiskey in half an hour and then drove to the house. This was 10 years before I became sober.

I entered the house and realized that Bernice had understated the situation. I found Dad curled up in a fetal position, crying. Mom did not want him in the house any longer. She had her cousins there who very much took her side in the fight. Dad was glad to see me and as I was helping him out of the house, one of Mom's cousins shoved us. That really made me mad. They had crossed the line and I let them know it.

"I'm going to take care of my dad," I said, "but when I get back you better be gone," and I meant it.

I drove Dad to the Blue Water Hospital in Goderich and had him admitted to the psychiatric ward. He was in the midst of a nervous breakdown and we needed to find out what was happening. Mom had been in the same hospital earlier in her life when she was having problems.

The doctors tested and evaluated him and prescribed only rest. No drugs, no electroshock treatments. Still, he was concerned about his mental state.

"Am I psycho, Doc?" he asked.

"No, Mr. McDougall. The only thing wrong with you is your terrible marriage," the psychiatrist replied. "There's nothing wrong with you."

What a relief for my dad, but also for Bernice and me.

As time rolled forward following his encounter with the lightning years earlier, my dad's manual dexterity and attention span were affected, which sometimes had humorous consequences. Before the accident, he was very capable around equipment and could do the thousand and one things that a farmer needs to do on a farm.

One day, Mom, Bernice and I went to town to buy things needed for Bernice's upcoming marriage to Gordon. Before we left, Mom wanted Dad to fix a linoleum tile that had come loose on the floor. He went to the shed for a can of Bulldog linoleum adhesive. It was cold out and the cement was unworkable. He set it on the stove to warm it up, with the lid on, but became distracted by something and forgot about it. When we returned home, Dad was frantically trying to scrape long black stalactites of linoleum adhesive from the kitchen ceiling. The can had exploded at about the same level as Mom did when she saw the mess.

In preparation for the wedding, Mom had all the kitchen cabinets refinished and they looked beautiful. People would be coming over to the house after the ceremony and Mom wanted the house to look good. Again, she, Bernice and I were out getting things for the wedding and left my dad at home. Around noon, he began cooking himself lunch. Again became distracted or dozed off and awoke to find his meal on fire. Hastily, he doused the flames and then aired out the smoky kitchen, but Mom's newly refinished cabinets were badly scorched. We returned home to find Dad sheepishly sitting in the kitchen waiting for the "Wrath of Marjorie" to rain down upon him. One wonders sometimes if these accidents weren't an inevitable byproduct of the nearly 40 unhappy, loveless years they spent together.

While Dad was in the hospital, Mom obtained a restraining order to keep him from returning to their house. We found a boarding house for him in Clinton and he settled down and began building a new life.

He and Mom finally took the advice I had given years earlier and divorced. Mom kept the house and Dad bought a trailer in Clinton, down the road from Auburn.

Mom never remarried, nor did Dad, but he began a wonderful relationship with a woman named Mary and they had several happy years together. They became quite well known in the community around Clinton.

Dad loved people but never managed to save money. It wasn't all that important to him. He used to tell me that what was important was the number of friends who would come to his funeral, the people who thought enough of him to come say good-bye when the time came.

He and Mary each had eccentricities that endeared them to the townsfolk. Dad was known as the "Turnip Man" and Mary became known as the "Bread Lady."

There was a turnip facility in Blyth, and they sold the turnips they couldn't sell to a store due to the size or blemishes for 50 cents a bag. Dad bought these "culls" and always kept a bag in his trunk. He would be chatting with someone in a store or on the street, tell the person to wait right there, grab two or three turnips from his trunk and make a little gift of them. He did this for years, hence the moniker "Turnip Man." Mary did the same thing with wonderful loaves of her home baked bread. She would hand them out to folks that she ran into in during her day, and both she and my dad became beloved by the community. Mary and Dad enjoyed the sulky races each week in Clinton, and every year since his death they hold a horse race in his honor. The winning horse receives a blanket with "Ken McDougall" stitched on it and that keeps the wonderful memories people have of the Turnip Man alive in the community.

Dad shared my love of cars and always looked forward to April when I came from Sudbury to take my car out of storage. He was in his 70s at the time and accompanied me to whatever barn I had my Trans Am stored for the winter. He would wear his winter parka and knitted toque and watch as I dug away the snow in front of the barn doors and chipped away the ice. My trips down to retrieve my car were always a big deal for both of us.

I'd put the battery back in and hook up the cables. Then I'd fire up the motor and pull the car out of the garage. Dad would climb in and the first thing he would say is, "Do you want to take the T-roof off?"

Had I agreed with his suggestion, he probably would have had the T-roof off, the windows down, but the heater on. The last week in April, Canada is not yet warm, so that would not have been a smart move, though I had done it before. So, I would say "No," and Dad would reply, "Well, let's go somewhere where I can buy you something for the car."

As I've said, Dad never had much money, but was blessed with a huge heart and was generous nonetheless. "Okay, Dad," I would say as we headed to a parts store, Canadian Tire. Invariably, I bought one of those 99 cent Christmas tree pine air fresheners and hang that on the mirror. Dad would give me a dollar for it. He felt good about it and so did I. It became a tradition between us.

After picking up the air freshener, my dad and I would ride around enjoying those first hints of spring and each other's company.

When my son took over the car a few years later, he cleaned it out and told me, "Dad, I can't believe how many air fresheners there were under your seat. It smelled like a pinery when I opened the door."

Shane didn't realize how they got there. It was a commitment that my dad had made. It was part of the bond between us, and brought back pleasant memories, which my son realizes today. He has a great love for his grandfather and has been blessed enough to remember him as a young boy.

After I quit drinking, I felt a need to tell Dad how much I loved him when I was a little boy. A counselor I knew at the time suggested that I write him letters but that I write them left-handed. The object was to slow down my thinking. Having to focus on printing with my wrong hand, she said, would enable me to write at the speed of my emotions, not my thinking.

This turned out to be a brilliant idea, and for the next couple years, Dad and I exchanged letters, me pouring out my feelings to him, laboriously printing like a six-year old trying to master the motor skill of writing, and my dad replying in his somewhat shaky hand. We never talked about it when we met or spoke on the phone; these were special communications we shared only with the written word. Writing gave us a solitude to express things we might not otherwise do in person. Dad wrote me about his life and his insecurities, success and failures. He also wrote about his steadfast love for his children. I kept all Dad's letters and they remain among my most precious possessions.

Then, on January 7, 1994, I received a voice mail from a girl I had a crush on in high school. She was now a nurse working at a hospital in Clinton. Hearing her name, my curiosity was piqued. Perhaps this was a message of love I longed for many years ago. As she continued talking, it became clear that the message was one of love, all right, but on another level. "If you want to see your dad alive, you better come home now," she said.

I dropped what I was doing, climbed into my car and drove eight hours to Clinton. It was a stormy night, but I would not be dissuaded. I arrived around 3:00 a.m. and went directly to the hospital. Dad was by himself in a room, dark except for the dim glow of a night light. He was dying. His breathing was shallow and faint.

"Hi, Dad. I'm here," I said.

"Allan," he said weakly and with much difficulty, "I love you. I knew you would come."

He took my thumb as I sat next to his bed. We didn't say much more. An air of finality pervaded the room, but it meant so much to me that I could be with my dad one last time and I sensed that it meant a lot to him as well. I sat there with him silently for a while and then took my leave so he could rest. The next morning, Dad passed away peacefully.

When I returned to his room, I saw my picture on the bed table at the far side of the bed. Dad or Mary must have placed it there when he was admitted to the hospital. Then, next to the picture, I noticed a bundle wrapped with a blue ribbon. I stepped to the other side of the bed and picked up the bundle. There were all the letters I had written to him five years earlier. He had saved every one and tied them up with a blue ribbon. As sad as the moment was, those letters signified that there was really nothing left to say between Dad and myself.

I have kept the letters and I cut a piece of that blue ribbon and tied it to my suitcase. I reconnect to my father every time I pick it up. I have

My dad, wearing his new Christmas sweater, about a week before he passed away.

to add though, that I have had much better luck reconnecting with Dad than I have with the nurse who made the phone call.

I think a lot about my father and mother and what a great relationship I had with both of them in the last years that they had on this earth. The bond I had with them was profound and beneficial because of all the tribulations that we had as a family. Hard work, effort, open-mindedness but especially forgiveness really brought us closer together.

My sister Bernice and I now have a beautiful relationship. For quite a few years, we lived in our own worlds. She had a young family. She was a teacher. I had my mining. I was a family man and we never saw each other very much. I feel bad today because sometimes I would go home to visit my parents and be drinking at night or go partying when my sister wanted to visit with me. Sometimes I'd be back home and only stop in to see her on a Sunday morning briefly before I drove back to Sudbury. I have since talked to her about that. I was young and foolish and didn't consider the relationship with her and never thought to tell her how much I care for her and love her and her family. I didn't show that in a very positive way when I was drinking. We never had words. It's just I never had much of an interaction with my sister. We do today and that is another blessing for which I am eternally grateful.

Bernice has told me on numerous occasions the importance of standing up to my mother and how that was the beginning of a much higher level of respect.

"You are the lucky one, Allan," Bernice said. "You got to deal with your demons with Mom."

I'll end this chapter by asking simply this, "What blue ribbon letters do you need to write to people in your life?"

CHAPTER 33

The Indispensability of Mentors

Whatever you can do or dream you can, begin it.
Boldness has genius, power and magic in it. Begin it now.
—Goethe

In 1996, I carried on with fairly regular attendance at AA meetings. Jim continued as my sponsor, though it had evolved into more of a very close friendship. He introduced me to a diverse circle of friends called the Mastermind Group. Every Friday morning, they met and discussed ideas from the famous book *Think and Grow Rich* by Napoleon Hill.

Still a perennial bestseller more than 70 years after it was first published, Think and Grow Rich contains the fundamentals of success that Hill distilled from interviewing some 500 of the most successful men of the day, a project he launched at the behest of industrialist and philanthropist Andrew Carnegie. Jim had observed my changes and the way I was reaching for new things in my life. He noticed my earnestness, my sobriety and my way of making things happen. So, he invited me into the group and I still maintain close contact with some of the people I met there.

Hill defined a master mind as "coordination of knowledge and effort, in a spirit of harmony, between two or more people, for the attainment of a definite purpose." Carnegie attributed the fortune he accumulated to the power generated by the staff of 50 men he surrounded himself with for the purpose of manufacturing and marketing steel. The combined intelligence of these 50 minds formed what Carnegie termed a "master mind" and Mastermind Groups began to form after publication of *Think and Grow Rich*.

Upon Jim's invitation, I became interested in the game of Mastermind and moving forward. I heeded the advice in the saying, "If you find that you are the smartest person in the group, then get a new group," and I had found a new one. There were around 12 to 15 of us in the group. Some were from AA. Some were from the Steelworkers Union and some were from management at INCO. Others were business people from the community. All of us had one thing in common: we were like-minded people seeking to better ourselves.

I retained my vision of becoming a motivational speaker and kept asking the God of my understanding, "How will I accomplish this? God, keep me open to new ideas, and as opportunities present themselves I will do whatever it takes to become a motivational speaker."

Having five years of sobriety is great, having even one day of sobriety is wonderful, but just having sobriety I didn't believe constituted enough success to give me sufficient credibility as a motivational speaker. People quit drinking every day, and that is a magnificent accomplishment. However, what is or *was* important in my case was not the fact that I quit, it's the fact of what I've done with the opportunities that have presented themselves since I quit. In my mind, quitting was just the catalyst for the change, quitting was not the change itself.

During this period, I was still working at the Creighton Mine amphitheater making presentations to miners before their shifts. I had great latitude in my work. It was gratifying to be trusted. I covered two mines simultaneously, the Creighton Mine and Crean Hill Mine, which was at another complex. My work was well received by the general office.

I was invited one day to the manager's meeting after Jim Ashcroft, the president of INCO Canada, heard me speak at the general office.

He asked me to attend the manager's meeting and I enthusiastically accepted. I went to my manager at the mine and told him what had happened and he said, "You sit beside me and I will take care of you. How come he invited you?"

"I have no idea," I said, "but I just wanted to tell you that I would be there."

I attended the manger's meeting, and the president told the managers of the different complexes about my work in the alcohol and drug office at EAP and about my training. Later, some people told me that he did that to give the go ahead for other managers to use me.

Some of the lessons to which I was exposed at my Friday morning Mastermind Group meetings had direct application to my role as a trainer. One of these was to under-promise and then over-deliver or, in other words, to go the extra mile.

Today, I still think of this when people come to any classroom where I deliver training. It may be the first time they have ever gone to a training seminar or it may be the only time. As trainers, we tend to become accustomed to a lifestyle of training especially when we are traveling to different companies or unions, and we can fall into a routine. For those who are receiving the training however, it may be the one time in their working lives that they will do a two day or week long training program, and they will definitely remember it. I always wanted them to remember the training as a positive experience. Under-promise and over-deliver.

When I conducted seminars at the union hall in Sudbury, I made sure to have both coffee and literature available in the morning. I went in at nighttime to set things up and people used to tease me that I slept and lived in the union hall. I was given a key and a pass to get in so I could do this preparation work. I would also come in an hour and a half before the class started. When people walked in I would welcome them and shake their hands. I didn't use name tags because I wanted everybody to know each other's names. I employed exercises to ensure that and my name recognition as a facilitator became as well-known as my recognition for being the guy who cleaned up that sand plant a few years earlier.

Not only did I study books on motivation, I thoroughly digested them. If you were to page through a copy of any of my books, you would see writing in the margins throughout. I highlight phrases and quotations and then write my thoughts in the margins and when finished, I put that book away. Books are the best teachers I have ever had because they are patient with me and there are so many lessons in them, but presented in a subtle, understated way. I put a book away for a couple years and when I take it up again, I can read two books at once: the book written as it was and the book as I digested it in the first reading.

Another thing I liked about this very eclectic Mastermind Group was that we took turns being chair of the meeting. We each had different topics to discuss pertaining to *Think and Grow Rich*. I belonged to that group for four years; some came, some left, others got what they came for and departed, but I became one of the core. Jim had essentially taken over this group and worked hard to ensure it was in a good position to help each of us.

We each had our individual goals for the month or for the week and we talked about these at the meetings. Then, during the week we'd call each other up and say, "Hey, how are you doing with your goals?" or "How can I help you?" If I had to write a paper for a university class, for example, someone would call and ask, "How is your paper coming along?" and that was enough to put me back on track and motivate me to do my best job on it. It was all done through the power of love.

One man in our group had a health issue, and as a consequence, his facial muscles were permanently constricted and he had, what I call a crooked smile. He was a financial genius and a superb motivational speaker.

He once told me, "Allan, I'm so scared to get up and speak in public because I have such a crooked smile. I'm scared to smile."

I thought about that for a couple of weeks. At a later group meeting, I said, "Peter, here's a tagline for you: 'Hi, I'm Peter. I'm the man with the crooked smile but the straight facts.'"

That was more than 10 years ago and Peter motivates people with learning disabilities and encourages independent living to groups that are challenged in some way. He does a great job and still uses that line I gave him. He tells people, "Proclaim Your Rarity." To me, that means to express the three things that people want to know about you:

1) Who are you?

2) What do you bring to the table? and

3) Why should we care?

That signature line of Peter's covers all three.

Once Peter mentions his crooked smile, his audience rests easy because they understand, "Wow, he recognizes this and he's not afraid to talk about it."

After the Mastermind Group digested *Think and Grow Rich,* we brought in other books. Each person could bring in a book, talk about it at the meeting and introduce it to others. I met someone through a friend who was on the board of the Templeton Foundation founded by Sir John Templeton. I brought in one of his books. Templeton was an icon in financial planning, but he also had spiritual aspects to his writing. I wrote him a letter about my life and how it had changed and thanked him for his writing skills, and he sent me an entire collection of his books, all autographed, with a very nice letter!

When I was working in the EAP office as a volunteer, Bob had a book on his desk called *Mission Success,* by Og Mandino. That book changed me profoundly. It was an easy read, and I liked his stories of how he overcame his struggles and went from rags to riches. At the back of that book there was a five or six page epilogue called "The Seeds of Success." At the time, I didn't have enough money to buy the book, so I hand wrote out "The Seeds of Success" in its entirety. Then I made a commitment to read them every morning for the next five years. I figured that would carry me past my five-year anniversary of sobriety. I carried those tattered papers in my lunch pail, carried them wherever I went and every morning, I took 10 minutes to read them. I still have those papers and they helped me considerably. The passage from which I quote here, expresses so beautifully what I attempted to do then and still do today—live one day at time and live it fully:

"I will face the world with goals set for this day, but they will be attainable ones, not the vague, impossible variety declared by those who make a career of failure. I realize that you always try me with a little, first, to see what I would do with a lot.

"I will never hide my talents. If I am silent, I am forgotten, if I do not advance, I will fall back. If I walk away from any challenge today, my self-esteem will be forever scarred, and if I cease to grow, even a little, I will become smaller. I reject the stationary position because it is always the beginning of the end."

I have most of Og Mandino's writings today. Around my 10th anniversary of sobriety, I wrote him to say how great an impact he had on my life. He replied with a note wishing me continued success as well as some autographed editions. It was wonderful of him to acknowledge my letter. It impressed me that a man of his stature would take the time to write letters and that is a lesson I have adopted. I strongly believe in the personal touch and taking the time out to write handwritten notes to people.

Some of the people in my Mastermind Group were attending Amway motivational seminars, and one morning as I was leaving to drive to Toronto to visit a friend, Jim said, "Al, here is a cassette tape I think you would like."

It was a 40 minute tape by a motivational speaker I had never heard of before named Les Brown. I made the four-hour trek down to Toronto and was utterly captivated by the sound of his voice. As I plugged the cassette into my tape deck, Les' message of hope plugged into my soul.

The name of the speech was "It Is Not Over Until You Win." He delivered it to a large audience at the Georgia Dome, and that talk literally gave me goose bumps. I played it over and over and over and over so often in my spare time, driving home from the union hall, driving back from making presentations at the mine, coming home from AA meetings, that the tape finally snapped. I still have that broken tape in my office and I will never throw that cassette away. I firmly believe that it fast tracked me in my progress and brought me to where I am today. I recently learned that I was supposed to have listened to the tape and then pass it on to another Mastermind Group member. I still owe him that tape!

Little did I realize that one day I would travel with Les Brown and become friends with him. I joined his speaking bureau, and he has opened doors for me which, when opened a crack, I was able to push all the way open. That all stemmed from the Mastermind group in 1996 in Sudbury when Jim said, "Here Al, here is one of my favorite motivational speakers, I think you will enjoy it." I am ever so grateful to Jim for his friendship and his support.

As my personal and professional life progressed, I began to establish a foundation for my life in motivational speaking: all the seminars that I took gave me the right to teach. I did health and safety training. I attended seminars on stress and many other courses besides my studies at the university.

In 1998, Bob retired from the EAP office and I began working there full time. For the previous six years, I had worked there as needs arose, but now I was there every day. Between then and 2002, I did tours of the other mine sites. In fact, the first thing I did was to tour every mine site and tell the people there on each shift that I needed their help to make the union's employee assistance program as valuable to the union and the members as it could be. The pay was much less than I made underground since there was no overtime or bonuses. The rewards however, were gratifying. My office helped many men into rehab and found sponsors for them from the union ranks and elsewhere.

In 1999, I began working part of the time in Pittsburgh, Pennsylvania. From then until 2005, I travelled between Pittsburgh and Sudbury, teaching communication skills in a leadership program while still running the EAP office in Sudbury. To help handle the work load in Sudbury, I brought in Don D. in 2002.

The International USW headquarters office in Pittsburgh had established what they called the Leadership Scholarship Program. Union members came from all over to attend a one week leadership training program and then returned home to implement what they learned. If they did well, they were invited back the following year for more training. The man who was my predecessor in the program had an opportunity to retire in 1999 and the international union headquarters asked me to come to Pittsburgh and teach public speaking and communication skills, an unbelievable request considering my background.

About half the people who came to lead seminars or to direct training were from academia, while the other half were off the shop floor. I made myself indispensable as the go-to guy for any logistical or administrative matters. I became known for my work ethic and delivered personal training as well. I much preferred the personal touch to a didactic approach, which is often aloof.

Having found mentors to help me in my own life, I opened up the program to staff training. I taught mentoring and life coaching courses and became well-versed in the art of facilitation and interactive education, but did not lecture.

In the mine, safety trainers came to lecture us about safety issues. This was back in the days of overhead projectors with transparencies.

CHAPTER 33 - THE INDISPENSABILITY OF MENTORS

The first thing I looked for as I sat in the audience was how many transparencies they had brought so I would know how long they planned to talk at, and sometimes down, to us. Our eyes would glaze over and develop the trout look, the eyes-glazed-over, mouth-open look.

I didn't want to be part of that adult educational model. I wanted to be part of something that was interesting and interactive. When I stand up in front of a group seminar today and talk about life experiences, I only have my own life to look at. However, when you add up the experience in years among the people there, sometimes there's 400, 500, 1,000, 2,000 years of wisdom in the room. So, why not tap into that?

Union leadership gave me the responsibility for teaching public speaking, which became extremely successful and a great deal of fun. It was truly memorable to come into a roomful of people in the morning who were scared of public speaking and witness the transformation in only a few hours. One of the benefits of living my life the way I had was that I could relate to them. I even disclosed my oral composition story. I never laughed at them and never thought that their fear wasn't real. Four hours into the module, they would stand and give a one or two minute impromptu speech and then talk about it and about their fears and experiences. It's wonderful to be in a classroom and see the lights come on in a person's eyes when they say, "Man, I can do that!" That in itself is worth all the evenings of preparation.

While I was working in the Creighton Amphitheater as part of my EAP involvement, I wrote a five-day stress seminar, which took me about 3 years to assemble. I was inspired to do it by the number of people coming into the Employees Assistance Program who were under severe stress. They were about to be fired for various reasons or were getting divorced, and I thought it would be a good idea to put together a program for them. I did extensive research and attended many stress seminars myself. I picked out subjects relating to stress and read about them and put together a program that the United Steelworkers adopted. It ran for five days and we introduced it at our District conferences.

It focused on the three areas of stress: social stress, organizational stress and physical stress. Physical stressors would be, for example, noise in the workplace or the poor lighting in the mine. Dust, gas, working in smelters and steel mills were forms of physical stress. For public work crews or road construction crews, snowplowing the highways in winter with traffic whizzing by constitutes stresses for them, and these are forms that are not normally considered.

Organizational stressors are factors such as shift work, mandatory overtime, or even part-time work, where the company doesn't have to pay benefits, which forces people to work two jobs to make ends meet. Working a night shift for seven days in a row and then moving to afternoons and then back to nights causes stress; the body's rhythms are thrown off and tires from all this shift work and has a hard time adapting.

Social stressors are another form. Statistics from a few years ago in Ontario showed that people spent 17% more than their income. In other words, they were piling up debt at a considerable rate. If I don't receive five or six unsolicited advertisements a week for more credit cards, free flights, free rooms, offers to consolidate debt on my email account, it is an unusually light week for spam.

Today, it is so easy to be caught in the web of debt. There are also the social stressors of keeping up with the Joneses. You don't want to have a car that doesn't fit your neighborhood.

I discovered that approximately 52% of first marriages do not succeed, 76% of second marriages do not succeed, but I have wonderful news: 93% of third marriages are blissful because, by then, the couples don't have any money left and are tired.

I didn't call my program "Stress Management," I called it "Stress

Awareness," and by now you can tell why. Possibly, it is the stressors in our environment of which we are not aware that can have the most negative effects on our health, our relationships, our work and our lives.

Through my work, I became increasingly involved in activities that would soon bring my life full circle with alcoholism.

BREAKING THROUGH

CHAPTER 34

RETURNING THE FAVOR

Hope is the thing with feathers
that perches in the soul
And sings the tune without the words
And never stops at all
—EMILY DICKINSON

IN 1993, BOTH THE UNITED STEELWORKERS AND INCO asked me to facilitate my stress awareness seminar. For the company, I held a day-long seminar every two weeks in the union hall classroom. For the USW, I held a week-long seminar twice a year in an educational setting outside Toronto. I would drive there, spend a week and administer the training. It was an interactive workshop called Finding Your Balance that taught how to live a life that has more meaning and experience less burnout. Believe you me, I felt qualified not only to write the seminar but to deliver it. I had lived 90% of the material!

As I was coming downstairs to the classroom one day, the Director of a national labor union said to me, "An employee of mine has a very, very serious addiction to alcohol. What could you do to help me?"

"First of all," I replied, "we'd have to set up an employee's assistance program for your union."

We sat down for a week and created an employee assistance program like the joint venture between the union and management at INCO. He brought his staff down to a training center. I spent two days figuring out how they would implement a progressive discipline system. This program would be helpful for people with addiction issues and the behaviors that stem from those.

I stressed that you have to love the person but hate the addiction. People with problems are not problem people. They are people with problems. Our job is to separate the two and find the root cause of the problem.

About a year later, the director called me again. "We have this one man who's in trouble," he said.

The trouble was alcoholism and he went on, "He's gone through procedures and the progressive disciplinary system. I remember that I once asked you what we could do to help this man."

"I'll go see him," I said.

I had a plane ticket in my hand that night and flew half way across Canada to meet the man in his home town. As I was flying out, his boss called him and explained that Al McDougall, on behalf of the organization, was coming to meet with him. Al was representing the organization on behalf of the Director, he was told, and was going to meet with him to help with his problems and to arrive at some decisions. The employee was told that he didn't have to quit drinking but if he didn't, there were other choices that he would have to make, such as retirement, or taking long-term disability, or whatever those options were. I would be there for seven days only to help this individual make some sound decisions.

I landed and headed to my hotel. Because the Director told him where I was staying, there was a red light flashing on my telephone when I arrived at my room. I wondered who that could be because no one knew where I was. Then I gave a little smile and thought to myself, "I could really relate to his fear and anxiety and being out of control." There was a voice mail saying, "Hi, my name is so-and-so, and I understand you're here to meet with me. Let's go for coffee."

We arranged to meet the next morning, and the first thing the man said to me was, "I don't think I have a problem with drinking. My two daughters just finished university with nursing degrees and we all visited Disney World as a family last year."

In his mind, he didn't have a problem so long as he could function as a father, pay the bills for his daughters to go to university, and as a family unit, have a vacation.

He hadn't descended to the level of whatever he imagined that an alcoholic was. His was the same as my definition of an alcoholic: someone who lays in ditches and flophouses.

"Listen, young man," I said, "I'm not here to determine if you're an alcoholic. Only you can determine that. I'm just here, on behalf of your employer, to talk about some of your work habits and how your personal life is affecting that. So, let's go to an AA meeting tonight and..."

Beforehand, I had contacted Alcoholics Anonymous in his city to find out where the meetings were and which ones were open meetings. The particular one I located was a closed discussion meeting.

We have different types of meetings in AA. We have closed discussion, which is members only. We have open speaker meetings, which are open to the public where a speaker talks about their experiences, strengths and hopes. We have different agendas at different meetings. They are all beneficial; it depends on what you want, or what you feel your need is at a particular time.

That night, we went to a meeting and John, as I will call him, was not very happy. I let John do all the work. John had to pick me up at my hotel and drive to the meeting in the pouring rain. It was mountainous, high hill country.

It's funny now. We both laugh about it, but he wasn't laughing that night, and I certainly wasn't laughing in the car with him. We were driving up some steep and winding roads with sheer cliffs overlooking the ocean. It was pitch black and heavy rain pelted the windshield. I looked out the side window and there was a big drop below, about 2000 feet.

"Hey, John," I said, "I bet you wish you could just stop this car and push me out the door over this cliff."

He just looked and me and said, "How did you know that?" Then he started to laugh, which broke the tension.

It's one thing to be honest and another to have gone through another person's experience already. You can put yourself right into his or her brain, emotions and shoes and be right with them. Nothing can buy that except experience. Textbooks can't buy it, which reminds me of an old saying, "You can't con a con."

We made it to the meeting and walked in. John moved as far away from me as he could to the other side of the room. In an AA meeting, everybody says, "Hi, my name is so-and-so, and I'm an alcoholic." Except John who said, from the far side of the room, in a low voice, "Hi, my name is John. I'm here because Al's here."

I thought that was hilarious and quick thinking on his part. Was he telling people that he was forced to be there because I was there? Or was he telling people that he brought me to the meeting because I needed help? I still smile when I think of that dark, wet, stormy night driving through the mountains.

I took away his company vehicle, company telephone and office key. I made him hand each of these over to me as a sign that this was really happening. I've discovered more through my own instincts than any textbook that you make more of an impression when the person has to physically give up something.

The next night, we were driving in his personal car to another meeting. I looked down and noticed a brand of whiskey advertised on a little plastic tag on his key ring. "Hey, John," I said, "I bet, just looking at you, that you enjoy Canadian Club."

That was the name on his key ring.

He turned ashen and blurted out, "My God, how did you know that?"

"I can just tell. I just know," I said nonchalantly. "I can see into people." I withheld from him for five years how I knew.

When doing an intervention, it's important to be cognizant of the surroundings. When I go into people's offices and talk to them about their problems, I look at the desk. I look at their walls. I see what is important to them. If it's old cars, for example, I get into the subject of cars. If it's sports memorabilia on the wall, I talk about the sport. I don't do this when I first go in, but later on in the conversation, I try to lower the tension a little bit, depending on how it is going.

My intervention style is to go in and for the first two or three days of the week, I give the person some options. I'm with the person and his or her family a lot those first days. I introduce myself to the family, and explain why I'm here. About the fourth day, I don't go near them. I let them have two days to think about it. However, my phone line is always open. I don't call them, but they are free to call me. I want to give them a break. My only contact is to arrange an AA meeting each night of the week.

I don't necessarily tell them I will be out of their life for two days. Maybe they are expecting something. Sometimes they aren't. For two days though, I leave them. This gives them some time to reflect and be with their families. They've also had some time to digest their options.

Believe me, they are all in denial. The denial, the anger, the sadness, the giving up the strongest relationship they ever had, which is alcohol, begins to churn inside them.

Sometimes they get angry. Sometimes they become resentful. Finally though, they come to some sort of acceptance. It takes time though.

A person can experience two or three of these elements at once. It doesn't always occur the way it is written up in textbooks.

Then, when I spend time with them during the last three days, I say, "I have a plane ticket for you to Ontario, where I live, for you to go into an in-house rehab, which is the one I went to. I can only talk about the one that I had personal experience with. It's your choice if you want to come. I'll meet you at the airport and we'll fly back together."

Usually, that statement generates extensive debate. "What happens if I don't go?" they ask.

I give them their employer's decision. "Well, if you don't go, these are some of your options."

This isn't a forceful confrontation. It's always suggestive, but it's leading as well, and I make sure that they know exactly what will happen if they decide to continue with their current lifestyle. That could include an early retirement or a long-term disability pension. Each case is different.

The day before we left, I told him, "Listen, John, your flight is at 7:00 in the morning. You meet me at the airport." Again, I put the onus on him to make the effort.

I said, "I'll be at the airport tomorrow, if you're there, that's fine, John, and if you're not that's also fine. These are your decisions."

I treated him with respect and dignity. I never want to let myself forget that I'm there to assist the person and his family. I'm also there to assist the organization, but never at the expense of the individual's dignity and respect. I've always said, "Never put someone in a corner without leaving them a doorway out to save face, because they're really hurting."

The next morning, I didn't know if John would be at the airport, but my instincts said he would be. His family brought him. John and I boarded the plane and flew back to Ontario. We drove four hours to the rehabilitation center and I helped him register. I spent the morning with him, made sure he was comfortable and then I left. I came back to visit twice a week. I had visiting rights because I'm the one who referred him and because of my EAP background. I'm also a past graduate of that facility. I can drive up and talk to the counselors as well. John had to sign release forms that I would be privy to some of his information. I didn't want to know all the facts and incidents of his life at the time, I just wanted to know how he was progressing over a period of a week or two.

John stayed for the 28-day program. They had a graduation the last morning to celebrate his success, which I attended. He talked about some of his experiences. Afterwards, I drove him to the airport. He boarded the plane and flew home to his family and his job.

While he was in the treatment center, I contacted the Alcoholics Anonymous inter-group and their counseling agencies in his home city and set him up with counseling. I also found a temporary sponsor to spend time with him for three or four months after his return to work. The organization gave him a few weeks off so he could readjust to his new world and the new ideas being presented to him, as well as give him time with his family.

John had to file a progress report with me. I acted on behalf of his CEO and kept myself informed of how he was doing in counseling and how many meetings he attended a week. I didn't take only his word for it; I talked to his sponsor as well.

I did a follow up visit with John three months later and did so every three months for a year. John has done very, very well. He hasn't had a desire to drink since way back in 1995. I'm extremely proud of him, but really, it is John's success, not mine.

I cannot take credit for someone else's success, much the same as I can't take the "blame" for someone else's choice to continue on with the same lifestyle and perhaps end up in an institution or die. I'm only a catalyst or an opportunist who has been sent to interrupt a person's life, to distract the person's thinking and make him or her look at their decisions and how these are having an impact on their lives and their families' lives.

John and I remained in touch, and on his fifth anniversary of sobriety, he asked me to come out to speak at his Alcoholics Anonymous group. This was held every Sunday at the local university amphitheater.

"Absolutely, I'll come," I said.

When I spoke at the meeting, I didn't talk about John's experience, I talked about Allan's experience, which is the only one I'm qualified to relate. John introduced me to the audience of around 200 by saying, "Five years ago, I met this man. I detested the ground he walked on. Today, I invited him back and I bless the ground he walks on."

What a magnificent testimony to a story of redemption and someone being able to change their life from detesting it to blessing it.

Some time after I first met John, the same director asked me to conduct another intervention. A vice-president had the same problem with alcohol.

Same scenario: I flew out, and arrived in town about 9 p.m. When I arrived at my hotel room, the red light on the phone was blinking. He knew what time my flight landed. I waited an hour and you can bet the phone was ringing, but I purposely didn't answer it. I finally picked it up on the 7th or 8th call and introduced myself, asked who it was and how he was doing. He told me "It's Jim. I'll be right in to see you."

He was pretty drunk by this time. Jim was a professional negotiator, and he was trying to negotiate the seven days of my life that I was about to spend in town with him and his family. The only problem was there was no negotiation on my part. I was there with pure intent and focus, not there to negotiate.

"No, no, Jim, you're not," I told him. "I've had a busy day. I've been in airports and planes all day. I'm tired. I'll see you in the morning and you get a good night's sleep."

"I'll be over to see you," he persisted.

"I won't be here," I repeated. "I'm locking my door and going to bed."

"Okay," he said, resignedly, "I'll see you at 7:00 a.m."

"No, I'll see you at 9:00."

"No, I'll meet you at 7:00," he insisted.

"Okay, how about 8 o'clock?" I offered.

"Great," said Jim. He thought he had won something and he had. He now had a bright spot in his life, whereas he'd been totally drunk for the last 7 or 8 days. "I'll meet you in your room."

"No, Jim, I'll meet you in the lobby."

"No, no, I'll meet you in your room."

"Okay, that's fine, Jim. I'll meet you at 8 o'clock up in my room at the hotel."

At 7:30 the next morning, I was outside having breakfast on the deck and at five minutes to 8:00, I saw Jim, who was a short man, taking giant six foot strides towards the elevator. I let him go past me. He didn't recognize me, since we'd only ever seen each other when I originally set up the employee assistance program with his director some time earlier.

Suddenly, I said, "Hey, Jim, what are you doing?"

I caught him off guard and he was bewildered. He had been drinking all night and blurted out, "Let's sit down here and talk."

"No," I countered, "but I'll go for a walk." So, we went for a walk. If I had my life to live over I would like to have been a hostage negotiator.

I explained why I was there. He already knew and said, "I'm not staying around here. I'm leaving. I'm going home. I don't need to talk to you. I'm calling my boss."

"I'm here on behalf of your boss," I told him, "and the boss is not taking your calls this week. I'm your boss."

Jim jumped in his car and, as I walked across the parking lot to go back to the room, he tried to run me down. His car roared up behind me, and I jumped between two vehicles, as he whooshed by, missing me by inches. I called the regional office of the company and asked for one of the partners to pick me up and drop me off at Jim's house.

"Absolutely not!" I was told. "He has a lot of fire power. He's got a machine gun in his garage. He's crazy when he's drinking. I won't drop you off and I suggest you not go in there, either." He refused to go up Jim's driveway.

"Okay, drop me off at the shoulder of the road close to his house," I said.

He dropped me off by the mailbox and I walked up the lane, knowing full well that Jim had a machine gun on a tripod in his garage. He was a gun collector. I walked up to the front door, stood off to one side and knocked.

"Jim, it's me, Allan."

He began hollering and screaming at me from inside.

"I'm not going away. You might as well let me come in."

He continued to holler and curse, but finally let me in. He made a cup of tea for me while he continued drinking whiskey. The house was a mess. You can imagine that his mind was just as much a mess.

"I'm here to stay," I told him.

He responded with angry threats of violence.

"I need to take your car."

He threw me the keys.

"No, no, no, Jim, you need to empty out the vehicle. You need to empty it out first."

I had seen his car. He worked out of it and he had stacks of papers and a computer in there.

"You have to clean out your car and put the contents in the garage."

Then I said, "Hand over the cell phone and hand me the car keys. I'm taking the car and taking your cell phone."

This made him even wilder. He continued to drink, but at the end of an hour or so I said, "Okay, Jim, I'm ready to leave. I'm exhausted. I'm exhausted doing this work. It's draining. It's very demanding."

You have to be in the moment in these interventions. You have to be aware of your surroundings.

Within two hours of this man trying to run me down in the parking lot, I was driving his car. That brought a smile to my face. I drove it for the week I was there.

The next day, Jim called me and said, "I've invited you to the house for dinner to meet my family."

"That's great, Jim. I'll be out at 6 o'clock."

I drove out, and of course, he had been tapering off his drinking, but not much. He tried to be civil to me and had ordered $100.00 worth of Chinese food. There was tons of Chinese food that evening. I ate and talked to his wife. She was so happy that I was there. Jim's brother-in-law told me, "My God, we were praying for somebody to come."

So, I knew that there had been a problem and the conversation with his family confirmed my suspicions. After dinner, Jim went outside to have a cigarette saying, "Come outside with me and talk."

We went outside and he said, "Well, I hope you'll leave now."

"No, I'm going back to my hotel. Thanks for dinner, but I'm not leaving the community."

"I just paid $100.00 for Chinese food and you're still taking me to meetings and back to Ontario for a 28-day rehab?" (We had discussed this with his family during the meal.)

"No," I said. "That's your choice if you want to come back with me, and if it's not, you're certainly welcome to stay here."

At the end of the week, I called him up and said, "Your flight is tomorrow at 8:00 am."

"Well, you got my car. Aren't you picking me up?" he asked angrily.

"No. You have to find your own way."

"Well, that's a fine fucking how do you do!" he snorted.

The next morning, Jim got on the plane with me back to Ontario. He was restless and agitated during the flight.

"You know, I've never flown sober," he said sheepishly.

I bought him a drink or two on the plane to settle his nerves. I drove him to rehab and about two hours after his arrival, he had an alcoholic seizure. It was terrible. I wasn't there to witness it but the doctors told me what happened. What saved me from having an alcoholic seizure in 1987 was the amount of food I ate, my age and the hard work I did in the mines.

Jim stayed an extra week in the hospital before his treatment program could begin. I visited him, went to his graduation, drove him back to the airport, set up counseling, went to visit him 2 months later, then again a month after that and Jim stayed sober.

In another intervention, during a medical exam at the rehab center, the doctors found the man had brain cancer and six months to live. I persuaded the company to put him back on the payroll so his daughter could get life insurance and benefits until she was 21 years old so long as she remained in school.

One Thanksgiving, I was headed from the U.S. to Canada. As I approached the border crossing, for some reason, I switched into another lane. I pulled up to Customs, the inspector looked out and I handed her my papers. She asked, "Do you have any tobacco?"

"I do not," I answered.

"Do you have any alcohol?"

"I do not."

She looked at me, paused and then looked more intently at me and asked once more, "Are you sure you don't have any alcohol?"

Normally I don't tell people about my history with my addiction. But here I said, "No, I do not. I have not drank for 20-some years."

Her eyes welled up and she began to cry. Through her tears, she said, "I've been praying for someone to talk to about my son's drinking problem."

What a wonderful opportunity to serve people. I don't know what made me get into that lane. It doesn't matter, I just did. I was there for 10 or 15 minutes. We talked and I looked in the mirror because I was wondering how many arguments or potential divorces I was creating in the traffic jam behind me. I couldn't hear husbands or wives or whoever talking, but I could just about read their lips. "I knew you shouldn't have gone in this lane!" "I knew there was that other lane you should have taken!"

At the end of the 15 minutes, when I had the information about her son, she reached out and shook my hand before I drove away. I often wonder if people are still talking about that strange situation that happened at the border way back on that Sunday years ago. When you are open and you don't even know you're open, to simply follow your intuition or your gut or your heart, sometimes there's a better purpose being served.

Those are some of the experiences I have had helping people deal with their alcoholism. Though I work today as head of USW's Emergency Response Team, I am still called on to help people struggling with alcohol, and I do so without reservation. As I said to the God of my understanding sitting in rehab in 1987 when I first had the dream to be a motivational speaker, "I'm not sure how to do this but I'll do whatever it takes. You lead me in the right direction and introduce me to people I need to meet."

It was all part of my dream. You just do what you have to do. Les Brown says, "You have to do today what other people won't do today to have the things tomorrow that other people won't have."

The job I have today is working with families that have just gone through loss of a family member due to a workplace fatality. Dealing with their sorrow has been tremendously challenging, yet motivating and refreshing. I believe I have the best job in the world to be in people's homes at one of the lowest points in their lives. They're reaching out for help and I'm there for them and they trust me to do my best.

I relate these stories only to demonstrate that change is possible. No matter the condition, something can be done about it. My life is a testimony to that. At one time, I was buried under emotional rubble at the bottom of an abandoned mine shaft still looking down on the rest of the world and sneering. If I saw a couple who looked like they had a loving relationship, I would think to myself, "They don't really mean it. They are cheating on the side or they beat each other at home when the doors are closed."

Once I realized that I needed to change however, help magically appeared. Goodhearted friends supported me with their kindness. Mentors came into my life with lessons that I applied to keep myself moving upwards.

Decency and willingness to help was around me all the time. I just needed to avail myself of it.

CHAPTER 35

REACHING FOR THE SPIRITUAL

*There's only one corner of the universe you can be certain of improving,
and that's your own self. So you have to begin there, not outside,
not on other people. That comes afterward, when you've
worked on your own corner.*
–ALDOUS HUXLEY

ONE OF THE THINGS I began doing right from the get go in my AA
meetings was to incorporate ideas that I was learning about and being
exposed to into my life. People mentioned books that helped them and
I would read those. People had certain behaviors and ways with dealing
with others that seemed to me to be positive, and I tried to emulate
these and make them my own. I looked for habits that were positive
and adopted them.

Again, I am a firm believer that anyone can own an idea. You can
take something you have heard or read or been told and adopt it as
your own. Try it out and see if it works for you. That is really the only
thing that matters. Does it work and more importantly, does it work
for you?

I begged people to show me different avenues of living and borrowed
ideas that I never thought of. I stole from people's minds and hearts
to claw, scratch and dig myself out from my personal cave-in that felt
deeper than any mine shaft I had ever entered.

After I had been sober for about 6 months, I overheard someone
talking about "retreats" so, of course, I became curious. At the time,
I was intently focused on fast-tracking my sobriety, so the idea of a

retreat appealed to me. I wanted everything yesterday, I didn't have the patience that I do today, and I wanted people to trust in me that I had quit drinking. I wanted to do all the work I could do as fast as I could do it. I was doing a great deal of philosophic, religious and spiritual study on the subject of self.

A Jesuit retreat house in the Sudbury area, called La Villa Loyola, set aside two weekends a year for AA member retreats. Some 30 or 40 AA members would convene there for a weekend.

There was a retreat master who coordinated the retreat, and it was a weekend to get together and talk about, primarily, the first five steps of AA. Also, to reflect upon how our lives had become unmanageable because of alcohol, how we came to believe that a power greater than ourselves could restore us to sanity, and so on. A retreat is a good time to get away and reflect.

Periods of silence for reflection and meditation were scheduled between guided seminars. A typical schedule would be to arise early in the morning, have breakfast, go back to the room for quiet time and read inspirational literature. Then, come out at 9:30 for the first 45-minute session, where somebody would discuss the first step of AA and how they applied it in their day-to-day living. A half-hour break followed which gave us time to reflect and do some writing. This pattern repeated twice in the morning and twice again in the afternoon.

Retreats were always on the weekends, so on Friday night we began with an opening session. On Saturday we had four seminars, and on Saturday night we'd have an AA meeting where people were selected to speak for five minutes at a time about why the retreat was meaningful to them. We would reconvene Sunday morning for an interdenominational church service and another closing seminar and leave for home at noon. It was always a very refreshing quiet time and I attended every year for the first 10 or 12 years of my sobriety. My schedule doesn't seem to allow for it now, but I do miss them.

I decided to use the occasion of that first retreat to do a juice fast. Where this idea came from I don't know. I went to the organic health food store and told the clerk what I was planning and he said, "Well, okay. Why don't you pick some juice, nothing from concentrate, pick some organic juice and do your fast."

I bought three quarts of sauerkraut juice because I liked sauerkraut as a kid. I had no idea what sauerkraut juice did to the human body, and I know some of you reading this are way ahead of me, but please remember I had been sober only six months and the fog hadn't lifted to a degree that I knew what I was doing.

I went to the retreat on Friday night. I didn't tell anybody that I had the secret to enlightenment in my duffle bag, just like I used to with booze. I was hiding this secret seed to fast-track success. That night, I drank a whole quart of sauerkraut juice. Now, the Jesuit retreat houses where I've been are very spartan. They don't have toilets in every room, so we had what I call a common throne room.

All day Saturday, I was in the common throne room. I knew it was a very spiritual retreat, because I was surely purged. The other indicator it was spiritual was because people kept coming in saying, "Oh, my God, who died in here?" I had a pair of LA Gear running shoes that had lime green trim and were very recognizable. Being the modest man that I am, when I heard the door open, I would lift my feet so no one knew who was in there having this spiritual experience.

The experience from that first retreat did not dampen my interest in their value, however. I found them very beneficial. I talked a lot on my retreats and always booked some time with a Jesuit father. I was raised in the Protestant United Church, not Catholic. My seeking out a Jesuit priest had nothing to do with the AA retreats. I just found that the Jesuits were very learned people.

I befriended one Jesuit priest during retreats over the years, and always took time to see him. One thing led to another in our conversations and he once asked me what books I was reading and what I was doing in my life and I told him.

He said, "I think a five-day silent retreat would be beneficial for you." I thought about it when I went home and the next time I came back, I asked him to tell me more about it.

"What you do," he said," is come to your regular weekend AA retreat, but when the other men go home on Sunday afternoon, you stay on until the next Friday. You would be in a room by yourself. You could leave to get your meals if you want, but you eat them in your room, or, if you are in a dining room, you eat at a table away from everybody else." He said that I could set it up however I wanted.

"Well," I said, "I would still like to continue to meet with you for 15 minutes every day in the morning with a question or two."

He agreed and that is how we continued. I was excited about the prospect. I had been sober for more than 10 years and I was really into changing my life (and still am today). My desire for change goes back to one of the original questions I had as I embarked on a life of sobriety, "Who am I?" It remains an ongoing quest as I evolve in my life.

That question really knotted me, not in a harmful manic way, but in an understated, powerful way. From Sunday school as a little boy, I remembered two things. One is the Biblical verse: "Ask, and it shall be given to you; seek, and ye shall find; knock, and it shall be opened unto you." The other is the ancient Greek phrase, "Know thyself."

Throughout my silent retreat, those quotations kept coming to the forefront of my mind. Every morning, I had 10 or 15 minutes with that Jesuit priest, and I asked him questions. Then, throughout the day, he would drop off articles, magazines or books on the topic of my question.

One day I asked him, "How can I become more open so I can fill myself with spirituality?"

"Allan," he answered, "if we knew how to do that, we'd fill it with something else. Just asking the question is enough."

I returned from that five day silent retreat feeling rested, focused and regrouped. I cannot tell you specifically what change occurred during the time; however, I can tell you that my life took off on a slow steady ramp upwards. A 20 percent grade ramp up, as we had in the mine. I continued to place one foot in front of the other, and life was very good to me. I became used to a normal day being an up day, not spectacularly up, just up. That was good enough for me.

I would suggest to anybody, whether in the AA program or not, to go on a retreat. There are all kinds of different retreats—for couples, for men, for women, and from my personal experience, they are very beneficial. Retreats offer ways to open up and jettison unnecessary mental, emotional or spiritual baggage. One final heartfelt suggestion: leave the sauerkraut juice at home. Trust me on this one!

Seminars were another avenue that I travelled down in search of recovery and growth. In 1991, I was at a seminar, the title of which was "Dying for Love." I thought that was a good title, "Dying for Love." Are we dying for love?

That seminar was about the issue of codependency and it resonated with me. I felt stuck during that period. I had just broken off a relationship and felt stuck.

At any rate, I followed up with the presenters of this seminar and attended a treatment center in Florida. I was there for 21 days, and they did psychological testing, health work and blood work on me. They talked about diet and about the harm that white flour and sugar do to a person's health. There were three sections at the treatment center: one for alcoholics, one for overeaters and one for codependents. I spent one week in the section for Alcoholics Anonymous and two weeks in the section for codependency.

Somewhere along the line, I learned about facing one's fears. One speaker I know talks about fear and says that anxiety occurs when facing one's fear. His formula to overcome this is to **F**ocus, **E**valuate, **A**ttitude and **R**espond. You have to: 1) focus on the problem, 2) evaluate it to see what the risk is, 3) determine your attitude, that is, what your mind is saying and 4) from there work out how to respond.

It brings to mind a little exercise to do with the word "attitude," and many reading this book may have heard about it.

First, write down the word "attitude" across a piece of paper. Underneath each letter, write the numerical order where it falls in the alphabet. For example: A is the first letter so that gets a 1, E is the fifth letter and gets a 5, etc. Fill in the other letters and then add them up and you will see how important attitude is. So, what kind of attitude are you bringing to the table? What's your intention? That's the bottom line: What's your intention when you perform an act?

Here is something I once read which succinctly and elegantly sums up the importance of attitude: "Attitude is the mind's paint brush. It can color a situation gloomy or gray, or cheerful and gay."

In an effort to find answers to questions that are important to me, I spent many hours in libraries and bookstores. In Sudbury, I had a Saturday morning routine: get up, have a little breakfast, go to the local Chapters bookstore, pick out a book that I heard someone recommend, go to the coffee shop, sit in a comfortable chair and read. It was a wonderful way to open my mind and enjoy a Saturday morning.

Another interest I developed during the early years of my sobriety and still have is astrology. However, it was at a deeper level than the daily horoscopes you find in the newspaper. I became very involved and had my chart drawn up with the exact date and time of my birth.

I wrote down the character traits of a Leo, both the positive and the negative. Then I did a self-assessment, something I learned during my time in the rehab center at Elliot Lake. I undertook a searching and fearless moral inventory of myself.

One of my mentors, Fred Flintstone, says, "You have to be you because everyone else is taken." I heard that on a cartoon show in the fog of a hangover when I was watching cartoons with my kids about 1978. I was lying on the couch with them one morning and I remember Fred saying to Barney Rubble, "Barney, you got to be you because everyone else is taken."

I was always interested in spirits, even the ones outside of a bottle, from my early days as a teenager in Auburn. I've gone to many psychics and they have played a role in my life. One of my friends said that he'd never met a man like me who, when he came to a crossroads in his life, would contact his higher power or higher self and consult with them and then move on to make sure that he was on the right spiritual path. My interpretation of that is he meant that I needed help for my self-esteem and assurance of moving forward with changes in my life. I knew I had to start believing in myself and my potential, but I couldn't see it myself. I had to learn how to find it.

Do you know what you bring with you? What's your potential? How many people reading this book have been told, "My God, I wish I had your potential." People have said to me, "I see something in you."

Back in 1988, when I was attending the labor college in Ottawa. I went to a coffee shop with some friends and there sat an elegant, well-dressed lady with a large magnifying glass on a stand beside her chair. Her name was Jocelyn.

I walked over and asked what she was doing. She said she was reading palms. I asked how much? She said $20. I didn't have much to spare in those days, but I took out my money and had my palm read. It's my highland Scottish background where we believe in laying on of hands, the therapeutic touch, healing of self, higher powers and gifted people. I believe that if a person is gifted, and many people are, if they use it for the betterment of humankind, then it will work out. If they use it for anything but the betterment of humankind, the gift will turn against them.

I sat down at the table, and Jocelyn traced the lines of my palm in ink. When I was done my hands were blue, and after peering through her huge magnifying glass, she said to me, "Your name will first become known nationally and then it will become known internationally." Then she looked at my hands and said, "Your seminars will be phenomenal."

I thought to myself, "Man, I just wasted $20! She clearly doesn't know who I am." I had just come out of a terrible bout with addiction, divorce, been disabled and was learning another job. I had been sober for a year and was proud of that but I thought, "This is way too much."

She stopped. She must have sensed my doubt, because the next thing she said was, "About a year, a year and a half ago, you came out of a terrific bout with alcoholism."

My heart stopped and I said, "Wow." Then she went on to tell me about traveling and speaking and books and all this wonderful life that I could only conjure up as happening to someone else.

I was grateful and thanked her when she finished. I was so hoping that these were true statements. The experience only reinforced my dream to become a motivational or inspirational speaker. I see a difference between them. I believe that an inspirational speaker will disturb someone's thinking and allow them to create an opportunity in their life for advancement. A motivational speaker continues to motivate people who have run out of steam. If you go by a gym the first two weeks of the year, it is packed. You can't get near the building. Three months later, and you see people parking near the door before they go in for their workout so they won't need to walk.

When I tell the story of my encounter with Jocelyn today, sometimes people say, "Allan, she put that idea into your mind and you just did it." The truth is: who cares? Is it nature or nurture? Who cares if it's innate in me and she discovered that if she brought that into my mind by telling me and I picked up on it.

Growing up in Auburn, there was a famous clairvoyant by the name of Mrs. McNichol. She lived in Millbank, a good 45-mile drive from us, and wrote many books. I still have some in my library at home. She was a retired nurse and was what is termed a natural clairvoyant. Mrs. McNichol and her husband lived in a big old house and whatever money people gave to her as donations, she would donate back to the Ontario Provincial Police College.

She had an uncanny ability to find things. She would touch part of a ring or a watch or wallet or something that was important to a person and she could see where they had lost things. She was so gifted that she would find the bodies of murdered people that had been hidden in a well or somewhere in the bush. She was quite popular in the area and I used to visit her. There were no appointments; it was first come, first served. Sometimes, Dad and I or Bernice and I would arrive at 2:00 in the morning and people would be parked on the street in front of her house. Then, at about 6 o'clock, her husband John would open up the door and people would rush in.

She was a wonderful, wonderful lady and I just fell in love with her. She was probably 65 years old when I was about 17. She told me many things, but one thing in particular that I remember, and which had a major impact on my life, she said when I wasn't there.

After I moved to Sudbury and drinking came to dominate my life, my mother and sister went to see her and my name came up. My mother said to Mrs. McNichol, "What will happen to my son Allan and his drinking?"

This was early on in my life. I was in my mid 20s which meant I still had 15 years of drinking ahead of me, and Mrs. McNichol looked at them and said, "Someday the sun will shine on Allan."

Talk about the power of words or the power of hope. No matter how far down the road I went with my addiction and the craziness, my mother and sister believed enough in Mrs. McNichol to believe that I would not die and would someday get out of that mess. Today I have. I can honestly tell you that the sun is clearly shining in my world today, has for quite some time and will continue to do so!

I looked into many alternative ways of studying myself. I studied numerology a little bit. I had a handwriting analysis done. I got my eyes checked by an iridologist for certain patterns that indicate things regarding my health. Astrology, numerology, reading and going to retreats. Had I been looking? Absolutely. Had I been searching? Absolutely. I don't think that astrology is the answer. I don't think that organized religion is the answer. I don't think that spirituality is the answer.

I don't think that any one thing is the answer, but I think choices are given to us in this world and we can study what is comfortable to us. It's all a piece of the gigantic jigsaw puzzle and we're all receiving the same message. We're just taking different avenues to get there. I walk through book stores and libraries and there are so many of my friends today who have books out. They're all about the same subject, but what will work for one does not work for another. There's TD Jakes, there's Les Brown, there's Zig Ziegler, Joel Olsten, Wayne Dyer; they're all communicating the same message but using different vocabulary. That's what I was doing; I was reaching out and searching for different things.

The sauerkraut juice didn't work well for me, but I have never stopped reaching out.

CHAPTER 36

OPENING DOORS

*Give to the world the best you have
and the best will come back to you.*
–MADELINE BRIDGES

BOOKS ARE WONDERFUL TEACHERS because they don't yell or scream or throw chalk at you or ridicule you. They sit there patiently, waiting for you to introduce yourself to them. One of my books returned the favor in a way that continues to have a positive influence on my life even today.

For years I had kept the message from that cassette of Les Brown's in my heart. His voice and message resonated deeply within me. When I attended Mastermind group meetings, we often talked about our goals and dreams. I said I wanted to meet Les Brown someday, never thinking that I would.

One day 10 years later, I was in my office in Pittsburgh. I had a copy of Les' book, *Live Your Dream,* on my desk. It was a large red hardback that I received from my sponsor Jim's widow, Barb, a few years after Jim passed away.

Barb had asked me to visit and was kind enough to ask, "What books would you like to have?" Jim was a book collector, always looking for *the* book. Nearly every second Mastermind meeting over the course of five years, Jim came in all smiles saying, "I have found *the* book. I have found *the* book."

The carrot of finding a magic answer kept him reaching out. As a result, he accumulated a vast collection of motivational and inspirational books. He loved Robert Schuller, so I took some of Robert's books and I took some of Og Mandino's as well.

Standing in Jim's library as I went through his books, I picked up *Live Your Dream* by Les Brown. I turned to Barb and said, "I'd like that book."

"It's yours, Allan," Barb replied without hesitation, and I brought it to Pittsburgh with me. One day, I was arranging my office and a member of the clerical staff happened by as I was pulling out some books and arranging my bookshelves.

"Oh, my God, is that Les Brown's book *Live Your Dream?*" Lee Etta exclaimed.

"Yes, it is," I answered.

"I have a friend who works with Les."

"You're kidding!"

"Yeah. She's been to some of his speaker trainings."

I had recently obtained my master's degree, moved to a new country and now this conversation transpired. I wonder what might have happened had Lee Etta not come in my office that day? Because I was getting ready to put the book on the shelf, she likely would never have seen it. That conversation might never have taken place.

It is like the time Jim was lying in the road that night preparing to die. The car that came along was not the one prearranged to kill him, it was a police officer. On top of that, it was a police officer who was a recovering alcoholic. The odds are astronomical when you stop to consider it—that policeman could have taken any road, Jim could have missed that all-important meeting by ten minutes, two minutes. Then Jim would not have had an impact on my life and I would not have affected other people's lives.

Lee Etta and I talked about Les Brown and I told her about my experience with the cassette of Les' talk so many years back. The next thing I knew, we were on the computer looking up Les Brown's website. I wrote down a phone number for his staff and noted a training seminar coming up in Orlando, Florida, the following month. The seminar was called Discover Your Power Voice. Excited, I called and signed up. Given my former lifestyle, I could rationalize the expense. If I could rationalize staying under the influence for 17 years, I can rationalize anything.

The next month, off I went to Orlando. I walked into the hotel and was nervous. There were probably 150 people there and we got together on a Friday night. Les walked in the room and it was magic. Here I was, in the same room with this man who had such an impact on not only my life but hundreds of thousands of other people.

Les stood up and introduced himself. He got the crowd laughing and made everybody feel comfortable. "We'll go around the room," he said, "and everyone will say their name, where they're from, and why they're here."

When it came my turn, I was nervous, even though I had been speaking in front of classrooms and seminars; it was quite different speaking in front of him.

"Hi. My name is Allan McDougall. I am from Pittsburgh by way of Canada," I said, "I'm here to meet the person whose message on a cassette tape entitled, 'It's Not Over Until You Win' resonated into my soul."

After the seminar everybody crowded around Les. I waited my turn and when we met, he hugged me and said, "You're my brother from another mother."

We all laughed about that, however, there was an instant connection. We share a closeness, Les and I do. He gave a wonderful seminar over the next three days. Afterwards, he talked about joining his Platinum Group. Either he or his staff interviewed those who expressed interest about becoming a Platinum Speaker. What would you get out of it? What would you bring to the table? They wanted to know.

I returned home and thought about it, and within three months, I was a member of Les' Platinum Group. I had to do much research into public speaking. I had to do some speaking in front of him and his staff. To become part of that group, you must have gained some credibility with him. That was a wonderful experience for me, a new and fantastic opportunity. I was out of the classroom setting and in a school without walls, learning from a mentor about public speaking and influencing, interrupting and disturbing people's thoughts. It was excellent training for me.

He held a training seminar every six weeks all across the United States. I would fly out on a Friday night and fly back Sunday afternoon. I met some wonderful people. It was a group of individuals trying to help one another become better speakers and help each other to achieve their goals. It was like a Mastermind Group of motivational speakers who have continued to help each other succeed. It is a "we" group, not a survival of the fittest, dog-eat-dog group.

One of the benefits of being a Platinum speaker was the opportunity to have interviews with Les. About 10 of us would fly into Chicago and go to his studio. There we would practice giving a one-minute speech, called an elevator speech. These consist of: Who are you? What do you bring to the table? Finally, why should I care? We rehearsed these and it became a way to communicate a powerful message effectively in a short time.

On one of those occasions, Les asked me, "What story has affected your life? Who has had an impact on your life the most?"

"Besides you?" I said.

"Yes, besides me."

I told him that Jim had, and when Les asked me why, I told him that Jim really helped me make some decisions about what I wanted to do with my life. By Les relaxing me and just sitting there interviewing me on a friend-to-friend basis, he brought that story out of me.

"There's your message," he said. "There's your message of hope."

Sometime later, I did a three minute speech on Jim's story and about my life. A woman approached me afterwards and said, "I really hope you get in touch with Mother's Against Drunk Driving in your state and volunteer to do work with them."

I did so, even though I never had a DUI, per se, since that one in 1984. I never was charged with criminal assault or vehicular homicide. I had never been involved in a DUI accident, though not through any brilliant planning on my part.

I drove to Harrisburg one day, and met with the Director of MADD for Pennsylvania. I sat with her and her staff and told a little bit of my story. It proved to be a great opportunity, because I was soon speaking every month to a group of people who had DUIs and were mandated to attend lectures as part of their parole and probation. There were probably one hundred to one hundred and fifty people from diverse backgrounds who had one thing in common: each had received multiple DUIs within a short period.

As a result of my talk at MADD, the director said, "I would like you to be part of the Allegheny County District DUI court system. We have a program for people coming in under these DUI convictions who have a choice to make: Do they want to do jail time or do they want to make a change in their life? There's an intervention we make. They are made to decide to do one or the other. If they follow the program for three years, they have a graduation at the court house."

A few months later, I went there to speak at a graduation. The courtroom was full of people who reached the milestone of three years continued sobriety. They had completed community work and attended counseling sessions to rebuild their lives. As the judge introduced me, I stood up and said, "This is such a pleasure for me. It is the first time ever that I've been able to speak from the front of the court room, not from the back."

Everybody laughed because they could relate. It was my way of talking with them, not lecturing at them. What can we learn from each other is the important thing.

That's a big part of the success of Alcoholics Anonymous. When you say at a meeting, "Hi, my name is Allan, I'm an alcoholic," everyone in the room can relate. It puts us all on a level playing field and establishes a pleasant atmosphere for conducting the meeting.

I continue to address these DUI groups today and when I speak to them, I try to impart a message of hope. I don't have a story to tell them about how DUIs affected my life, per se, but I try to give them a message of hope. That's a realistic hope and that's the best drug there ever was—hope. Leaders are dealers of hope!

However, it has to be realistic. If all it took was positive thinking, we would all be skinny, rich and beautiful. There's much more to changing a life around than positive thinking. It is a process, not an instantaneous flash.

Remaining positive plays a part, but it wasn't only positive thinking that transformed me to where I am today. If I could do it, from my very humble beginnings, honest to God anyone can do it through work, dedication and diligence.

"What makes huge success is an accumulation of small successes." What makes 25 years of sobriety, what makes 15 years of marriage or 40 years of employment in a company is simply taking it one day at a time.

At another speaker training program, two men sitting in the audience approached me after I had finished my 3-minute speech, "Allan, we would like have lunch with you."

Coming from my background, I said to myself, "Great" I'm always open to new opportunities and ideas. It's the HOW of being successful: honest, open and willing.

We went for lunch and one of the young men was doing his thesis on people overcoming adversity. He had a connection with a university and wanted to make my story into a documentary for a film festival.

Whoever thought that this empty shell of a man who didn't know who he was and whose greatest fears were "Who am I?" and "Will anyone like me when I quit drinking?" such a short time earlier was being interviewed by this ambitious university student wanting to make a documentary about him and the value of his life? It was quite humbling.

On the way down the chute to my personal hell, doors closed behind me. Cave-ins blocked my way. Bridges burned to the ground and my life got darker and darker. Ultimately, I had to admit that I did it to myself. By contrast, on my ride up, my life has become a serious of doors opening, opportunities offered and bridges built even across the oceans.

Another opportunity came to me when I was speaking along with Les Brown in the UK. Everything about it was exciting. The flight over was exciting. I took a week's vacation and we spent four days providing speaker training. We spoke at the Nigerian Consulate, and I delivered a talk about leadership. I spoke on how their leaders affected other people's lives with the decisions they made in their professional roles.

The next morning, we taped a BBC talk show that was to air in many countries about overcoming adversity, about achieving success and about living true to your dream. To walk into a TV station and be interviewed on a morning show, I got chills up and down my spine. It was electrifying. By remaining sober, I'm excited about life. While I was addicted, I was never truly excited about anything.

There's a world of difference between being childish and being childlike. I was childish when I was in my addiction, and now, by just believing, I'm childlike. That is growth, that is development, and it will continue. I'm going to change, hopefully until two days after I pass on. I'm just too busy to stop changing the day I die.

The day after our taping, we went for dinner and then we were on our way to a presentation at Westminster Common Hall, which stands two miles from Buckingham Palace. We walked into the magnificent theatre and I went through the ritual that I began 15 years ago when I started to conduct seminars. I go into the room early and assume an attitude that I own the room. I take possession of it. I walk around the theater touching the back of every chair and say a short prayer, "God of my understanding, whoever is sitting here today, I want them to receive some good direction or something that's meaningful for them from this seminar." I walk to the next chair and do that at each chair because I need all the help I can get to deliver the help I want for others.

As I went from seat to seat in the theatre, I could feel the electricity and see the energy in the room. This was before anybody else arrived. About six or seven Platinum Speakers, as well as Les, would be on stage. The theater was too large for me to touch all the chairs, so I went to every section of the theater and touched the guard rail and said a blessing for everyone who would soon be sitting in those seats. Perhaps I picked up this ritual subconsciously from the days when I went on retreats. I learned that the retired priests and nuns living there would pray for those coming to an upcoming retreat. It doesn't really matter where the idea came from, I find that it works and is something others may want to try as well.

As I climbed the steps to the stage to deliver my speech to the audience, I could feel grooves that had been worn in the treads from centuries of use. My feet were trodding the same steps as Ghandi, Churchill and Charles De Gaulle. What a place for a guy like me who had climbed out of a ditch. It was breathtaking.

I delivered a speech and again, there was someone in the audience who came up afterwards and said, "I'd like to meet with you sometime. I have a radio show that is aired in Spain. I'd like you to tape a show with me to air on Christmas Eve and New Year's Eve because during that time, many people are depressed and lonely. Some have suicidal thoughts."

I agreed and asked the person, "What kind of focus do you want me to put on this presentation?"

He had a great idea in response. "Why don't you think about a song that's important to you and talk about your life around that song," he suggested.

I reflected on it and saw that my life has had two parts. I asked him if I could have two songs, one pre-June 3rd 1987 and one post-June 3rd. He thought that would great. I decided that my first would be "Nowhere Man," by the Beatles, their song about a nowhere man, living in a nowhere world with no plans. It captured me perfectly, drifting from what I thought was happiness to escapism from 1950 to 1987, 37 years of being a real nowhere man. It has been said that some of us die at the age of 30 but do not get buried until we are 80.

I put a great deal of thought into my second song, which was "Hero," by Mariah Carey about the hero inside of each of us. Whether you're speaking to one or one thousand, be a hero, be a light in this world of darkness. Be a dealer of hope!

The morning of my return flight to Toronto I was at Heathrow Airport about 6:00 a.m., sitting there with half a dozen other Platinum Speakers. We were exhausted because we had been up until all hours the night before. When we get together, we are excited and motivated, so we don't sleep much. We stay up talking and sharing our success stories in between the seminars, building new relationships and helping each other.

At any rate, I was dead tired. A woman came over from the airline counter and said, "I'd like to see your boarding pass, sir."

I thought it had something to do with my passport or my seating arrangement or something. I handed it to her and she went back to her station. A moment later, she came back and said, "You're upgraded. You've been upgraded to executive business class."

"Wow," I said. "Thank you. Is that because of my frequent flier miles or something?"

"No. It's because you're dressed for executive business class."

The guy sitting beside me grumbled, "Man, I wish I'd been dressed up today."

That was a wonderful flight home because I got incredible service. I had a reclining seat and I was dog tired. We had a fabulous breakfast with champagne and orange juice. I always said that God has a sense of humor. When I was drinking, I couldn't afford to fly. Now when I'm flying, I can't afford to drink, and never the twain shall meet. I had the orange juice by choice.

Later, a flight attendant asked, "Anything you want for lunch?"

"Absolutely," I replied.

"Here's a menu."

I ordered lunch and said, "Please wake me when it's lunchtime."

It's amazing how opportunities come to you when you least expect it. Here I was, sitting in an airport, prepared to take my coach seat that I had bought for economic reasons and next thing I knew, I was upgraded because I had on dress slacks and a blazer. That is a lesson that I'll never forget. The lessons that I've been taught, I'm willing to share with others under the power of love, not the love of power.

All these are wonderful opportunities for which I'm truly grateful and I'm open to anything that will come to me. However, it is just as important to sit down with some guy on the street who is having a bad day and ask, "How can I help you today," or "What can I do for you today?"

I was walking down the street one day in Pittsburgh, and there was a man sitting on the street corner beside an ATM machine looking for a handout. I was coming back from a meeting and had a suit on. As I walked past him, he said, "Here comes a Philadelphia lawyer," to which I replied with a smile, "And this is going to cost me money."

We both laughed and had an instant connection. I was at the ATM machine, and he was sitting there being very polite and not in my face, so to speak. He was using the Law of Attraction, not promotion, which I try to live by. He wasn't being aggressive or assertive, just sitting there, but he was definitely down on his luck.

I took my money from the ATM machine. It was all twenties so I said, "Don't leave. I'll be right back."

I went inside a 7-Eleven nearby and got some change, returned and put some paper money in his cup. He looked at me and said, "Oh, my God, folding money," and he took it out of his cup and put it into his pocket.

Then I did something that I had never done before. I reached my hand down and said, "Hi, my name is Al."

"Hi, my name is Terry," he replied, as he shook my hand.

"You know, this was me 15 years ago," I said. "I was one drink away from sitting where you are today. I'm not here to preach, I'm not here to judge, but I made a decision one day about 15, 20 years ago to go to Alcoholics Anonymous. Whatever you want to do with that money is okay by me. It's yours. That's not the reason I said that. I just hope you have a great day."

With that, I left. The sun seemed to shine just a wee bit brighter.

I went for lunch and when I came back past the same spot, he was gone. I had a wonderful day wondering, well, did Terry go to a meeting or did he go to the local establishment to buy some booze. Either way, I thought that possibly I had given him a little message of inspiration or hope with the handout.

Lo and behold, I was walking down the same street about a month later and there he was in his spot. As I walked over, he said, "Oh, my God, there's that lawyer guy. You look like a lawyer."

"How you're doing?" I asked. "Would you like to go for lunch?"

As you may not know, people on the street usually work in teams of two. So I knew there was someone else around who worked with him because when they receive handouts, they each only had to collect half as much to get enough for a bottle.

I said to Terry, "Well, I don't know where your friend is but invite him, too."

"How'd you know about that?" Terry asked.

"I told you, I have had some experience on the street."

Terry waved to his buddy and called him over, and I met Randy.

Terry, Randy and I went to a bagel shop and walked in. The manager immediately came over and said, "You two aren't allowed in here. I kicked you out two days ago for eating all the samples and for bothering people."

"Excuse me, sir," I said. "They're with me."

I could see the embarrassment leave Terry and Randy. The manager said, "Well, that's fine, but just . . . ."

"We don't need to hear that, sir," I interrupted. "They're with me."

The three of us sat down and had an enjoyable lunch. I've been doing that every two or three months since. They're real people and we talk about real issues. I never talk about where I came from very much or the changes I made. They know the change I made. I don't need to talk about it. I always say, "Beware the holy person who always tells you how holy they are." Terry and Randy don't need to hear what I did. They see the difference. They see the difference that I'm not living in the street or I'm not at the mercy of other people's whims about whether to give them money or not or a free handout at a bagel shop.

Sometime later, I was back up in Canada talking to someone and she said, "Oh, Al, the way you live on the edge of the street, you've got to be careful. They'll stab you."

I thought to myself, "Well, maybe they would, however, if they did, I'd see it coming. Not that someone would say something like that with a knife in my back."

These two friends of mine and I just laugh and joke about these different situations and opinions that people have. We happened to have that common denominator of being addicted to booze at one time. Their time is now and my time was in the past. By living one day at a time and not drinking today, I know that I will go to bed without feeling sick and will I wake up in the morning without a hangover.

One day a time, that's all we have.

BREAKING THROUGH

CHAPTER 37

The Promises of Recovery

*The law of harvest is to reap more than you sow. Sow an act
and you reap a habit, sow a habit and you reap a character,
sow a character and you reap a destiny*
—James Allen

Alcoholics Anonymous is famous for its Twelve Step program and
many organizations have adapted the model for their own programs.
Numerous widespread compulsions or addictions have led to variations
of the AA Twelve Step model, from narcotics to overeating, gambling
and others.

While not so well known as the Twelve Steps, there are promises in
the AA Big Book, also numbering twelve, that I repeat here:

> If we are painstaking about this phase of our development,
> we will be amazed before we are half way through. We are
> going to know a new freedom and a new happiness. We will
> not regret the past nor wish to shut the door on it. We will
> comprehend the word serenity and we will know peace. No
> matter how far down the scale we have gone, we will see how
> our experience can benefit others. That feeling of uselessness
> and self-pity will disappear. We will lose interest in selfish
> things and gain interest in our fellows. Self-seeking will slip
> away. Our whole attitude and outlook upon life will change.
> Fear of people and of economic insecurity will leave us. We

will intuitively know how to handle situations which used to baffle us. We will suddenly realize that God is doing for us what we could not do for ourselves.

Are these extravagant promises? We think not. They are being fulfilled among us—sometimes quickly, sometimes slowly. They will always materialize if we work for them.

Even as I read them again, many years after my initial introduction, I still get a wonderful feeling. The endorphin release that I receive from reading the promises reminds me of another situation in my life. When I received my first copy of the Big Book of AA in 1987, I tore out the page where the promises were written and taped it to my refrigerator.

One day back in the early '80s, I was walking down the street in Sudbury. I had $300 or $400 in my pocket. My wife and children were away for the weekend. I had no responsibilities at home. I had money in my pocket. I was walking down the street, dead sober on a Friday afternoon after work and I had the weekend free. I had the same feeling, this rush through my body. I was on my way to have a drink or twenty, I had no time to be home. I got the same rush from reading the promises.

There are a number of reasons I should have remained sober that Friday afternoon in Sudbury. One, I would have saved several hundred dollars. Two, I would have saved considerable anguish. Three, I would have avoided a hangover, and four I wouldn't have been sick Sunday and Monday. I was so sick that Sunday, I'll never forget it. I could hardly get out of bed and I couldn't function. Friends came over to party but I wasn't in a partying mood. My wife came home with the kids Sunday night and it was just a mess. I think back to that Friday afternoon, when I was dead sober on my way to drink. Today, I know that I no longer have to go through that sickness anguish again.

"If we are painstaking about this phase of our development, we will be amazed." I *am* amazed. I'm totally amazed at where I am today. I say this out of humility not out of ego. (There is a good acronym about what ego is. Ego stands for <u>E</u>asing <u>G</u>od <u>O</u>ut.) Simplicity is profound, it really is. I learned that I could handle AA's "one day at a time" concept. If I don't drink today, I will not become drunk and I will not have a hangover.

I jokingly tell people that there's a downside of being sober. The downside is that when you wake up in the morning, that's as good as you will feel. Some days, I would wake up in the morning and feel as though I had to die to start feeling better. My worst days today are much better than my best days when I was drinking.

That freedom they talk about in the promises is hard for me to describe. About a year into my sobriety, I was driving and a police officer pulled up behind me. When I saw the lights come on, I said, "Oh, my God," and that old panic about being caught driving drunk hit me until I realized, "Hey, I'm not drinking. I'm not!" It may sound ironic but what a pleasure it was to be pulled over.

The officer came over as I rolled down the window. "Do you know, sir, that your signal light is not working on one side?"

"Thank you, officer. I had no idea. I will get it fixed tomorrow."

"Have a great day," he said and walked back to his cruiser.

That experience was amazing to me, that I was able to continue on my way instead of heading off to a police station.

Every year close to the Christmas holidays in Sudbury and across most cities in Canada, police officers set up traffic stops to catch people who have been drinking. The first year I was sober, I went out looking for one because they were giving away driver's license holders that read, "Thank you for being a sober driver."

I couldn't find one and it was frustrating. All those years I tried to avoid them and here I was looking for one and couldn't find it. Another night when I did find one, I pulled up to the line and felt proud. I rolled the window down, and the officer stuck his head in and asked, "Have you been drinking?"

"No, sir. I've been sober six months. I haven't had a drink since June 3rd."

He busted out laughing. He had a "Who's this guy?" look on his face, but I was so proud. I was 38 years old but had retained a childlike enthusiasm. It was fun. I'm a perpetual teenager. People say I look younger than my years and I say, "Yes, because I'm very immature." Maybe that's the magic, not living logically every day. Just living. That's the freedom, simply to be living.

The second promise of AA is, "We will not regret the past and wish to shut the door on it." I certainly do not wish to shut the door. It's like driving a car: the size of your rearview mirror compared to the size of your windshield gives a comparison between your past and your future. Where you came from is behind you, but when you look out the windshield and see the vast, expansive sky and the trees, that's your future.

When you are driving and looking out the windshield, you're living in the present. You have to be in the present to be attentive to what is coming down the highway or to look into the future. My driving instructor told me way back in 1966 that periodically, you have to look in the rearview mirror to see what's behind you. I emphasize the word periodically. The past is there; it's a part of me and made me who I am today. It's part of my story. However, I do not regret the past nor do I wish to shut the door on it. I like to open it from time to time to take a peek.

I believe that the size ratio between the rearview mirror and the windshield provides a good guide of how much time we should spend inspecting our past. It has to be checked from time to time but not so much that we drive off the highway of life.

I've worked through my issues. They were what they were, and I never want to forget that. I always want to retain that nucleus within me. I remember what it was like so I don't get too cocky or too egotistical. I've heard of many people who went back to drinking after twenty years of sobriety. After twenty-three years, I still listen to the stories of those who made that decision because it keeps me focused day to day.

The AA program has taught me that we're never fully cured; the disease can go into remission. Medical people have told me that also. If I went back drinking today, my liver would be as affected as if I had never quit. Is that true? Is it not? I don't know. I'm not a medical doctor, and never professed to be. Hearing that though, keeps me aware of how fragile life is. I have one more drunk in me but I don't know if I have one more recovery.

The third promise is, "We will comprehend the word serenity and we will know peace." I don't think I ever knew the word serenity or understood it. I was always on edge. There was always a knot in my stomach that something bad would happen. I feel blessed to know that serenity today. I heard that word serenity at my very first AA meeting. Over the years, by following the 12 Steps, plus seeking outside help, journaling and living one day at a time I have found periods of serenity.

Near the start of my sobriety, I kept a journal called "My Spiritual Journey." It is a leather-bound book and I reviewed it from time to time. During those first couple of years, I was focused on things that weren't serene in my life. I was working towards serenity. Then, I realized that it would take the rest of my life. That has helped me become more serene about finding serenity. I am reminded of the saying, "Your ship comes in under calm waters."

I am content with taking a lifelong journey. It took me a long time to build a tolerance for the amount of alcohol that I could drink. Nobody becomes an alcoholic overnight. We may have the alcoholic's mindset long before we take a drink. I didn't arrive at the capacity to handle a .328 blood alcohol content reading and still function by having one drink a week for twenty years. It took a dedicated commitment to become that capable a drinker.

I used to have an idea about being able to drive better when I had a few drinks under my belt because I was more focused. That's not true at all, but it was one of my dangerously silly ideas. Stinking-thinking when mixed with drinking leads to disaster. I'm so grateful for the serenity I have found. That, and the sense of peace that everything is as it should be. Of course, some days life is not the way I want it to be, but then again why should I think that I could have it the way things should be just for me. It's not about me.

Any time I feel that way, I HALT. That is an acronym I use to help keep me on track:

Hungry: When is the last time that I ate?
Angry: Is there someone/something I need to work with/on?
Lonely: When is the last time I reached out?
Tired: When is the last time I slept properly?

Promise number four is, "No matter how far down the scale we have gone, we will see how our experience can benefit others." When I was sitting in rehab in 1987, I heard a speaker. Listening to him planted the seed that one day I could be a speaker and an author. I've kept that seed alive for 24 years. That's well over 8,000 days, or more than 200,000 hours. That's a long time to nurture one seed. But I kept it, I watered it, I never forgot about it. I knew in my heart of hearts that even though I was far down the scale, I could help other people. I could relate my experience, strength and hope to others, and therefore, my life would not be without value.

There's a story about a gentleman who is lying on his death bed. The door opens. His vision is dim and he sees shadowy figures coming towards him. He is elated and cries out, "Oh, my God, Oh, my God. My friends from high school and college have come to say good-bye. What a wonderful thing! I'm so glad to see you."

They approach and he notices that their faces aren't smiling and their eyes aren't happy. Then, one shadowy figure leans over and whispers solemnly, "No, sir, no. We have not come to say good-bye. We were your hopes. We were your dreams. We were your goals that you had for such a promising life years and years ago when we knew you, but you deserted us. We have not come to say good-bye. We have come to die with you."

As the saying goes, "Live full, die empty."

Promise number five is, "The feeling of uselessness and self-pity will disappear." I learned the first week or two of AA that is a growth experience not to indulge in self-pity.

Bob and Dave said to me early on, "Allan, the experience that you're going through right now will make you one of two things. It doesn't matter what else you do in life, this is as simple as it gets: You'll become a bitter person or a better person, and that choice is absolutely, unequivocally, up to you."

Uselessness and self-pity make a very bitter person as far as I'm concerned. I choose to be a better person.

The next promise is, "We will lose interest in selfish things and gain interest in our fellows." That's what the fellowship of Alcoholics Anonymous taught me. I now know what I don't know and surround myself with people who know what I don't know. Learn from each other and learn from your experiences, your strengths and your hopes. Is the glass half empty or half full?

I'm of Irish and Scottish background: one half wants to drink and the other half is too cheap to buy. I said that in a seminar one time and a guy came up to me and said, "I'm terribly offended by you saying that Scottish people are cheap."

"If you remember my speech, sir," I replied, "I never said which was which." I got a kick out of that. The point is to gain interest in our fellows. If you want to help yourself, help someone else.

I was on my way to a Les Brown speaker training one Saturday morning. I had clothes with me in a garment bag and there was a great deal of traffic at the airport, so they rerouted us through an alternate security checkpoint. It was a different route for me and I was out of my usual pattern. I was in a hurry and went through security, came down the escalator and when I arrived at the gate, I realized that I had left my garment bag back at the security area. It was the middle of winter and I had heavy clothes on.

I asked the gate attendants if I could leave my briefcase and carry-on there and they said, "No way."

I jumped on the tram back to security. When I arrived, I saw two escalators coming down, but none going up. I looked around and there was no elevator and no stairs. I had on a big leather jacket and was holding my carry-on bag and my briefcase. I stood there and wondered, "Now what do I do?"

I waited for the traffic coming down the escalator to clear and up I started. I ran up the down escalator, going against the flow, against convention. People were amused at my predicament and smiling at me. When I got to the top I was pooped. My legs felt like they weighed 200 pounds each.

A security guard at the top who had been watching me said, "I would have bet money that you wouldn't make it."

I grabbed my garment bag, hurried back down, caught the tram again and made my flight. I tell you that story to illustrate this: what's your commitment to your commitment? Those circumstances could have been a roadblock for me. Two escalators coming down, I'm going up. No elevator, no stairwell, and the only way to get to what I needed was to take one step at a time up those escalators.

Is what you are facing an obstacle or is it an opportunity?

"Self-seeking will slip away," is the next of the promises. It's about how to help others and yourself at the same time. A person's whole attitude and outlook upon life will change is the promise. There was a time that I was planning to die, but I was too much of a coward. Now, I truly want to live.

Perhaps, I was always into living on the edge, driving fast cars, for instance. I hung around with a friend in the village who had a 1959 Ford Fairlane, black and white. We would speed along on the gravel roads and literally, sail over the hills. We never knew what was on the other side, whether there were cows, a tractor or sheep. Often, horses or farm implements used the roads. My friend's goal was to lift the car entirely off the ground and we were often quite successful.

High speed chases, being a miner, drinking myself to the brink of death, that is where I took myself. I don't want to live on the edge of death anymore; I want to fully embrace life today. "Our whole attitude and outlook upon life will change," the promise reads, and mine certainly did.

Another promise is: "Fear of people and of economic insecurity will leave us." Believe you me, I've lived life when I didn't have very much money. I lost a lot of money. After my divorce settlement, I couldn't afford to go back to the lawyers to have it changed. When my wife and I originally made it, I was still working underground and making much better money than I was a year later when I hurt my back and left the mine for good. I look back today and see that as a blessing, because even though my family suffered in many other ways, they always had money coming in.

I took my daughter Marcie shopping one Christmas in Sudbury, and there was a big campaign running at the time directed at dead beat dads. Family Services had billboards up along the roads and posters in the mall about dead beat dads. As I walked through the mall with my daughter, I saw these posters and didn't have to shrivel inside or feel guilt or embarrassment because I paid my financial obligations to my family.

Today, I have everything that I need in life. I may not have everything I want and that's a good thing, because I need to have goals and dreams. However, I know that the economic security will always come.

The truth is I had life backwards when I was drinking. Later, I realized that God was doing for me what I could not do for myself. While in rehab, I said, "God, if I am to be an author and a motivational speaker, I need Your help. I don't know what to do; I don't know how to do it. But I'm open to anything that You can give me, to help me find my way."

Then the Big Book continues, "Are these extravagant promises? We think not. They are being fulfilled among us. Sometimes quickly, sometimes slowly." Then comes the most important sentence, "They will always materialize, if we work for them."

Robert Frost wrote, "Something we were withholding made us weak, until we found it was ourselves." In my weakness, I reached out for help and by doing so, I found my strength. What an incredible paradox. While almost everyone would agree on the importance of a healthy self-image, few of us understand how to acquire one or how the one we now possess was created in the first place.

Our self-image is exactly what it says; it's the image that we have of ourselves made up of ideas that we have formed over the years. As Les Brown says, "Don't let someone else's impression of you become your reality."

In our childhood, we are accepting of ideas. If our parents were loving and supportive, it helps us to develop a good self-image. If we were ridiculed in school or abused at home, we may adopt a less positive self-image. My definition of self-image is "what we believe about ourselves." If we made a habit of dwelling on life's inevitable disappointments, we have made disappointment a central part of our image. What you focus on the most or what you fear the most will become your reality. Ultimately, we have to take responsibility for ourselves and our condition. I had to take responsibility for my situation. Long ago, I learned that the subconscious mind will accept any thought about yourself that you regularly think, whether it is true or not. That idea will eventually become part of your self-image.

As I mentioned earlier, Fred Flintstone said, "You have to be you because everyone else is taken." We are unique individuals. No one else has your thoughts, your ideas or your way of doing things. Not only do we have to recognize our uniqueness, we have to proclaim it.

I have learned that acceptance is the answer to all my problems. Bob showed me something on acceptance from the Big Book of AA during my first weeks of sobriety. Acceptance is the answer to all of my problems today. When I am disturbed, it is because I find some person, place, thing or situation, some fact in my life, unacceptable to me. I can find no serenity until I accept that person, place, thing or situation exactly the way it is supposed to be at that moment. Nothing, absolutely nothing happens in God's world by mistake.

Until I could accept my alcoholism, I could not stay sober. Until I could accept life completely, on life's terms, I could not be happy. I need to concentrate, not so much on what needs to be changed in the world, as what needs to be changed in me and in my attitude. Keeping that in mind, the role of acceptance becomes more easily understood.

I have always rewarded myself on the anniversaries of my sobriety. On my first anniversary, I had a white sports coat made that I wore to accept my medallion. For my five year anniversary I decided to buy myself a Trans Am. I bought it sight unseen from my friend Stan. I called him one day and said I would like to buy something for my anniversary. He found it for me at an auction and I went down to pick it up. My son still drives it today and it has more than 400,000 miles on it.

As I wrote earlier, I drove the Trans Am during the summer but put it in storage in winter. I bought old cars for the winter from Stan, cars that he'd take in on deals.

One winter, I was driving an old '85 Mercury Topaz. One April, I drove from Sudbury down to Auburn to get my Trans Am, and I was so happy because I would be teaching at an educational seminar for a week after I visited with my family and retrieved my car from storage. It was going to be a wonderful week.

Around midnight, I stopped to gas up and was on a back road, two hours from my parents' home. The heater in this Topaz had not worked all winter. I was bundled up in a winter coat and had a toque on my head. About a mile from the gas station, the car became warm. I said to myself, "God has a sense of humor." Here it was the end of April and no longer very cold and the heater came on.

I pulled over to take my jacket off because I would now have a comfortable ride with the heater running, something it never did in 40-below weather. I took it off and tossed it in the back seat. Next thing I knew, the car stalled. It had been a tremendous car all winter. At 35-below it started with no problem. Now it stalled.

I opened up the hood and a sea of flames leapt up. The whole engine was on fire. I quickly shut the hood and vividly remember saying to myself, "I really don't need this at this time."

There was another gas station right across a roadside ditch. The attendant came out and I ran over to tell him to call the fire department.

Acceptance entails being able to act in the moment and to have presence of mind and focus. I said, "Well, whether the car burns or not, I need my materials and my clothes next week." I began removing boxes of training materials from the trunk and putting them by the side of the road, away from the car. Not much goes on out in the country even on a Friday night. However, even at midnight a car fire really does attract a crowd.

I couldn't believe how fast the car burned; it was mostly plastic. Parts were melting off it and then, it started to roll down the shoulder towards a roadhouse next to the gas station. The woman who owned the bar and grill came running out; a burning car rolling towards your establishment is quite an attention getter.

She began screaming, "Who owns that car, who owns that car?" I said to myself, "Do you think I'm putting my hand up? When this car is rolling down towards your place of business?" It reminded me of a Viking funeral pyre ship when they buried their fallen warriors at sea.

Thankfully, the car stopped and died before it reached her roadhouse. The police showed up, and the volunteer fire department came and put the fire out. I had people offer to take me home, saying that I could stay the night with them. Some, I thought would be adventurous and others I declined immediately when I saw who they were. I'll leave the imagery up to you. The police looked at my car and it was totally destroyed.

I sat in the cruiser and did some paperwork, and it was such a delight to be in the back of a police cruiser not under the influence and being charged with a DUI. They treated me very well. One said, "Mr. McDougall, you don't look very worried about that car you just lost."

"Look at it. Look at that car," I replied. "Would you be worried about it?" All that was left were the rims and some steel.

The police officers were laughing and asked, "Do you need a ride somewhere?"

"No," I said. "I'll call my sister."

They transported my materials and clothes inside the gas station, which had a little snack shop. I called my sister at 1:30 a.m. and said, "Hi, Sis. What are you doing?"

I couldn't remember the last time I had asked her to help me out of a jam. I thought her son would be up at night and he could come get me. Brotherly love and sisterly love being what it is, she jumped in the car and drove two hours to take me home. The next morning I picked up my Trans Am and continued on to the training site.

Sometimes we have to practice acceptance quickly. I thank God that no one was hurt.

I'm grateful to be alive because I have the opportunity to do anything. I'm not saying that I will get everything I want, but I have the freedom to try. There are so many things that I can do today with the freedom that was offered me in the promises of AA. I don't have to allow my negative behavior of the past to dictate, for example, what I should or should not do today. I have the freedom of choice and that is a very valuable freedom.

These are just a few examples of the opportunities promised through AA and how these translated, not only to the world outside me, but also to my inner life. I had to learn to love myself. There is power in love. One of the powers I have gained is the ability to choose my thoughts. Only I can determine what I do with this power. I've chosen to take a risk by stepping out and writing this book.

Something that made a big impression on me during my first year of sobriety, and continues to today, is the Prayer of Saint Francis:

> *Lord, make me an instrument of your peace.*
> *Where there is hatred, let me sow love.*
> *Where there is injury, pardon.*
> *Where there is doubt, faith.*
> *Where there is despair, hope.*
> *Where there is darkness, light.*
> *Where there is sadness, joy.*
>
> *O, Divine Master,*
> *grant that I may not so much seek to be consoled, as to console;*
> *to be understood, as to understand;*
> *to be loved, as to love.*
> *For it is in giving that we receive.*
> *It is in pardoning that we are pardoned*
> *and it is in dying that we are born to Eternal Life.*
>
> *Amen.*

CHAPTER 38

LIFE AS A ROCKET RIDE

Live and let live is not enough; live and help live is not too much.
–ORION E. MADISON

DRUNK OR SOBER, one aspect of my life that has never changed is my love of cars. For my 15 year anniversary of sobriety, I planned to reward myself with a 1966 Shelby Cobra 427 that I hired a mechanic to build. Today, I still drive that Shelby, but the car came with an experience that proved to be a milestone as significant as the one it was meant to commemorate.

I paid the man $30,000 to build my dream car. I trusted him to do a good job but it turned out that he used the money as part of a shell game he was running. For three years I would visit his shop and he would tell me, "Here is your car. It is coming along."

The next day, another customer would come into the shop and he would say the same thing to them. He was a con artist of a high order.

He had car bodies and motors in his shop as well as parts lying around. I had given him $30,000 but nothing was forthcoming in return. It finally began to dawn on me that I was being taken to the cleaners. At first, I was in denial. This couldn't be happening to me. Then, I got angry and had revenge on my mind. After that, I became sad. I had told people I was having this car made and was so excited. It was embarrassing to be a grown man, sober for years and be conned so thoroughly. I was trusting. I was childlike and got taken. I would tell my friends who asked about it, "Yes, my car is coming."

This saga went on for years. I was traveling a lot at the time, and because his shop was off the beaten track, I could not always check on him. Still, there were times that I simply did not want to see him because I knew he would lie to me and lead me on some more.

Had I still been drinking, I don't know what I would have done, but it would not have been positive. Likely, I would have sought refuge in my bottle and the episode would have given me one more reason to lie in my ditch and look down on the world.

Now though, I had sense enough and strength enough to take action.

I contacted a lawyer who wrote the man a letter. Mr. Con-man was used to that and it did nothing. Then I spoke to people in the community and asked them, "Have you ever heard of this man?"

"Oh, yeah," they said, "sure, we know him."

I said that I had a problem with him.

"Hey, take a number and get in line," they said. "There's probably thirty people ahead of you."

Before the fiasco was over, I met, no exaggeration, twenty-five people who had the same problem. Some had just walked away, some had given him $5000, and some had given him $10,000. Some, like myself, had given him $30,000 and some of those just walked away in embarrassment. Some people got half of their car, some people got none and they all were fed a steady diet of lies.

I decided that I wouldn't give up, so I went to an AA meeting in the community. I talked to some fellows there and they knew him, too. As a result, somebody knew somebody who knew somebody who had a tow truck. Five years after I made a deal with him to build me the car, I went to his garage and he happened to be away at the hospital that day. I retrieved the fiberglass body, an engine and some parts for my car and that was what I received for my $30,000.

As I drove down the road afterwards, I had tears in my eyes and thought, "This isn't the vision that I had. I thought I would have my son with me and we would be driving down the road in a 427."

The 1966 Cobra is an iconic, absolutely beautiful car. All I had was a gray body with an old 427 that needed fixing up and some parts on the back of a flatbed. What a sign! I can still recall the disappointment; it was a very sad day.

The disappointment fueled my persistence and diligence however, and I brought people together who had also been defrauded, and the man was charged. I made a commitment to be at every court appearance that he was at even if it was remanded and even though the court was five hours away from where I lived. I wanted to be the last person he thought about before he went to bed and the first person he thought of when he woke up in the morning.

The twenty-five of us formed a network over the internet and set up times to meet. Over coffee, we had counseling sessions of a sort.

By remaining diligent and with persistence, we brought him down. He went to court, was tried, convicted and received his sentence. I won't mention his name because it's a done deal and today, honestly, I have no resentment towards him. I did the best that I could with what I knew at the time. This became a lesson for me that, no matter how far down I went again, I would never think of returning to my drug of choice.

I relate this story also to make the point that just because one quits drinking doesn't mean that one lives the rest of his or her life on a pink cloud. I've had terrible disappointments since I quit drinking, but my behaviors, thoughts and actions towards those disappointments are much different than they would have been had I reached for another bottle of whiskey or another case of beer. I still would have woken up with the problem, but I'd have a hangover and be short more money.

Fortunately, I later met a street rod mechanic, Terry Edwards, who not only rebuilt my Shelby, he rebuilt my faith in human beings. I met Terry through the contacts I had made in the area, a town called Wasaga Beach on Lake Huron. After that traumatic experience, you can imagine the doubts and anxieties I had dropping my car off with another complete stranger. Terry turned out to be a poster boy for honesty and integrity, the complete opposite of the other man who lived a life of deceit and ruined people's hopes. Terry worked on my car in his shop, Street Rod Services, in Wasaga Beach; he kept in frequent contact to update me on his progress and did a wonderful job. What a happy ending to what would have been a terrible disappointment otherwise.

When I worked underground, the back of our duty belts contained

My 1966 Shelby Cobra that Terry built for me, a gift I gave to myself in celebration of 15 years' sobriety.

a D ring to which we hooked a lifeline whenever we worked near any opening deeper than six feet. These lifelines were made of a woven fabric and were flat, maybe an inch wide, and very strong. They were drop tested with weights to ensure they would save a miner's life who fell from a ladder or stumbled down a chute. At either end of the line a snap hook was attached to the line that was looped through the hook and stitched back on itself. One hook attached to a timber or stable point where we were working and the other hook snapped onto the D ring on the belt.

Any system is only as strong as its weakest link, and on our lifelines, that was the stitching that held the snap hooks to the line.

For many years of my life, I had nothing that represented a lifeline. Perhaps, I could have developed one had I been able to sink some roots as a child. That did not happen, and I tumbled down an emotional mine shaft and fell headlong for many years. By the grace of some higher power, a lifeline was tossed to me just before I hit bottom.

In those early days and weeks without alcohol, that lifeline was, at most, a few gossamer threads. Every AA meeting I attended added another stitch and another fiber of fabric to the line. The great people I met in AA helped me learn how to hook the line securely to myself. The mentors who came into my life—my sponsor Jim, the Mastermind Group members, Les Brown and the people I met in his network to name only some—opened my mind and my heart, letting me find the stable rocks between which to string the line.

The result was a certainty of myself that began to grow with each milestone in my life: 90 days of sobriety, my first alcohol-free year, telling my story in front of the class at the community college, returning to school to further my education, reconnecting with my children, my retreats at La Villa Loyola, finally standing up to my mother and forming a new relationship with her, the blue ribbon letters I exchanged with my dad, the relationships that helped peel layer after layer of pain from the core of my being, my addiction intervention training, the help I was able to give to others when they were in the same condition I was once in; all these and many other life experiences I have had since 1987 have given me the personal strength to deal with challenges in life positively, not run from them as I did for so many years.

The night Marcel pinned me to the fence with a knife at my throat, I felt no fear and came away from the experience with stronger stitches in my lifeline. The situation with my Shelby Cobra would have ruined me when I was drinking, but living a life of integrity for years gave me the strength to obtain a measure of justice for myself and others who had been harmed.

In the 1930s, Dr. William Silkwood studied the progressive deterioration of alcoholics in the psychiatric ward of the New York hospital where he worked. A pioneer in the field of alcoholism research, he observed the pattern that most alcoholics follow of climbing on and falling off the wagon, and he concluded that until the alcoholic experienced a fundamental psychic shift, there was little hope of recovery.

Yet, once this change had taken place, by whatever means, the person who earlier seemed doomed suddenly found himself able to control rather easily the desire for alcohol.

My weakest moment occurred the day I sat in that rundown Sudbury bar and my body rejected the booze. The psychic change I was literally dying for began with the postcard I received from my son Shane during rehab. From that moment, my weaknesses began to transform into strengths.

Many of the stories in the second half of this book are milestones in my recovery. For me, they validated the growth I had made emotionally and spiritually. They added stronger stitches to my lifeline and helped me find inside myself the stability I had never known.

That is the story of my struggles with alcohol. For years, alcohol was the solution to my problems. Like many supposed "solutions," it created more problems than it solved. My "solution" destroyed my marriage, it harmed my children, it ruined me financially and nearly ruined my health.

The lessons I learned can be applied to many people who are at a crossroads in their lives and who need to make a change. The need for change may stem from the abuse of the bottle or a needle, from a dysfunctional relationship or a broken home, from a situation at work or, as in recent years, from the lack of work. My life today revolves around helping people to deal with and overcome whatever adversity they are facing. Many people are stuck in jobs where they do only enough not to be fired while being paid just enough by their employers not to quit. Other adversities arise out of this delicate but dangerous balance.

In 2005, the USWA and the PACE Union merged to form the USW. As a result, an Emergency Response Team (ERT) program was formed to deal with various issues such as workplace injuries or fatalities. In 2006, the International Steelworkers Executive Board asked me to head this new department. Working in the EAP office, I already had years of experience in helping people deal with situations in their lives that had spiraled out of control, so they knew I was well suited to head the ERT.

Many working class professions are as dangerous as mining and when a union member is seriously injured or killed on the job, I am there as soon as I can make it to help the family deal with their trauma and if necessary, to ensure they can secure good legal representation.

My life has been transformed by taking on this role. I have been drawn into the realm of crisis counseling and I find myself providing assistance when a family is at their lowest possible point. There are now 35 people in the ERT department, spread across the U.S. and Canada, who can leave their regular job at a moment's notice to assist a family after a workplace tragedy and who can provide assistance for up to a year after the accident.

One day, I received a call from a local union two hours north of Pittsburgh. A man had been crushed to death at a factory. The man worked the night shift, and his wife received a call at 4:30 that morning saying not to expect her husband home because there'd been an accident and he had broken his leg. The people at the factory had no idea how to tell this woman the truth so they were making up stories. They said they would call back and later when they did, said it was a broken leg with complications. They didn't know what to tell the woman who was nearly frantic with worry. Finally, her son drove to the factory and learned the sad truth that his father had been killed.

I was delayed in Pittsburgh and could not arrive until that evening around 8:00. Neighbors were in the house and I was invited in. The man's widow was more concerned for my comfort than her own loss and offered to make me coffee. We went to the kitchen and she said, "I am so grateful today."

That puzzled me. "But how?" I asked.

"I feel so blessed today," she continued. "You know, blended families are not always so blended. We were married for five years, the second marriage for us both, and some months ago, started talking about renovating the house. It became contentious and there were many heated debates and arguments.

"Well, last night we went out for dinner and a movie before he went to work, and he told me that he loved me. We hadn't said that much to each other lately. Those were the last words he said to me and for that I will always be grateful."

Despite the unforgivable way the factory handled the news, she had the grace to rise above the sadness of the moment and see a bigger picture.

If there is any lesson I have learned it is that there is always something that can be done about a situation. When someone is facing a tough spot in the road, I like to count myself among the people who can inspire others to initiate the actions that will take them to a better place.

As I realized when I faced my own tough situation many years ago, I alone can do it but I can't do it alone.

About Allan

A POWERFUL SPEAKER AND TRAINER, Allan McDougall is founder
and President of AM Public Speaking, which specializes in personal
and organizational empowerment. Powerfully dynamic, he integrates
proven strategies into personalized programs. His real life experiences,
energy and captivating style, influences, motivates, educates and
inspires audiences to take the action required to change their lives for
the better.

As well as being a sought after keynote speaker, he delivers seminars
to a wide range of audiences on:

- Alcohol Intervention
- Relapse Prevention
- Crisis Counseling
- Overcoming Adversity
- Self Development
- Conflict Resolution
- Stress Awareness
- Success for Life

For more information about Allan, his seminars, workshops,
recorded lectures, workbooks and materials, or to schedule him as a
keynote speaker, please go to:

www.AMPublicSpeaking.com
Email: allan@ampublicspeaking.com
Phone: 724.496.0460

ACKNOWLEDGMENTS

It took me approximately one year to write the story of my twenty-four year dream. I have to say this acknowledgment page has by far been the most difficult.

I have stated that this book has taken a toll on me—not the recollections, some very sad, others extremely funny—not the dictation, not the editing or proofreading. The toll on me was the twenty-three previous years when I lived my life in such a way that it would be a story worthy of being told.

Saying that, who do I acknowledge? My mind is a sea of faces, names and voices that propelled me forward, some deceased, some still with us and some who were born after June 3, 1987, when I stopped drinking.

I truly hope that everyone who has impacted my life will take a measure of satisfaction in the fact they have all played a role in this book.

It has often been said that you are only as good as the people you surround yourself with. I can truly state that this is true of my life.

To all who have helped me, you know who you are. Thank you from the bottom of my heart.

I also wish to acknowledge the support of several people in bringing this book to life: Dan Koon for his collaboration and editing, Carrie Cook for her design work and CarolLee Kidd for her transcriptions. Thank you all.

Appendix

20 Question Assessment

On the first day of my sobriety, I answered this 20 question assessment, which was originally developed in the 1930s by a doctor who was working at Johns Hopkins University at the time. The answers I gave on that day follow each question.

1. Do you lose time from work due to your drinking? YES.

2. Is drinking making your home life unhappy? YES.

3. Do you drink because you are shy with other people? NO.

4. Is drinking affecting your reputation? YES.

5. Have you ever felt remorse after drinking? YES.

6. Have you gotten into financial difficulties as a result of your drinking? YES.

7. Do you turn to lower companions and an inferior environment when drinking? YES.

8. Does your drinking make you careless of your family's welfare? YES.

9. Has your ambition decreased since drinking? YES.

10. Do you crave a drink at a definite time daily? YES.

11. Do you want a drink the next morning? YES.

12. Does drinking cause you to have difficulty in sleeping? YES.

13. Has your efficiency decreased since drinking? YES.

14. Is drinking jeopardizing your job or business? NO.

15. Do you drink to escape from worries or troubles? YES.

16. Do you drink alone? YES.

17. Have you ever had a complete loss of memory as a result of your drinking? YES.

18. Has your physician ever treated you for drinking? NO.

19. Do you drink to build up your self-confidence? YES.

20. Have you ever been in a hospital or institution on account of drinking? YES.

If you have answered YES to any one of the questions, there is a definite warning that you may be an alcoholic.

If you have answered YES to any two, the chances are that you are an alcoholic.

If you have answered YES to three or more, you are definitely an alcoholic.

The Progressive
Diseas

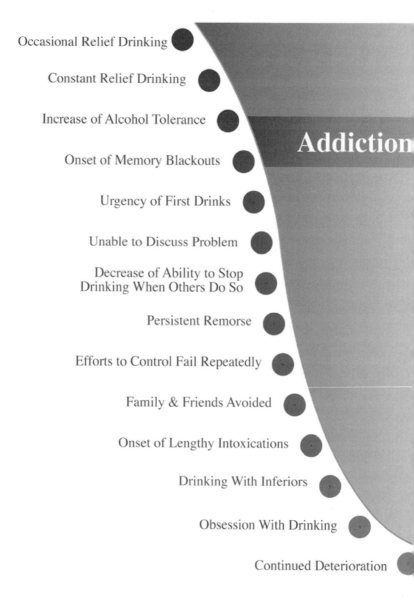

Occasional Relief Drinking

Constant Relief Drinking

Increase of Alcohol Tolerance

Onset of Memory Blackouts

Addiction

Urgency of First Drinks

Unable to Discuss Problem

Decrease of Ability to Stop
Drinking When Others Do So

Persistent Remorse

Efforts to Control Fail Repeatedly

Family & Friends Avoided

Onset of Lengthy Intoxications

Drinking With Inferiors

Obsession With Drinking

Continued Deterioration

Alcoholism

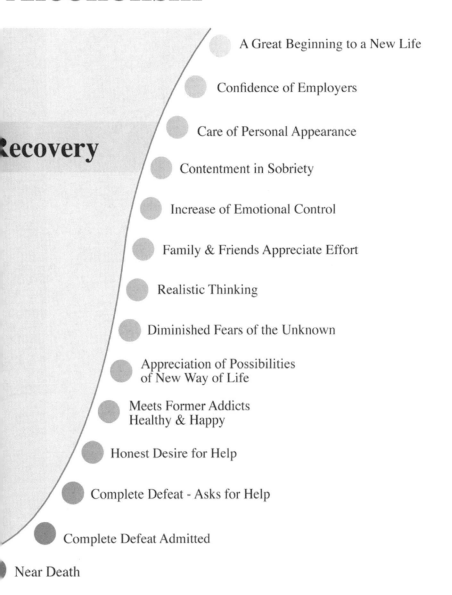

Recovery

A Great Beginning to a New Life

Confidence of Employers

Care of Personal Appearance

Contentment in Sobriety

Increase of Emotional Control

Family & Friends Appreciate Effort

Realistic Thinking

Diminished Fears of the Unknown

Appreciation of Possibilities
of New Way of Life

Meets Former Addicts
Healthy & Happy

Honest Desire for Help

Complete Defeat - Asks for Help

Complete Defeat Admitted

Near Death

My old teacher, Mr. MacKay wrote the following poem, which I include here in his memory.

SUCCESS

Success is what we aim to reach
As we stand on the brink of life,
Something to have, something to be,
To win a name in the strife.

How false are the visions that fly
Before the eager eyes of youth
Success hides behind wealth and name
Their barriers conceal the truth

Success is not to amass wealth
By just grinding out of brothers.
Gold which is not righteously yours,
But the honest food of others.

Success is not to win a name
To be placed on memory's page.
That will not perish with the clay,
But endure from age to age.

Success is not to have the world
Bow lowly, humbly at your feet.
To climb the steep ascent of fame
Which the fickle mass can greet.

But in the simple path of duty,
Perform your task with utmost care.
By the common forge of labour
A kind thought for others share.

Scatter little beams of sunshine
In a brother's cup of pain
Kindle little sparks of kindness,
Be the rainbow in the rain.

All the needy, poor and helpless
Will your humble efforts bless.
And on the day of reckoning,
God will crown you a success.

Duncan MacKay